revolutions, nations, empires

revolutions, nations, empires

conceptual limits and theoretical possibilities

Alexander J. Motyl

COLUMBIA UNIVERSITY PRESS   NEW YORK

Columbia University Press

Publishers Since 1893

New York   Chichester, West Sussex

Copyright © 1999 Columbia University Press

All rights reserved

Library of Congress Cataloging-in-Publication Data

Motyl, Alexander J.

Revolutions, nations, empires : conceptual limits and theoretical

possibilities / Alexander J. Motyl.

p.   cm.

Includes bibliographical references and index.

ISBN 0-231-11430-3 (cloth). — ISBN 0-231-11431-1 (pbk.)

1. Revolutions. 2. Nationalism. I. Title.

HM281.M667   1999

303.6'4—dc21   99-17430

Casebound editions of Columbia University Press books are

printed on permanent and durable acid-free paper.

Designed by Chang Jae Lee

Printed in the United States of America

c 10 9 8 7 6 5 4 3 2 1

p 10 9 8 7 6 5 4 3 2 1

To Joseph Rothschild

contents

God is in the trees.

—Thomas Merton

Certain old men said, "If thou seest a young man ascending
by his own will up to heaven catch him by the foot and throw him
down upon earth, for it is not expedient for him."

—*The Sayings of the Fathers*

preface

Revolutions, nations, and empires are big themes, but this is not a book about an even bigger theme: how the three interact. That they do seems obvious enough. Nations are constituent parts of empires, and the formation and demise of empires almost invariably involves national movements and nationalist agitation. So too revolutions and empires frequently go together, with the former seemingly leading to breakdowns of the latter, and the latter, in the guise of imperial collapse, promoting the former. Revolutions and nations are also connected—just consider the large number of revolutionaries who were nationalists and of nationalists who were revolutionaries—although, surprisingly, this connection remains underexplored in the social science literature.[1]

My goal in this book is more modest: to sketch some ways of thinking about revolutions, nations, and empires. Indeed, I hope to demonstrate the obvious—that only by drawing clear lines around these concepts can we hope to incorporate them in our empirical and theoretical canvases. In that sense, revolutions, nations, and empires are merely vehicles for a larger argument about the centrality of concepts to theory and theory building. The structure of each of the book's three sections is therefore identical—first I discuss the concept, then the theories, and finally the theoretical implications of the proposed reconceptualizations—and each chapter is informed by the arguments concerning conceptual indeterminacy and theoretical underdetermination developed in the introduction. Empirical data appear mostly in the guise of conceptual referents that illustrate a theoretical point.

Chapter 1 proposes an unoriginal definition of revolution as rapid, fundamental, and comprehensive change and underlines the obvious—that revolution is but one of many ways for societies to change. Chapter 2 dissects Theda Skocpol's flawed book, *States and Social Revolutions*, and uses it as a pretext for addressing the question of whether revolutionary theory—as well as theories of revolution—can be predictive.[2] My answer is no. Chapter 3 provides additional reasons for declining the revolutionary bet by examining "postsocialist pathways" in general and those of Ukraine and Russia in particular.[3] Chapters 4 through 6 perform a similar kind of deconstructive operation on nations and nationalism. If we define both concepts without reference to causal factors, there is no reason to think that nations and nationalism cannot be found in the distant past and in the future. In particular, chapters 4 and 5 take issue with the choice-centered, well-nigh voluntarist views of "constructivists." Finally, chapters 7 through 9 argue that empires, as peculiarly structured political systems, presuppose neither choice nor imperialism and that the forces that promote such systems are both present and likely to remain with us for some time to come.

These explorations rest on three related claims. First, in drawing boundaries around sets of properties, concepts transform clusters of properties into the bounded entities that then serve as the empirical referents of theories. Without concepts empirical data do not exist in any meaningful sense. Second, as the building blocks of theories, concepts are the key to theoretical coherence and robustness. A conceptually incoherent study is ipso facto theoretically incoherent, and no amount of empirical richness can obscure that the data collected lack structure and thus have nothing to say. Third, conceptual boundaries define the range of claims that a theory can make. Conceptual limits imply theoretical possibilities and, more important, theoretical impossibilities.

If we recognize that concepts, referents, and theories are incestuously related, it follows that how concepts are bounded—how they are defined—is not just a matter of casual, or abstruse, concern. Rather, it is part and parcel—indeed, the *central* part—of theorizing. Defining, in this sense, is already *proto*theorizing. In Giovanni Sartori's words, "Bad language generates bad thinking; and bad thinking is bad for whatever the knowledge-seeker does next."[4] Seen in this light, this book is an attempt to come to terms with the challenges—and flaws—posed by positivist social science on the one hand and postmodernism on the other. I fully appreciate that I am placing the two in binary opposition to each other. Although this maneuver does injustice to many of their nuances, it enables us to stake out a coherent theoretical space between what, to my mind, are the unrealistic aspirations of the former and the anarchic implications of the latter.

Despite my often vigorous criticism of existing approaches, I stress that the conceptual frameworks and theoretical alternatives developed in individual sections work only insofar as they offer not unreasonable ways of looking at revolutions, nations, and empires. I emphatically do not claim that my approach is the only correct one or that it explains everything. To the contrary, I am fully persuaded that all theories are inadequate and that the least inadequate theories are, when taken on their own terms, equally good or bad. Were theories clerics, they would all be whisky priests. Like all attempts at theorizing, mine are stabs. I trust and hope, however, that with some degree of conceptual clarity they will not be futile stabs in the complete dark.

Although I have addressed many of these conceptual, theoretical, and empirical themes in other works, this book brings these strands together and attempts to weave them into one cloth. Parts of some chapters draw on substantially rewritten parts of previously published articles or chapters: *Sovietology, Rationality, Nationality: Coming to Grips with Nationalism in the USSR* (New York: Columbia University Press, 1990), chap. 3; "The Modernity of Nationalism: Nations, States, and Nation-States in the Contemporary World," *Journal of International Affairs* 45 (winter 1992):307–23; "Inventing Invention: The Limits of National Identity Formation," in Michael Kennedy and Ronald Grigor Suny, eds., *Intellectuals and the Articulation of the Nation* (Ann Arbor: University of Michigan Press, forthcoming); "Concepts and Skocpol: Ambiguity and Vagueness in the Study of Revolution," *Journal of Theoretical Politics* 4 (January 1992):93–112; "Structural Constraints and Starting Points: The Logic of Systemic Change in Ukraine and Russia," *Comparative Politics* 29 (July 1997): 433–47; and "Thinking About Empire," in Karen Barkey and Mark von Hagen, eds., *After Empire*, pp. 19–29 (Boulder, Colo.: Westview, 1997).

The number of people who contributed to the thinking, puzzling, rethinking, writing, and rewriting that have gone into this book is enormous. To all—and especially to Rajan Menon and Ronald Suny—I am grateful. Special thanks too, for their inspiration, to John Armstrong and Giovanni Sartori. Finally, I thank all the scholars with whose excellent work I take issue, conceptually or theoretically. Without their thought-provoking contributions to various intellectual debates, for better or for worse, I would have little to debate.

revolutions, nations, empires

introduction: concepts and theories

If it walks like a duck and it talks like a duck, it's a duck.

John Searle is surely right to insist that a material world really exists—and is unwittingly assumed to exist even by those who would deny its existence—and that, regardless of where the world begins and ends, the rest involves the "construction of social reality."[1] We construct, or constitute, social reality by means of concepts, which Giovanni Sartori defines as "the basic unit[s] of thinking. It can be said that we have a concept of A (or of A-ness) when we are able to distinguish A from whatever is not-A."[2] Conveying an "abstract property shared by some substances and not by others," socially real concepts do not just point, as perhaps in the natural sciences, to physically bounded material things.[3] Socially real concepts do have referents, but these referents are coherent clusters of properties that may or may not be found within the boundaries of some already formed entity.[4] We could not, even in principle, collect the empirical referents of revolutions, nations, and empires and place them—like real ducks—into infinitely expandable bags. The problem is not that such bags would be too small for such an endeavor; rather, we could never seize the objects and actually move them from one place to another, from a physically bounded "here" to a physically bounded "there." The same limitations apply to seemingly more manageable, "smaller," socially real entities such as actions, decisions, and choices.

Like real ducks, however, conceptually bounded, coherently clustered, and thus socially real referents, whether micro or macro, *do* exist—they are *really* real or as really real as everything besides atoms and molecules—because the properties they possess create a boundary that marks them off from the rest of the world.[5] Choices, for instance, exist, not because they are preformed things but because we can arrange something called alternatives, speech acts of the "I choose" variety, and subsequent behaviors in the appropriate bundles. By the same token, the concept of the nation has an ontologically real referent so long as the defining characteristics we ascribe to

the "nation" can be identified in the world; if and when they can be so identified, the empirical referent necessarily exists, without necessarily having
existed in some ontologically prior, tangibly material sense as a bounded
thing. People do run through streets, guns do get fired, prisons do get razed,
and monarchs do lose their heads, but only through an act of conceptual
will are such disparate real events roped together to "become" a revolution.
We also know that cultural differences and power differentials exist, but
only the concept of, say, empire can draw a line around such different facts
and join them in a meaningful category. Robert Cox's claim that "the state
has no physical existence like a building or a lamp-post; but it is nevertheless
a real entity" is exactly on the mark. He is, however, just as off the mark
when he says that the state "is a real entity because everyone acts as though
it were"—a claim that shifts the ontological rootedness of the state from the
concept to popular behavior. But he is back on track when he argues that
the state "is a real entity . . . because *we* know that real people with guns and
batons will enforce decisions attributed to this non-physical reality" (emphasis added).[6]

From this philosophically "conceptualist" perspective, concepts "create"
socially real entities but not willfully, not haphazardly, and not out of thin
air.[7] Concepts are somewhat like paintings. Both define a reality as they depict it. Canvases collect clusters of properties within a spatial frame and, in
so doing, depict coherently related *collections* of properties that define, illu-
minate, and reveal the entities being painted. People and objects exist on canvas, but in existing on canvas in specific ways defined by artists, the pictorial
representations of people and objects are more than mere reflections of their
external appearance. This statement seems obviously true of the abstract
portraits of Oskar Kokoschka and Amadeo Modigliani, but it is no less true
of the superrealist close-ups of Chuck Close, the flattened bottles of Giorgio
Morandi, or the traditional representations of Rembrandt van Rijn.[8]

Similar in many respects to Jonathan Turner's and William Outhwaite's,
this argument presupposes the validity of some form of holism.[9] Although I
do not deny the reality of individual entities such as choices, decisions, and
preferences—how could I without contradicting myself?—I see no reason to
deny the reality of social entities. When examined under a conceptual mi-
croscope, they are the same kinds of entities with the same kinds of limitations. Both individual entities and social entities can be grasped only by
means of concepts, and neither exists in quite the same way that atoms and
cells and rocks and even human beings do. If individual entities are *really* real,
so too are social entities. And if the latter are not—because they are too fuzzy

conceptually, somehow too immaterial—the former are not. That individual entities are "smaller" than social entities and "closer" to flesh-and-blood human beings in no way endows them with a privileged ontological status. Seeming proximity to nerve endings and capillaries is not the same thing as being the mass of nerve endings and capillaries; a persuasive connection still must be established between the nerves and, say, the decision. As the ongoing debate regarding consciousness suggests, that is a terribly hard nut to crack.[10] Indeed, the closer one approaches the living human being, the more one is obliged to delve into the invisible world of psychological entities—hardly a less daunting task than dealing with mere societies.[11] Moreover, the case for proximity unjustifiably assumes that the smaller "distance" must entail a "smaller" number of intermediate causal steps, whereas the number of steps, like the number of points, between any two points can be infinite.

In addition to presupposing equal reality, my position rests on a claim of equivalent methodological validity. Arthur Danto notes that the truth claims of what he terms methodological "socialism" may or may not successfully be translated downward, into methodologically individualist truth claims, which in turn may or may not be translated upward, into holistic ones. If the former translation *can* be performed, so, obviously, can the latter. And if the former *cannot*, the latter cannot. Either way, each system of truth claims is, *ceteris paribus*, as valid, or as little valid, as the other.[12]

DEFINING DEFINING AND DEFINING

Because theories consist of concepts arranged in some supposedly causal fashion, specifying the concepts of *A, B,* and *C* and distinguishing them from not-*A*, not-*B*, and not-*C*—or simply defining them—must be the starting point of any theoretical enterprise. But how do we define *defining*? Following Sartori's lead, we know that it is not describing and that it decidedly is not explaining. W. V. Quine suggests that definitions are best defined as translations: the *definiens* permits us to disregard the *definiendum*, because it—the definiens—provides an alternative, and presumably more specific, set of words purporting to seize the same concept.[13] Definitions are thus semantically equivalent statements of the "*A* is *B*" variety, such that any sentence containing *A* could be written with *B*, and vice versa, without any change in meaning. In contrast, descriptions are of the "*A* is *a, b, c*" form, whereas explanations have the "If *X*, then *Y*" form and posit some kind of causal connection between *X* and *Y*.

When smuggled into definitions, descriptions produce either poor translations or, far worse, distortions in meaning. Descriptions have causal implications if features *a, b,* and *c* are written in a "time-specific" manner that limits the object described to a certain period and thereby confines explanations of it to that period as well. If we define nationalism as a specifically nineteenth-century ideology, we are willy-nilly forcing explanations of nationalism to be rooted in phenomena—such as industrialization, modernization, and the like—also found in the nineteenth or, perhaps, the eighteenth century. Smuggling a straightforward explanation into a definition is even more egregious a causal sleight of hand and can be written as "*A* is (If *X*, then *Y*)" or "(If *X*, then *Y*) is *B*." Both maneuvers resolve the problem of explanation by definitional fiat and are akin to including synthetic elements in analytic statements. Writing in this spirit in his now classic volume, *Political Order in Changing Societies,* Samuel Huntington on the one hand defines revolution as participation exceeding institutionalization and, on the other, attributes revolution's occurrence to participation's exceeding institutionalization. As German nursery tales put it, *"Und wenn sie nicht gestorben sind, dann leben sie noch weiter."*[14]

Charles Tilly also provides a striking example of a definition-qua-explanation. He defines revolution as consisting of a revolutionary situation—when contenders and power holders are balanced—and a revolutionary outcome—when that balance is resolved in favor of the revolutionaries. Tilly includes both cause and effect in his definition but without stipulating which part of his definition is the revolution and therefore which is cause and which is effect. He compounds the problem by inconsistently using the concept of the "state," which is both a Weberian organization if modern and little more than a lord and his vassals if premodern. Because his definition is indistinguishable from an explanatory scheme, and because his theory does not distinguish between causes and effects, Tilly's key argument, that "the possibility and character of revolution changed with the organization of states and systems of states; they will change again with future alterations of state power," rests on two vague devices—the state and revolution—combined in what amounts to a grand historical narrative of contestations between rulers and their challengers.[15]

CATS, DOGS, AND ZOOS

We can, as the postmodernists realize, construct any concept we like. No semantic Leviathan can tell us how to think or how to talk. Indeed, no one can stop us from developing our own, possibly incomprehensible language, if that is what we want to do. If our goal is to communicate, however, we generally develop and/or use concepts that are intelligible and useful. We could, for instance, insist that empires really are red things that go quack, but unless we embed that concept in an intersubjectively accessible system of invented meanings, we should not be surprised to learn that no one will understand us and, more important, that such a concept has little use in the study of, say, Rome. We therefore prefer blue to "grue," as in Nelson Goodman's example, precisely because blue helps us cope with the world as it is constructed and grue does not.[16]

Intelligibility and utility are relative notions. Some people will fail to understand or appreciate even the best crafted concept, and all concepts will be useful for some projects but not for others. We maximize intelligibility and utility by recognizing that they are functions of conceptual clarity and conceptual consistency. To be sure, perfect clarity and complete consistency are unattainable goals—because concepts are defined in terms of other concepts in a process that ultimately resembles an endless spiral—but there are degrees of lack of clarity and inconsistency, and less of both is surely preferable to more.[17]

Although concepts are constructions, they are not, as in some Dadaist poetry, serendipitous constructions. Concepts can be more or less vague and more or less ambiguous, whereby vagueness concerns the sharpness of the connotative boundaries between concepts and ambiguity addresses the denotative boundaries of their empirical referents.[18] Concepts can also, as Sartori points out, be self-contradictory "cat-dog" amalgams—a point I return to shortly—whereas some, such as institution, the state, and bargaining, appear to be zoos.[19] Consider in this light the concept of internal war.[20] If war refers to a condition of hostility between two political organizations with the appropriate Weberian characteristics, whatever can "internal war" be? Two states cannot be involved in a condition of *internal* hostility. Substate entities can, of course, but because these entities may be virtually anything—husbands, wives, friends, lovers, classes, groups, genders, clubs, movements, parties, gangs, and so on all fit the bill—internal war ends up referring to every form of conflict that is not explicitly between states. And that is both too vague and too ambiguous.

As minimal vagueness, minimal ambiguity, and minimal inconsistency make for maximal conceptual coherence, the best one can achieve conceptually, although hardly perfect, is not quite as bad as postmodernists would have us believe. In any case, we have little reason to take the postmodernists too seriously on this score, because, their useful admonitions notwithstanding, their concepts often resemble crudely essentialist contrivances. "The Other" may as well be a Platonic form, always and everywhere present for ostensibly nonsubstantialist entities to "negotiate" and "interrogate" as they define and redefine themselves relationally. "Discourse" is no less of a Thing. Even if discourse is only about discourse and if words are only about words, they are decidedly not empty signifiers with no empirical referents: quite the contrary, they must refer to something that, on closer inspection, is stable and immutable enough to warrant being referred to consistently and coherently. As a result, Others and Discourses are not just ontologically real in the language and logic of postmodernism. As they are virtually all that is real, they almost necessarily become portrayed as reified, fetishized, and anthropomorphized world-historical personalities of Napoleonic dimensions. Like heroes in history, Others and Discourses drive reality in a way that few positivist independent variables ever could.[21]

CONCEPTUAL IMPERIALISM

Because concepts consist of chains of concepts, they can only fall into different "semantic fields" and have a variety of meanings. Because any concept will always have a multiplicity of competing definitions, the quest for "the" meaning of, say, revolution is fundamentally misguided and inevitably frustrating. At best, we can argue for or against a meaning, we can engage in debate, and we can try to make our meaning intersubjectively comprehensible, if not acceptable, to others. But that is all. Definitions change with time, place, and profession, and for Lenin, Khomeini, Barrington Moore, and me to share the same understanding of revolution would be remarkable. Friedrich Nietzsche recognized this long ago: "All concepts in which an entire process is semiotically concentrated elude definition."[22]

Such conceptual pluralism has important implications. First, if we distinguish between terms, which are words and, as such, mere sounds or marks, and concepts, which are units of thought, it follows that the presence of a term—at some time and in some place—may, but need not, imply the presence of the concept and its referent. By the same token, the concept and its referent may be identifiable, but the term may be utterly absent from the language of the historical actors. We are not only free to approach history in general and the history of revolutions, nations, and empires in particular from our own vantage point, with our own language, and our own concepts but we have no choice but to do so. The result, for better or for worse, is, as Russell Hardin puts it, that

> contemporary anthropologists speak a language virtually no one else speaks—certainly the peoples they study do not speak it. Many sociologists cannot even understand their own vocabulary—the people who are their subjects have no chance. Psychology is almost entirely about ununderstood influences on the self and unperceived motivations. Economists also speak a rarified language. . . . Hence, virtually all social and psychological theorists are together in their problem of using theories and vocabularies that defy the thoughts of those whose actions they are supposed to explain.[23]

Second, although it may be interesting to investigate the understandings, representations, mentalities, images, and other self-reflective dispositions of historical actors and to ask why they perceived their reality as they did, it is impossible—contrary to Leopold von Ranke, who recommended that history be written *"wie es eigentlich gewesen sei"*—for us to recreate or experience it, because we can never break out of our hermeneutic circle and enter theirs. Indeed, even if we could definitively establish how historical actors used certain terms, logic would dictate that, if we were truly determined to use these terms in a historically contextualized manner, we purge our language of *all* terms and *all* meanings foreign to the period about which we are writing. To be fully consistent with this requirement, we would have to write in the language and with the meanings of the historical actors we are writing about— surely an impossible project if ever there was one.

Geoff Eley and Ronald Suny's injunction—that "the discourses of politics of earlier times must be understood and respected in their own particularity and not submerged in understandings yet to be formed"—therefore amounts to the impossible demand that scholars adopt some ahistorical Olympian vantage point and, after purging their thinking of all "understandings not yet formed," write in the language and with the meanings of the societies they study.[24] Eley and Suny's recommendation also amounts to the dubious claim that revolutionaries, nationalists, and imperialists are the best judges of how to think and talk about revolutions, nations, and empires.[25] How they think and talk has obvious implications for how scholars should think and talk, but it would be as questionable to privilege their discourse as it would be wrongheaded to consider fundamentalists and populist demagogues the ultimate authorities on religion and democracy. More important, writing as if we were in their shoes would actually undermine our ability to comprehend history. As Arthur Danto has shown, the conceptual distance imposed upon us by the passage of time makes historical understanding possible.[26] Precisely *because* our perspective is rooted in the future, we can invest the past with meaning and not merely randomly chronicle bygone events. The fact of the past, like the fact of difference, demands that we practice not conceptual laissez-faire but a conceptual mercantilism bordering on imperialism.

A CONCEPTUALIST APPROACH

If the entities we study and hope to explain in the social sciences are constructed conceptually, they exist if and when their defining characteristics appear, or can be identified, in some time and place. Revolutions or nations or empires exist whenever their defining characteristics—A, B, and C—are clustered in some time and space. The task of a theory, then, is not to explain "the" nation, "the" revolution, or "the" empire—or "the" choice, "the" decision, "the" action, or "the" desire—as if they were material objects that could be scooped up and placed in large bags but to account for the "coming together" or "existing together" of the properties A, B, and C. Such a conceptualist approach, which is *analytical* in the exact sense of the word, breaks things down into their components and claims that the things can be best understood by closer examination of the components.

Such an approach to revolutions, nations, and empires has at least two consequences. First, if we avoid smuggling time-specific descriptive or causal elements into the set of defining characteristics, we have, a priori, no reason to think that revolutions, nations, and empires can exist and emerge *only* in some particular historical period. That they may seem to be empirically confined to certain times and places means only that their defining characteristics could in fact be identified in those times and places. We cannot conclude therefrom that these same characteristics can be identified only in those times and places and, conversely, that they cannot be identified in other times and places. A conceptualist approach draws clear conceptual boundaries around entities and, in so doing, removes them from the grip of specific historical contexts.

The very title of John Armstrong's *Nations Before Nationalism* illustrates this point. Because Armstrong argues that "nationalism can be defined as the contention that the organizing principle of government should be unification of all members of a nation in a single state," he can also claim that, "although not unknown in earlier centuries, as a dominant credo and organizing principle this contention did not become salient until the generation of 1775–1815. These dates therefore constitute, in my opinion, the single decisive water-shed in the historical development of ethnicity and nationalism." Note how, by avoiding definitional circularity, Armstrong is able simultaneously to ac-knowledge the reality of "nations before nationalism" and the fact that na-tionalism "took off" in the early nineteenth century.[27]

Yael Tamir also appreciates that "when the reasons for the emergence of feelings characteristic of these relationships are mistaken for the typical fea-tures themselves, an inadequate definition [of the nation] results." She there-fore defines the nation in explicitly nonnationalist terms—as a "community whose members share feelings of fraternity, substantial distinctiveness, and ex-clusivity, as well as beliefs in a common ancestry and a continuous genealogy." Tamir is then in the position to argue that "nationalism is not the pathology of the modern age but an answer to its malaise—to the neurosis, alienation, and meaninglessness characteristic of modern times." By logical extension she could also argue that, just as these feelings and beliefs can come during modern times, so they may arise before or after them.[28]

Second, and equally important, an analytical approach to entities in gen-eral and revolutions, nations, and empires in particular implies a very differ-ent theoretical project from that usually undertaken. In effect, our task, in ex-plaining some entity, Y, is to propose a theory, not—strictly speaking—of the "If X, then Y" variety but of the "If X, then (A,B,C)" variety, where (A,B,C) represents the set of Y's defining characteristics. Y can then emerge in a vari-ety of ways, as

1. (A,B,C), a "ready-made" cluster, or in "parts"
2. $A + (B,C)$
3. $B + (A,C)$
4. $C + (A,B)$
5. $(A,B) + C$
6. $(B,C) + A$
7. $(A,C) + B$

The characteristics to the left of the plus sign represent "add-ons" to existing defining characteristics that in each case also belong to the set of initial con-ditions underpinning the theory.

As we know from Ernst Nagel, initial conditions are the conditions, x, y, and z, under which, and only under which, a theory of "If X, then Y" can hold.[29] Put differently, they are the conditions without which theoretical propositions cannot be true or, for that matter, even false. "Science," according to Quine, "normally predicts observations *only* on the assumption of initial conditions" (emphasis added).[30] As such, initial conditions subsume but are not identical to necessary conditions. Inasmuch as theories without initial conditions are either groundless predictions or elaborate tautologies masquerading as natural laws, theories with different initial conditions are different theories, even if they all claim to be explaining the same (A,B,C).[31] If our goal is to explain the emergence of (A,B,C) as a ready-made cluster, the initial conditions will be some x, y, and z but not A, B, or C; in all the other variants, however, the initial conditions will include some combination of A, B, or C. Thus, for $A + (B,C)$, B and C belong to the initial conditions; for $B + (A,C)$, A and C are part of the initial conditions, and so on.

THEORETICAL LIMITS

Because each variant listed rests on different initial conditions, it follows that a unified theory of the "If X, then (A,B,C)" variety—incorporating variants one through seven—is unattainable even in principle. Theories one through seven, however, are not unattainable. That is the good news. The bad news is that, because all theories consist of concepts that rest on concepts and so on, "partial" theories will still fall far short of their limited explanatory ambitions. Even partial theories cannot generate the sufficient condition, or cause, of something, simply because the ultimate indeterminateness of concepts militates against specifying the exact boundaries of so omnipotent a variable.[32]

Although sufficient conditions are theoretically useful only if constituted precisely, necessary and facilitating conditions retain their utility even if bounded fuzzily. Recall that in variants two through seven the terms to the right of the plus sign represent both the initial and necessary conditions of the respective theories. Even if we can never quite pin down the exact conceptual boundaries and empirical referents of A, B, or C, we do know that their absence—which is far easier to determine than their exact presence—makes the emergence of (A,B,C) impossible. By the same token, because the presence of necessary conditions only enables but does not require (A,B,C) to occur, their inescapable fuzziness need not preclude our claiming that, with A, B, or C *more or less* in place, the probability of (A,B,C)'s occurring is somewhat greater than zero.

However true, this second claim would be almost trivial were it impossible also to argue that that probability might be increased by the facilitating conditions of A, B, or C. Although probability and probabilistic theories are hardly the straightforward notions we often assume them to be, isolating the facilitating conditions of, say, A is at least equivalent to asserting that yet another theory of "If Q, then A" exists. The latter theory, although subject to all the constraints I have discussed, has the effect of making A's occurrence possible. Should three such theories—for A, B, and C—exist, we can argue for the increased likelihood of A, B, and C and thus for the increased likelihood of their clustering as (A,B,C). Significantly, this line of argument presumes that the theory of "If Q, then A" (or B or C) is more established, more valid, more rightly taken for granted than the theory of (A,B,C) with which we are grappling. Because theoretical validity is, as should be clear by now, a tenuous notion in the social sciences, we are in effect asserting that, for the purposes of demonstrating (A,B,C), we shall assume "If Q, then A," "If Q', then B," and "If Q'', then C"—with all the many caveats already noted with respect to "If X, then (A,B,C)" appended here as well. One more limitation should, alas, be noted: although facilitating conditions may increase the probability of something's occurrence, we have no way of specifying just how great that increase will be.

Just as conceptual clarity rests on conceptual clarity, so too does theoretical robustness rest on theoretical robustness (and, lest things are insufficiently complicated, on conceptual clarity as well). As these chains have no logical starting point, we are trapped within something resembling a vicious circle.[33] Although we may therefore never be able to explain why things happen or why entities emerge, the alternative is neither despair, nor irony, nor thick description. Postmodernists are correct to point to intertextuality as a reality, but they are wrong to suggest that conditional causal claims or theories cannot be constructed. As a matter of fact, inasmuch as theories are made and not found, intertextuality is the precondition of theorizing. We can surely argue why things cannot happen or why entities cannot emerge (because of the absence of necessary conditions) as well as when and under what (facilitating) conditions they are more or less likely to happen and emerge. In place of theoretical certainties we do have theoretical impossibilities *and* theoretical possibilities.[34] In this case, as in most cases, satisficing is quite satisfying.

FROM CONCEPTS TO THEORIES

As theories are elaborate semantic chains that, perforce, share in the vagueness and ambiguity that concepts inherently possess, much of what we claim to know about the world is inevitably tainted by the ultimate indeterminacy of the concepts we use and thus can only be at most a rough approximation of reality. Stephen Hawking makes a similar point even with respect to the theories used by physicists.[35] Because concepts and referents are inextricably related to each other, theoretical closure of the sort to which positivism aspires is impossible, and theory "testing" cannot be about matching theories with supposedly nontheoretical or preconceptual facts and seeing whether they fit. Thus the positivistically inspired social-science approach to evaluating theory—demonstrating how rival theories do not explain certain "puzzles" and how one's own invariably does and concluding, q.e.d., that one's own must be superior—cannot be correct and it is certainly unproductive. Indeed, the endlessly inconclusive debates, the circular recurrence of once-dead theories, and what Jeffrey Alexander terms the continued "centrality of the classics" also suggest as much.[36]

The postmodernist response to this conundrum is to suggest that everything goes, that, because all theories and nontheories consist of strings of indeterminate concepts, all theories and nontheories are equally persuasive narratives; that no criteria for separating the better from the worse exist; and that even the natural sciences, which use their own language, are ultimately little different from other forms of writing. No one, I submit, *really* believes this last proposition: certainly no one acts as if this proposition were believed. When experts reconstruct the steps that led to some catastrophe—the derailment of a train or the crash of an airplane—and when illustrators then depict those steps in some magazine, we view their cumulative efforts not just as another stab at creative storytelling but as a probably accurate account, with real-life implications for us as well, of why and how so many people lost their lives. As a result, we adjust our behavior: we avoid certain airlines, change our vacation plans, or have a double martini on board. Alternatively, whoever truly believes that science is little different from poetry must embrace "Sokal's hoax" as a perfectly legitimate expression of postmodern science and thus deny the ontological reality of everything but narratives. This view, as cynics and pragmatists might point out, invariably dissipates in the hothouse of academic politics when tenure, promotions, and similarly nondiscursive issues intrude on texts.[37] Jacques Derrida's decidedly nondiscursive tussle with a prominent university press, in which both sides claimed to know just what their contract *really* said, comes to mind.[38]

In the final analysis, postmodernism subverts itself by resting on a binary opposition that implicitly endorses an unusually extreme form of positivism. Accordingly, abstract entities cannot be ontologically real because, as the earlier discussion of painting intimated, only words on the one hand or materially bounded, physically tangible objects on the other can constitute the legitimate realm of the social sciences. Such a stance rests on a curiously antiquated premodern notion of the sciences. If physics and astronomy may usefully refer to entities that are not visible, while frequently using utterly imagined concepts to great effect, surely the social sciences have no reason to insist on far more rigorous standards.[39] Just because we cannot "see" something, just because something is not observable, does not, as various critics of positivism have pointed out, mean that "it" is not real.

A THIRD WAY?

If both positivism and postmodernism offer us little guidance for evaluating theories, is there perhaps a more-than-residual space—a median, and not a mean—situated somewhere between the two extremes that does? That social science theories consist of strings of concepts and that theory construction must begin, and perhaps even end, with the formation of clear and consistent concepts that hang together suggests a simple, though strangely underused, method for testing theories in a theoretically plural and underdetermined world.[40] Before even contemplating the question of whether theories "fit the facts" and explain what they purport to explain—an undertaking that, as I have suggested, is unlikely to settle the score among several contending theories—it behooves us to ask whether theories, when taken on their own terms, make sense conceptually, that is, whether they consist of concepts that make sense, on their own and in conjunction.

Concepts cohere, or fail to do so, in three ways. As I have already noted, they may be defined so vaguely and so ambiguously as to lose their connotative and denotative power. Second, concepts may be used differently throughout a text, thereby endowing the terms appended to them with different meanings. Inconsistent usage results in a moving target; worse still, it produces atheoretical narrative, because without the conceptual contours that make theory possible all that is left is the writing. Most worrisome, and least appreciated, is that, because concepts necessarily rest on concepts, different concepts—even if properly defined and consistently used—may rest on incompatible conceptual premises.

Recall that the definition of a concept consists of concepts with meanings of their own. Although the possibility of extending this process ad infinitum has obvious implications for the ultimate indeterminacy of concepts, more important for present purposes is that the lower-level meanings underlying a definition also presuppose certain assumptions. These primary beliefs—called "ontologies" by Stephen Gaukroger—overlap with Imre Lakatos's "hard core" and arguably are irrefutable.[41] They cannot be proved; they are simply assumed. That said, we cannot just assume anything. The assumptions that constitute an ontology should not be an arbitrarily scrambled hodgepodge. As Karl Popper notes, the "system of axioms must be free from contradiction, . . . independent, i.e., it must not contain any axiom deducible from the remaining axioms," and it must be sufficient and necessary for the "deduction of all statements belonging to the theory which is to be axiomatized."[42]

Contradictory assumptions matter, because they can be used to prove anything and therefore everything.[43] A prize-winning article by James Fearon and David Laitin illustrates the point. Fearon and Laitin explicitly emphasize that they will not treat ethnicity and ethnic groups as a given that precedes the individual: "We informally sketch a theory of interethnic peace and violence that starts from individual-level problems of opportunism rather than from group-level animosities."[44] Before the sketch is over, however, they violate their injunction by smuggling ethnic groups into the argument, quite literally as dei ex machinis: "Ethnic groups can provide a partial solution to this problem for their own members."[45] Indeed, they even claim to know that "ethnic groups are frequently marked by highly developed systems of social networks that allow for cheap and rapid transmission of information about individuals and their past histories," and that "ethnic groups cooperate to take advantage of each side's superior information about the behavior of individuals within the group, and this leads to the containment of interethnic violence."[46] Having added primordialist group premises to their methodologically individualist assumptions, Fearon and Laitin have little difficulty explaining both why ethnic violence occurs *and* why it does not—in a word, everything.

Manifestly false assumptions also matter, not so much because they are wrong but because false premises may contradict the true ones that comprise the taken-for-granted background knowledge. Rational choice theory frequently falls into this most elementary of traps by assuming that maximizing utility is the essence of human psychology. If utility is defined in material (and therefore theoretically elegant and parsimonious) terms, the theory assumes what science has shown to be inadequate or false. If utility is defined broadly (to encompass any number of values and norms), contradictory preferences inevitably become part and parcel of the hard core of rational choice.

Whatever the assumption, rational choice theory succeeds—mirabile dictu—in proving everything.[47]

Finally, even ill-fitting assumptions matter, because, by serving as the lower-level meanings of conjoined surface concepts, A and B, they transform their conjunction into a cat-dog—and thus to nonsense—even if A does not appear, at first glance at least, to contradict B. Consider the currently popular notion of the "ethnic security dilemma," which International Relations (IR) theorists frequently invoke to explain ethnic conflict. On the one hand, how a security dilemma can characterize intergroup, and not interstate, relations is not at all clear, because the dilemma's existence is premised on a condition of anarchy—in a very precise IR sense of the word—that can only fail to characterize the circumstances in which ethnic groups, even hostile and warring ones, exist. Anarchic circumstances are not necessarily anarchy. On the other hand, even less clear is how an ethnic group, as a large and inchoate collection of people, can face a security dilemma. As ethnic groups are not states or anything like unitary actors with one set of goals and one voice, such claims as "the 'groupness' of the ethnic, religious, cultural and linguistic collectivities that emerge from collapsed empires gives each of them an inherent offensive military power" are simply incomprehensible.[48]

The concept of the "marketplace of ideas" is no less of a cat-dog. A marketplace is a specific location where commodities are bought and sold, where money is exchanged, and where the law of supply and demand presumably determines prices. Ideas are also specific things: they circulate, they acquire greater or lesser popularity, their supporters compete for prominence. Although the marketplace metaphor is appealing to liberals who would like to think that the freedom to debate, like the freedom to buy and sell, results in the best or most efficient outcomes, it is hard to see just how ideas can be like commodities, how they can be bought and sold and with what, and how they can respond to the supposed economic laws of the market.[49] The metaphor may be analytically suggestive, but on its own it amounts to an insufficiently coherent research agenda.

THEORETICAL PLURALISM

If the concepts comprising a theory manage to avoid the most egregious pitfalls I have outlined, they fit, and the theory, because it is conceptually coherent, is valid. The theory's usefulness, however, especially compared to others, will depend on its ability to provide, on its own terms, a persuasive conceptual framework for as large a number of empirical settings as possible. "Theories and empirical data," according to Scott Gordon, "function as complementary implements of investigation, and the only rules that must be followed are that theories should be coherent and logically sound, and articulate with observation data that are objectively obtained and properly processed."[50] A theory "$C^1, C^2, C^3 \ldots C^N$" (where each C stands for a concept and its referent) should, ideally, tell the whole "just-so story" of, say, the set of all revolutions, R. Of course, it will not. So long as the conceptual scheme applied to some revolutionary story contains all the C's, however, with extratheoretic concepts P, Q, and S thrown in as well, second best is still quite satisfactory. Less satisfactory are stories containing P, Q, and S in addition to only some C's or those containing all or most C's but arranged in the "incorrect" order—C^2, C^1, C^4, C^3, and so on. In effect, a theory $C^1, C^2, C^3 \ldots C^n$ is "good" if it applies, in maximally unadulterated fashion, to as many stories of R as possible. Inasmuch as rival theories will, in all likelihood, be as "good"—if, perhaps, differently applicable—we inevitably are left with several more or less equally good theories of R.

Albert Camus illustrates this point in *The Stranger*. The first half of the book provides us with a blow-by-blow, almost clinically emotionless account of the days preceding Mersault's killing of the Arab. We "know" the facts. Mersault's trial, however, produces three competing theories of his behavior. The prosecutor claims that the killing was a premeditated act of murder; the defender argues that it was the product of emotional strain; Mersault attributes it to the sun. Given what we know about the facts, each account is plausible, each is persuasive, and each, incidentally, is repeated in any number of contemporary murder trials. No less significantly, that the prosecutor's version prevails has rather less to do with its intrinsic believability than with his emotional delivery and rhetorical tricks.[51]

Better theories may differ from worse ones in consisting of concepts that fit, but if theories are well-crafted conceptually all their elements—assumptions, concepts, and referents—will fit tightly because they will have been chosen, modified, and adjusted to fit tightly. And if well-crafted theories are human constructs that are made to explain only what they claim to be able to explain, we cannot tell whether social scientists paint bull's-eyes around gun shots or actually shoot at the targets. Johan Galtung's claim—"*If the hypothesis fits, then it fits*; and if the degree of confirmation is maximum, then so much the better"—goes still further, even suggesting that the better a theory, the *less* susceptible it is to refutation.[52]

Thomas Spragens takes Galtung's argument to its logical conclusion, speaking of the "inescapable ultimate circularity of all human thought—a circularity which can be repressed only by confining inquiry to proximate questions and denying the dependence of these proximate questions upon irreducible presuppositions." Indeed, Spragens finds that "because epistemology is inherently reflexive—that is, it is thought about thought, to the point of infinite regress—it can finally rest only upon self-confessed circularity which will be 'paradoxical' or upon an affirmation of certainty which will be dogmatic. There are no other alternatives." Although Spragens suggests that the "choice between these two ultimate paradigms must itself be a matter of personal judgment," he prefers the "former alternative, self-confessed paradox . . . because it incorporates and accepts its own contingency. As Robert Merton has suggested, this justification of knowledge resembles Munchhausen's feat of extricating himself from a swamp by pulling on his own whiskers. But the alternative resembles standing on thin air, a tenuous basis for laughing at Munchhausen's efforts."[53]

To acknowledge, as I have done, the validity of Spragens's circularity thesis, or what Quine calls "holism," is to accept two far-reaching epistemological positions.[54] First, the truth value and meaning of theoretical statements have no sense outside some theory. Because we cannot apprehend the world in a manner that is unmediated by mental processes, truth and meaning are immanent qualities of theoretical understanding and have no independent ontological reality of their own.[55] As Quine puts it, "Truth is immanent, and there is no higher. We must speak from within a theory, albeit any of various."[56] Second, theoretical holism and conceptual contingency force us to the conclusion that theoretical pluralism, or "theoretical anarchism" in Paul Feyerabend's words, is an inescapable condition.[57] That is, it is perfectly normal—and not an aberration caused by the truculence of social scientists—for there to be many competing theories of reality. There is no one correct theory, and to think otherwise is to engage in what Douglas Chalmers calls "totalitarian thinking."[58] Once we accept this proposition, however, we are forced to realize that, other things being equal, there can be no intrinsically theoretical reason for accepting or not accepting, developing or not developing any one well-crafted theoretical framework as opposed to another. If that is so, deconstructionists have a valid point in insisting that theories—regardless of whether they are "metanarratives" deserving of what Jean-François Lyotard kindly calls "incredulity"—are forms of writing—texts, narratives, or stories—that may be adjudged in terms of literary criticism. Donald N. Mc-

Closkey dissects the "rhetoric" of even the most scientific of social sciences, economics, whereas Berel Lang performs the same operation on the most objective of the lot, philosophy.[59]

If theoretical pluralism is the inevitable condition of the social sciences, so too are debate, disagreement, and dissensus. Should such pluralism be lacking, should consensus or theoretical hegemony rule, this condition must be due to some intervening force or forces that impose consensus from outside the intellectual domain of the social sciences. If instead of a hundred flowers blooming, only one does, we may rightly conclude that some gardener—and not the forces of nature—is at work. In other words, dissensus is "natural," whereas consensus is not. Dissensus is reflective of a free discipline; consensus is not. Although dissensus may not therefore be termed "good"—I fully appreciate that I am flirting with the is/ought fallacy here—consensus surely is "bad," and hegemony unquestionably is "worse."

Seen in this light, that the neorealist paradigm has been dominant—and, arguably, still is dominant—in International Relations is a sign, not of theoretical sophistication but of theoretical poverty. In contrast, that comparative politics is, as Gabriel Almond has pointed out, riven by disagreements is, I submit, a sign of vitality.[60] The seemingly inexorable march of rational choice theory is thus a genuine cause for concern, whereas the triumph of the market—as economic reality, policy goal, theoretical presupposition, and ubiquitous metaphor—verges on calamity.

I. REVOLUTIONS

chapter 1. revolutionary change

At one point in Peter Weiss's play, *The Persecution and Assassination of Jean-Paul Marat as Performed by the Inmates of the Asylum of Charenton Under the Direction of the Marquis de Sade*, the inmates sing, at first mournfully and then excitedly:

> Marat we're poor and the poor stay poor
> Marat don't make us wait any more
> We want our rights and we don't care how
> We want our revolution NOW[1]

The song is stirring, and we may even commiserate with the Parisian poor, but what exactly do the inmates want? And how could we ever tell that they got it? Their lyrics imply that revolution involves moving rapidly from poverty to entitlement. Without revolution the poor will stay poor. Without revolution rights will not be had. Without revolution the wait will continue. The clues are tantalizing, but why believe madmen? Surely, we can do better if we consult eyewitnesses or the revolutionaries themselves.

The testimony of the former presumably carries weight because they were there. Someone who was present during the storming of the Bastille or the Winter Palace actually saw the Parisian sans-culottes or the Bolsheviks attack and seize the buildings. Someone who was present at Louis XVI's beheading actually saw the guillotine swoop down and severe the monarch's head. Eyewitnesses may not have seen everything, of course, and their personal interpretation of events will be unavoidable, but their presence at a scene gives them access to what most people would call privileged information. We are fascinated by the memoirs of Nikolai Sukhanov and François René de Chateaubriand precisely because they claim to remember things they saw.[2]

So far, so good but, alas, not quite good enough. We may admit that eye-witnesses witnessed stormings, beheadings, and the like, but how are we to know, without accepting their word on faith, that they were actually witness to a revolution? They may emphatically insist that they really did see a revolution; after all, they were there. "Where?" we might ask. "At the storming, at the beheading, at the mass rallies," they might answer. Are, then, a storming, a beheading, and mass rallies a revolution? How do the eyewitnesses know that? Why is a storming not enough? Or, perhaps, only a beheading? Or, finally, mass rallies followed by the threat of a storming and a behead-ing? How are we to know that the ten days experienced by John Reed really "shook the world"?[3]

Our eyewitnesses might then point to the revolutionaries: "It is they, the stormers, the beheaders, and the ralliers, who made the revolution. Speak to them." And we do, but once again we are likely to be frustrated. If the self-styled revolutionaries insist that they are better eyewitnesses than mere eye-witnesses, we will be entitled to wonder why. If they respond by claiming that their unmediated involvement in beheadings, stormings, and rallies qualifies them as better eyewitnesses, we may willingly grant that they real-ly were better eyewitnesses to beheadings, stormings, and rallies—or, per-haps, only to some of the goings-on frequently associated with beheadings, stormings, and rallies—but not necessarily to revolution. "When actors de-scribe their action as revolution," notes Andrew Arato, "they are generally referring to the coexistence of experience, event, and structural change. Since they may be mistaken about structural change, it is impossible to determine the presence of revolution by focusing solely on revolutionary involvement, experience, anxiety, or labeling."[4] Our revolutionaries may re-join that, unlike mere eyewitnesses, they enjoy a truly privileged status. *They* have access to revolutionary theory. And the theory identifies revolution by telling them how to bring it about. But how would a theory of revolution help us determine whether we are in the presence of a revolution? Because theories presumably explain things, they cannot be of much help in answer-ing our question: after all, they already presuppose the very thing we are try-ing to ascertain.

Only two courses of action are left: to seize the phenomenon directly or to rely on our pretheoretical wits. The first alternative can work only if the phenomenon we hope to grasp impresses itself automatically, presumably with exceptional clarity and directness, upon our senses. An explosion might be such an impressive occurrence; a sudden intense flash of light or a power-ful earthquake might also fit the bill. A particularly heartrending beheading or an especially dramatic storming may also have the capacity to grab our senses and not let go. But how could a revolution have such an effect? And even if it could, how would we know that it was a revolution and not, say, the beheading or the storming that so moved us? Even if we acknowledge that the world was shaken, just what, exactly, did the shaking?

Mark Lilla captures just these ambiguities in discussing the revolutionary import of the sixties in the United States:

> Although we know *something* happened then, we still don't know what it was or even when it began. Was the Berkeley free speech movement the beginning of the end? Columbia '68? Woodstock? Or was it, as Larkin mused, the sexual revolution of 1963, between the end of the *Chatterley* ban and the Beatles' first LP? The conservative use of the term "the Sixties" is imprecise, but there is probably no precise way to mark a cultural revolution—no tennis court oath, no storming of the Bastille, no beheading, no Thermidor. Still, we all recognize a before and an after, and we are all still groping for the meaning of what happened in between.[5]

EXPANDABLE BAGS AND SEMANTIC FIELDS

We can exit this cul de sac by abandoning the language of presence and accepting the premise that revolutions are not actually "out there," like mountains shrouded in mist. "Revolutions are not," writes Stan Taylor, "naturally-defined phenomena comparable to those studied in the natural sciences."[6] Revolutions do not exist as materially tangible three-dimensional objects, in the sense that we say that rocks and trees and airplanes exist as physical things. We can throw, touch, or board the latter, we can use all or some of our senses to comprehend their physical reality, but we cannot do the same for revolutions. We cannot, like homicide investigators, draw a chalk line around a revolution, nor can we place it in an infinitely expandable bag. We cannot touch it, taste it, or for that matter even see it. Naturally, many eyewitnesses to revolution claim to have seen it, but in reality what they saw was events and processes and people and things that, together, are called revolution.

Is revolution just a name, then, one that we apply more or less randomly to things that otherwise have nothing in common? The solution to our conundrum is not to seek refuge in nominalism but to recognize that, although revolution clearly is a word, it is also a concept that groups certain properties within defined boundaries and thereby distinguishes the resulting cluster from other clusters. How, then, do we go about defining the concept of revolution? The obvious starting point has to be by not reinventing the wheel. Although we may have no reason to believe eyewitnesses and revolutionaries, neither do we have any reason to dismiss their hunches, experiences, and impressions out of hand, especially if we treat them as metaphors, similes, and analogies masquerading as protodefinitions.[7]

Mao Zedong noted that revolutions were not a "dinner party, or writing an essay, or painting a picture, or doing embroidery"; Crane Brinton termed them fevers; for Karl Marx they were "the driving force of history"; Charles Tilly called them traffic jams.[8] Mao's metaphor, like Brinton's, tells us that revolutions are not genteel things, that they are disruptions of routine, of tradition, of the normal course of events—that they are, in a word, upheavals. Marx's metaphor suggests that revolutions move history, that they are powerful engines of historical development, of, quite simply, change. Tilly's metaphor points to obstruction, frustration, blockage, disorder—in a word, turmoil.[9] (When a heavily accented gentleman, standing on a busy Brooklyn street corner, said to me, "Sir, you are making blockage!" did he accuse me of subversive activity? Presumably not. But who knows: he did resemble an old bundist.)

The three metaphors locate revolution in different semantic fields—those of upheaval, change, and turmoil. If so, revolution may be conceived of as a type of upheaval (sudden, mass), a type of change (rapid, fundamental, comprehensive), or a type of turmoil (sustained, all encompassing). If revolution is situated in the realm of upheaval, its semantic cousins are rebellion, revolt, uprising, and insurrection. If it is in the realm of change, they are reform, transition, transformation, and evolution. Finally, if revolution is a type of turmoil, semantically related concepts are breakdown, anarchy, chaos, and riot.[10] Everyday language reflects these understandings. We speak of revolutionary hair products and revolutionary banking innovations, of revolutionary electoral results, and of permanent revolutions. Innovations represent significant breaks with the past; electoral landslides reflect a popular upheaval against incumbents; permanent revolutions are conditions of chaos.

The notion of a sudden mass upheaval entails only the eruption of activity and, as a concept, is unconcerned with outcomes, such as change, or with conditions, such as turmoil. Scholars who speak of revolution in Nicaragua in 1979 or in Eastern Europe in 1989 generally have upheaval in mind.[11] In contrast, rapid, fundamental, and comprehensive change is concerned with outcomes only, as if it were measuring the distance traversed by some entity between times t and $t + n$ and, as a concept, not asking how or why that distance was traversed or what the consequences of change are. Thus students of "revolution from above," as in Stalin's USSR or in Hitler's Germany, are fundamentally interested in the magnitude of change.[12] Finally, the notion of sustained, all-encompassing turmoil refers to the coming asunder or falling apart of things—indeed, of life—and, as a concept, is unconcerned either with the upheaval that may have preceded the falling apart or with the change that may eventually result. Scholars who claim that the Soviet Union underwent a revolution in 1989–1991 seem to have just this kind of turmoil in mind.[13]

However one chooses to locate revolution—and one may of course opt for different semantic solutions—it should be evident by now that revolution may not be transformed into some combination of these and thus into a cat-dog (or the equivalent of a "driving force with fever"). One example illustrates the moral hazard involved. William H. Sewell Jr. rechristens revolutions as "events" and then defines a "historical event" as "(1) a ramified sequence of occurrences that (2) is recognized as notable by contemporaries, and that (3) results in a durable transformation of structures."[14] Even if, against my better judgment, we grant the legitimacy of Sewell's distinction between events and occurrences, his threefold definition still falls into a series of conceptual traps. First, Sewell's events are classic cat-dogs, combining occurrences (or upheavals) with transformations (or change). Second, in proffering such a beast, Sewell effectively confuses definition with causation. And third, by insisting that occurrences must be recognized as such by historical actors, Sewell undermines his theory. Giving equal time in his theoretical framework to the conceptualizations of contemporaries and of scholars opens the conceptual Pandora's box discussed in this chapter and the introduction—lest we forget, as William Outhwaite elegantly puts it, the conceptions of agents are not "necessarily viridical"—and thereby places an impossibly heavy additional burden on theorists already straining under the weight of theoretical inadequacy.[15]

REVOLUTIONARY CHANGE

Like many other scholars—as diverse in their theoretical approaches as Andrew Arato, Christoph Kotowski, and Theda Skocpol—I choose to place revolution within the semantic field of change.[16] I do this for two reasons. First, I would like to believe that the study of change is more interesting, because it is richer and more variegated than the study of upheavals or turmoil. Upheavals and turmoil seem largely to be the handiwork of actors from below (the Great Proletarian Cultural Revolution may be one exception). We do not as a rule think of them as being brought about from above or from outside, unless we hope to argue that popular discontent is really the work of outside agents engaged in vast conspiracies. Although a concern with "froms"—from below, from above, or from outside—is a concern with causes and not with the actual entity being studied, that upheavals and turmoil are hard to imagine as being rooted anywhere but "below" suggests that the research agenda implied by both is relatively narrow. In contrast, revolution as change, like change itself, connotes no one source, reason, or cause of the change. Things change for many reasons, and revolution as change permits us to accept as equally valid causal candidates structures, institutions, attitudinal dispositions, and actors. There is no reason that we should not be able to countenance the possibility that revolutions occur as a result of international conditions or economic structures, relative deprivation or rational calculation, or revolutionary agitation or action from above.

One more point of contrast exists between revolution as change and revolution as upheaval or turmoil. Although we can and do ask what the consequences of upheaval and turmoil are, most often we confine our interest to the question of how and why they began and ended. The internal structure of both upheavals and turmoil—they emerge, they persist, they end—may have something to do with scholarly concern with beginnings and ends. Change, including revolutionary change, also begins and ends, but change also begs, even if not necessarily, the question of its consequences. We want to know whether the change is likely to be permanent; we ask whether its effects are likely to be good or bad. Indeed, these very concerns manifest themselves in political debates concerning major overhauls of, say, the tax system or of health care. For students of revolution as change this means that they can—and perhaps even should—ask whether revolutionary change can succeed in creating as stable and good a society as nonrevolutionary change.[17]

UNPACKING REVOLUTION

Naturally, revolution is not mere change, if only because that would reduce it to life. I have therefore defined it as "rapid, comprehensive, and fundamental change."[18] Let us unpack this definition by examining first the notion of change. I suggest that change is best conceived of as the difference between an entity, A, at time t and that "same" entity, now A', at time t + n. Change is the degree to which A' differs from A.[19] Entity A may be changing and may no longer recognizably be A, but until it is settled as A', until it comes to rest as A', it is conceptually impossible to argue that change, and not the process of changing, has taken place. "Changing" or "things-in-changing" are more accurately described as turmoil; as things fall apart, change per se has not yet occurred.[20] Only after things have fallen apart do we know that change has indeed occurred.

Consider now the concept of comprehensiveness. I suggest that comprehensiveness is best understood as referring to the breadth of change, to the number of spheres of life that change affects. If many spheres change, the change is comprehensive. If few change, it is not. Clearly, something claiming to be absolutely comprehensive must be tantamount to life, so insisting on absolute comprehensiveness as a defining characteristic of revolution has no point. But where do we draw the line? Do we focus on individuals and their souls, on spheres of public life, or on both? There are two reasons for confining our enquiry to public spheres.[21] First, determining what is "really" going on inside individual human beings may be impossible; in contrast, we can "see" change on the outside. And second, although most revolutionaries eventually want to create a "new man," they generally recognize that the way to get there is by changing the conditions of life.

The dimensions of public life that comprehensive change ideally affects are—and it goes without saying that these categories overlap—four in number: the political, the economic, the social, and the cultural.[22] Genuinely comprehensive change therefore would touch on the polity, the economy, the society, and the culture. Are three out of four still comprehensive enough to be "comprehensive"? I think so. Two out of four realms, however, appear to be insufficient to merit the label—or at least that is what common sense dictates to me. Appending the qualifier "more or less" to the modifier is perfectly valid so long as we tend, as a rule, to err on the side of more and not of less.

But revolution is not just comprehensive change. If it were, life would be revolution, insofar as change of some kind is always affecting politics, economy, society, and culture. It is, after all, a truism that nothing stands still. So we want to insist that the comprehensive change also be fundamental. And "fundamentalness," I suggest, refers to the depth of the change taking place within the political, economic, social, and cultural spheres. The most fundamental kind of change affects structures and institutions; less fundamental change relates to policies and behaviors; least fundamental, or perhaps not fundamental at all, is change affecting people and personnel. (Naturally, one could just as easily claim the opposite, on the ground that structures are human constructs and therefore epiphenomena.[23]) Thus change in government personnel is change, but it is not fundamental. A change in the very nature of the government—its regime and the institutions and structures that underlie it—is. So too a change in a society's class or ethnic structure would be fundamental, as would an overhaul of a value system or a transformation of the mode of production.

Must we also argue that the degree of fundamental change in each dimension of change—politics, economy, society, and culture—be the same? Indeed, must there be fundamental change in each category for revolution to be said to have occurred? It seems reasonable to soften the requirement, as we did with comprehensiveness, and to insist that "more or less" fundamental change occur in, say, at least three of the four dimensions. Thus a regime change (clearly fundamental), a "managerial revolution" (fairly fundamental), and a change in the system of social status (more or less fundamental) would probably suffice to make the whole package of change revolutionary. Inevitably, here as before, a large gray area consisting of instances of change will remain the source of dispute.[24]

There is, finally, the question of time. The last two hundred years have certainly witnessed comprehensive and fundamental change in every country of the world, but we would not want to say that these two centuries represent a revolution.[25] Clearly, we have to insert a temporal element into the calculation, and revolutions surely are things that occur "rapidly." But how rapid is rapidly? One year? Five years? One generation or two? And whose standards of rapidity do we use—our own or those of the society undergoing change? Perhaps what was rapid for medieval Christians would seem to take eons for contemporary Americans. On the other hand, Weiss's inmates may be asking for too much in demanding a complete overhaul of society "now." As I have already argued, scholars have no choice but to impose their own definitions on reality, so only they can determine what they mean by the modifiers they attach to nouns. Obviously, an appeal to common sense would not be inappropriate here. Anything that takes more than about five years—more or less—does not seem all that rapid, at least to me. Should varying degrees of fundamental and comprehensive change be rapid, revolution will be located in the top righthand corner of the grid that appears in figure 1.1.

The procedure to follow in identifying revolutions and revolutionaries is mindbogglingly simple and, for obvious reasons, does not involve asking the

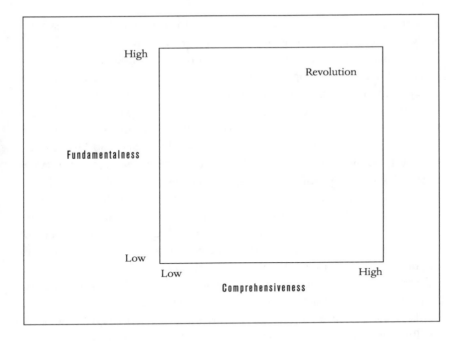

FIGURE I.I
Rapid Change and Revolution

latter for their opinions. Instead, wherever and whenever we find rapid, comprehensive, and fundamental change, we have identified a cluster of properties that make a revolution. There is no reason that we cannot term Mün-
ster's short-lived Melchiorite utopia in 1534–1535 as much an instance of
revolution as Stalin's Russia.[26] In both cases—here a city, there a country—
rapid, fundamental, and comprehensive change took place. By the same
token, if such change were to take place in an empire, we would be justified
in identifying a revolution there too.

In turn, whenever and wherever we encounter people who promote or
implement rapid, comprehensive, and fundamental change, we are in the
presence of revolutionaries. Such people may call themselves revolutionaries
or they may not; they may wear white shirts and silk ties and receive hefty
salaries or they may dress in army fatigues and live off the land; they may use
the terminology of revolution or they may not; they may, finally, consciously desire something called revolution or they may not. Che Guevara "looked"
like a revolutionary—are jauntily worn berets mandatory attire?—and he
may have lived and died for "the revolution," but as little reason exists to reify

his sartorial and terminological preferences as to agree with Ronald Reagan's acolytes that his fiscal policies amounted to a revolution.

Inasmuch as our concepts define revolutionaries, self-identification, sartorial inclinations, language, and intent are completely irrelevant to whether rapid, fundamental, and comprehensive change should be termed a revolution and someone promoting it a revolutionary. If the policies of change in, say, the postcommunist states involve rapidity, fundamentalness, and comprehensiveness, they must be termed revolutionary—no less revolutionary, I submit, than those of Stalin, Hitler, or Mao Zedong. By the same token, the proponents of such change, be they Helmut Kohl, Yegor Gaidar, or Vaclav Klaus, must be considered revolutionaries—revolutionaries *malgré soi*, perhaps, but revolutionaries nonetheless.[27] Two prominent "white-collar" revolutionaries endorse this point. According to Henry Kissinger, "If the definition of a revolution is fundamental change in the economic and political system . . . then what we are trying to engineer in some of these countries [such as Indonesia after the financial crisis of late 1997] is clearly a revolution."[28] And Jeffrey Sachs obviously realized that the title of his book, *Poland's Jump to the Market Economy*, and of its first chapter, "What Is To Be Done NOW?" were variations on well-known Maoist and Leninist themes.[29]

TYPES OF CHANGE

Let us compress fundamentalness and comprehensiveness into one dimension, "difference," and assign it to the x axis. If we then assign "time" to the y axis, we can locate different rates of change—and these are by no means the only ones that can be identified—as shown in figure 1.2.

Note two painfully obvious points. Systems, societies, and polities can change in many ways, and, a priori, we have no grounds for privileging one form of change over the others. As even a superficial reading of the historical record shows, most—and possibly all—systems have experienced the entire repertoire of change. Consider the United States. The American Revolution was, by the definitional standards proposed earlier, more of a transition. Most of the nineteenth century witnessed varying degrees of reform, whereas the period during and after the Civil War resembled a cross between a transition and a transformation.[30] Finally, the twentieth century experienced multiple reforms and transitions, occasionally amounting—as, perhaps, in the 1930s and 1960s—to transitions bordering on transformation. At

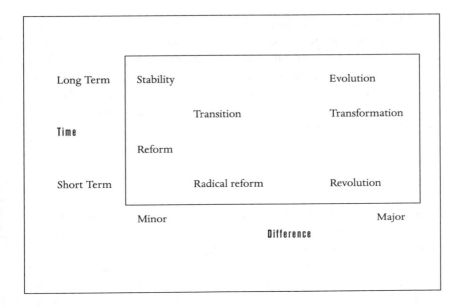

FIGURE I.2
Types of Change

no time, arguably, did the United States experience a genuine revolution, although none would, I think, deny its having "evolved" enormously—and positively—in the last two hundred years. In addition, the two most impressive Western-initiated systemic changes of the twentieth century, in post–World War II Germany and Japan, were not revolutions—indeed, Alfred Stepan consigns them only to the category of "externally monitored installations" of "redemocratization"—but transformations entailing less-than-rapid fundamental and comprehensive change.[31] In both countries the American and/or Allied authorities instituted a broad array of systemic changes—political, social, economic, and cultural—in the course of the occupation. Some changes, such as partial elite replacement, transpired rapidly, but most were only put into place legally and then permitted to run their course institutionally under the watchful eye of the occupiers.[32] East Germany, in contrast, *was* revolutionized by the Soviets.[33]

Although revolution is far more dramatic than reform or transition, there is no reason that, ceteris paribus, the repeated application of reforms or transitions should not, in the medium to long run, result in greater permanent change than revolution—which is simply to say that, although revolution may be the surest way to bring about major change quickly, it is not the only way to bring about major change. Nor is it necessarily true that rapid, fundamental, and comprehensive change is intrinsically superior to other forms of change even in the short run. Quite the contrary, a good case can be made that the costs of such change are so high as to be perhaps too high. As I argue in the thought experiment that follows, one such cost may be the abandonment of democracy, because, contrary to the conventional wisdom, revolution and democracy cannot go together.[34]

SQUARING CIRCLES

Because revolutions involve extremely high rates of change, as measured by the degree of difference attained over time, the rate of expenditure of "resources"—assumed for the time being to be uniform in character—required to sustain revolution is necessarily far greater than that needed to sustain reform, transition, or transformation. These three types of change may actually be as expensive, or perhaps even more expensive, than revolution in terms of the *total* expenditure of resources required, but revolution necessitates a far greater intensity of resource expenditure. Political elites that choose to embark on revolution must therefore be especially well endowed for their project to take off and succeed.

We know that resources are not uniform. Material resources involve providing or withdrawing instrumental incentives; coercive resources entail using violence and compulsion; normative resources involve appealing to patriotism and other values.[35] Determined revolutionaries will want to possess all three in abundance. Democratic revolutionaries, on the other hand, will have to be choosy. Presumably committed to heeding the voice of the people and promoting freedom, democrats will refrain from physical coercion, and they may downplay negative material sanctions as being coercive as well. Because material rewards and legitimacy will, ceteris paribus, form the core of their resource package, democratic revolutionaries must be unusually wealthy and popular in order to succeed at revolution, and their wealth and popularity must remain substantial for as long as some definitionally satisfactory combination of political, economic, social, and cultural structures, institutions, policies, and behaviors undergoes rapid change. Should something go wrong—Murphy's Law may offer sage guidance here—democratic revolutionaries will have to compensate with still greater resource expenditures. By the same token, should their legitimacy decline, their material resources will have to grow, and vice versa.

We do know, however, that no revolutionaries—even those in charge of states—come to revolution with endowments of fabulous resources. Nondemocratic revolutionaries may and do use coercion to acquire material and additional coercive resources. Democratic revolutionaries do not have this option. They either have to be wealthy and popular at the outset, or they have to acquire wealth and popularity in the course of the revolution. But note the paradox. Although well-endowed revolutionaries should have no difficulty adopting revolutionary paths, they will also have no reason to do so. Not only is their status exceptionally legitimate and solid but any society that could generate such elites cannot be in need of revolutionary change. Should such revolutionaries be foolhardy or fanatical enough to attempt to revolutionize it anyway, popular resistance would seem to be inevitable and successful popular resistance highly likely. If so, the democratic revolutionaries will have to choose between revolution and democracy.

What if the revolutionary democrats are less than fabulously wealthy and wondrously legitimate? Indeed, what if they are—like most revolutionary elites—only moderately endowed with resources and legitimacy? Doing their bidding will pay off, and therefore generate passionate followers and true believers, for a minority of the population at best. Why, then, should the rest of the people get on board? The spontaneous dynamic described by Timur Kuran does not apply, because there are, by definition, no sanctions for not joining a democratic cause presumably reflective of actual popular preferences.[36] Only additional material incentives and/or greater legitimacy can induce people to sign up. The former is unlikely to be forthcoming, as revolutionary change can only upset settled routines and produce at least temporary drops in economic efficiency and output. Although the latter will suffer as a result, it might be bolstered, temporarily at least, by self-legitimizing public relations efforts. But these too are not cost free. There seems, in sum, no reason to expect the relevant resource endowments of less than wealthy democratic revolutionaries to increase once the revolution has begun. What are our revolutionaries to do? Abandoning revolution is one option. The other is persisting despite inauspicious circumstances. Authoritarian methods of resource extraction then appear to be unavoidable.

Stephan Haggard and Robert Kaufman show that even "simultaneous economic and political liberalization"—and not full-fledged revolution—appears to be unsustainable for reasons similar to those I have just adduced. Discussing reform efforts in Nigeria and Mexico in the late 1980s and early 1990s, they conclude that these cases suggest that "the strategy of pursuing political and economic reforms simultaneously results in a highly unstable equilibrium, and that governments are likely to be pushed toward one of the other two stylized sequences" (viz., either democracy first or economic reform first).[37] In a similar vein, Leslie Armijo, Thomas Biersteker, and Abraham Lowenthal discuss the "incompatibility" of democratization and economic reform. Thus

> the democratizing politician may find the implications of economic liberalization particularly distressing owing to three structural characteristics of economic reforms. First, although adjustment's costs pinch immediately, its benefits lag. . . . Second, the costs of adjustment tend to be unevenly distributed. . . . Third, even those who are potential or even probable beneficiaries of reform are unlikely to realize it.

Last but not least, "just as democratization can undermine economic reform, the process of economic reform can turn crucial social actors against democratization: the unavoidable costs of economic reform are likely to lead to increasing political opposition from those who feel them most."[38] Finally, Dennis Quinn and John Woolley provide compelling indirect evidence for my argument. Using extensive empirical data, they show that a "democracy's performance will reflect *both* the risk aversion of its citizens *and* their desire for increased wealth. . . . The way in which democracies will differ from dictatorships is that democracies will seek either low volatility growth strategies or higher volatility strategies that are unusually well-compensated by higher rates of growth."[39] In a word, even if a case could be made for the theoretical compatibility of democracy and revolution, the empirical reality seems to be that democracies simply are *not* revolutionary.

STATES OF NATURE

For many contemporary revolutionaries, both in and out of office, the mismatch between goals and resources is a nonproblem, because democracy and the market do not have to be created and, least of all, imposed; they simply emerge. According to Sachs:

> The problem of reform is mostly political rather than social or even economic. Society accepts the need for change and is ready to slough off the brutality and artificiality of the communist system. This is especially the case when governments take care to provide targeted relief

for the most vulnerable groups in society. Many of the economic problems also solve themselves: markets spring up as soon as central planning bureaucrats vacate the field.[40]

John Mueller is just as emphatic:

> The transitional experience in many of the postcommunist countries
> and elsewhere suggests that democracy as a form of government and
> capitalism as an economic form are really quite simple, even natural,
> and, unless obstructed by thugs with guns, they can emerge quite eas-
> ily and quickly without any special development, prerequisites, or
> preparation. It seems to me that democracy is fundamentally about
> leaving people free to complain and that capitalism is fundamentally
> about leaving people free to be greedy. Either emotional quality, it
> seems, can be stifled easily, and neither is terribly difficult to inspire.[41]

Like run-of-the-mill revolutionaries, Sachs and Mueller address objections to
the revolutionary project by claiming that, because the goals of the revolution—in their case, the market and democracy—are "natural," the change
involved in attaining them is necessarily simple. The revolutionary problematic discussed by Otto Kirchheimer is defined out of existence, because, if
obstructionist forces are swept away, both the market and democracy simply
spring up. "Confining conditions" are impossible by definition because nothing
about the revolutionary project and its relationship to the real lives of real men
and women could possibly be construed as out of sync.[42] Other revolutionaries make the identical argument: human nature is such and such; a variety of
social, economic, or political forces deny it; and once the revolutionaries have
swept these forces away, nature will take its course. And if it does not, then, as
Daniel Cohn-Bendit and Gabriel Cohn-Bendit mused several decades ago, it
must be that "the workers . . . failed to seize their opportunity" because they
were "overwhelmed no doubt by the unexpected vistas that had suddenly
opened up before them."[43] In all such instances, as Dietrich Harth points out,
revolutionaries effectively hark back to the functional equivalent of a golden
age, a time, real or imagined, when the good things in life were in abundance
and thugs were absent.[44] "Man was born free," intoned Jean-Jacques Rousseau,
"but everywhere he is in chains." Why not, then, exert just the right amount of
"political will" to incline him to be what he is anyway—free?

   Although revolutionaries of all stripes are entitled to believe that their
goals, and only their goals, are natural, it is important to appreciate that, even

if they are right, *revolution* is anything but natural, except in the most trivial sense of the word, and it is certainly not simple. If anything, what I designate as evolution and stability are. As rapid, fundamental, and comprehensive change, revolution necessarily upends lives and—insofar as institutions presumably bring some regularity, order, and simplicity to life—revolution, by its very "nature," is antithetical to living normally, naturally, and simply.

No less important, we have no reason to believe the modern revolutionary's argument that the market and democracy are natural. Putting aside that the very question is more normative than empirical, the case for naturalness presupposes definitions of both—leaving people free to complain and be greedy—that are grossly inadequate. At best, such conceptualizations apply to all nontotalitarian forms of life and thus are too expansive to be useful; at worst, they are misleading distortions of the historical record that, in suggesting that it all boils down to emotional qualities, deny history, institutions, culture, structures, and just about everything else.[45] If the case for naturalness presupposes this much confusion, we might be well advised to opt for simplicity.

chapter 2. revolutionary bets

If, as I argued in the introduction, the social sciences necessarily are theoretically pluralist undertakings, particular theoretical approaches or paradigms will characterize schools of thought, or communities of scholars who share certain assumptions and concepts. Some schools may be better than others, some may be worse, but, a priori, nothing about schools qua schools suggests which are which.

Revealingly, Jack Goldstone at one time distinguished among three "generations"—and not schools—of scholars studying revolution. The first, typified by the work of Crane Brinton, Lyford P. Edwards, and others, had a morphological focus and attempted to trace the "natural history" of revolutions.[1] The second, the exemplars of which were Chalmers Johnson, Ted Robert Gurr, and Samuel Huntington, focused on the behavioral determinants of revolution.[2] The third, represented by Theda Skocpol, Ellen Trimberger, Jeffrey Paige, Barrington Moore, S. N. Eisenstadt, and Goldstone himself, saw the causes of revolution as historical and structural.[3] The "new points of analytic emphasis" for third generation theorists were, according to Goldstone,

> 1) the variable goals and structures of states; 2) the systematic intrusion, over time, of international political and economic pressures on the domestic political and economic organization of societies; 3) the structure of peasant communities; 4) the coherence or weakness of the armed forces; and 5) the variables affecting elite behavior.[4]

Because most third-generation scholars would probably agree that Skocpol's *States and Social Revolutions* exemplifies their approach, analyzing her concepts critically is an excellent way of addressing their concerns (and of puncturing their hubris). More important, it will permit us to get at the very essence of, and thereby evaluate, the revolutionary project itself. That a fourth generation appears to have emerged in recent years—such scholars as William H. Sewell Jr., Said Amir Arjomand, Ronald Suny, and the later Goldstone, who are concerned with integrating culture, ideology, and discourse with structure—may have obvious and not unwelcome implications for the third generation's conceptions of uniqueness and self-worth but will not, as we shall see, affect the raison d'être of this exercise.[5]

JANUS-FACED STATES

Skocpol calls her theoretical approach "structural."[6] Central to that project is the interaction between horizontal and vertical relationships, or structures, and how it brings about revolution. The first set of structures refers to interstate relationships, which Skocpol, like most International Relations (IR) theorists, takes to be conflictual inasmuch as they involve sovereign states in an anarchic world. The second refers to relationships between and among classes, and these too Skocpol—now arguing in the Marxist mode—takes to be conflictual.[7] Her central task is to connect both structures in a manner that does not hinge on human volition.

Skocpol purports to pull this trick off by means of the "state," which she insists is "Janus-faced." She defines the state in Weberian terms as a set of "administrative, policing, and military organizations headed, and more or less well coordinated by, an executive authority" and claims that states interact in classic IR fashion.[8] This proposition appears at first glance to make intuitive sense. We know from experience that internal and external factors interact somehow, and we know from IR theory that various ways of theoretically expressing this interaction exist.[9] Skocpol's innovation is to use the state as a device for translating truth claims about external politics into truth claims about internal politics, and vice versa. Such a maneuver necessitates that the term, *state*, have one meaning and that Skocpol use it uniformly in both sets of truth claims. But this she signally fails to do. Instead, her state designates two entirely different concepts. The Weberian state is a set of domestic institutions involved in the administration, exploitation, and policing of a territory. The state of IR theory is really a shorthand designation for the elite, the government, or state officials. Elements of the Weberian state may make policy decisions; in contrast, the entire IR state makes such decisions.[10] Briefly, Skocpol's solution of the internal-external problematic is purely assertive—embracing and not resolving the conceptual contradictions on which it rests.

Having landed in such a muddle, Skocpol proposes a dialectical exit by means of "potential autonomy," a mysterious quality that enables the class-dominated state to rise above its limitations and act as if it were an international relations elite.[11] The implied logic is as follows. Were the state not at all autonomous, it would possess no capacity to rise above the interests of the dominant class. Were it completely autonomous, Skocpol's insistence on the importance of class structure would be irrelevant. Were it relatively autonomous, we would not expect the state ever to overstep the bounds—however large or small—of its relative autonomy, because relative autonomy implies as much consistency in state behavior as complete autonomy or no autonomy.[12] The potentially autonomous state, however, purports to partake of international relationships *and* seems to be grounded in class relations as well. Ostensibly, its autonomy is sufficiently autonomous to involve the state in international structures as well as sufficiently potential to root it in class structures.

Skocpol's contrivance might have worked had the state endowed with autonomy been one entity and not two. Instead, potential autonomy only papers over the contradiction between the two sides of Skocpol's Janus-faced state. The Weberian state is enmeshed in class relations and may have the potential to be autonomous in appropriate circumstances, but the IR state is by definition always autonomous on the world stage. In essence, each of Skocpol's states enjoys a different kind of autonomy as well as a different degree thereof. An obvious solution would be to choose between the state as elite and the state as political organization, an approach Skocpol understandably eschews. As either of these alternatives, the state could be imagined as potentially autonomous. The elite state could "change its mind"; the organization state could have a set of coherent interests that might on occasion require resolute self-assertion. A state that is both, however, can only resist a systematic, intersubjective understanding.

Because the conceptual chasm between these disparate concepts of the state is bridged in a theoretically regressive manner, Skocpol's theory of revolution suffers severe damage.[13] Recall that revolution, according to Skocpol, presumably occurs after states are weakened by international crises such as wars and when peasants exploit state weakness to engage in upheavals. But which state suffers harm in the international arena? Although the IR state involves the country in war, only one component of the Weberian state, the military, loses it. Because we have no obvious reason to expect the government, bureaucracy, or police to be equally debilitated, peasants have no reason necessarily to rebel.[14]

Although Skocpol's potentially autonomous state does little to enhance her theory, it does—as we would expect from a cat-dog—fulfill a useful narrative function. An independent variable of such unpredictable nature transforms the theory into an act-by-act recounting of when and how potential autonomy manifested itself and of the enormous impact such an uncovering must have had for class and international relations. But a potentially autonomous state is also the ideal literary hero. Though bound to the dominant class structure, the state rises up from time to time and attempts to transcend its limitations, only to collapse tragically, exhausted by its noble exertions. Like Hegel's world historical personality, Skocpol's potentially autonomous state can do virtually everything, but only its creator, Skocpol herself, can ever divine it.[15]

FUZZY REVOLUTIONS

As I noted in the introduction, there are at least two cardinal rules to follow in defining concepts. The first is that definitions should not be causal statements. The second, which is shockingly commonsensical, is that one's use of concepts should be consistent throughout a text. Skocpol violates both rules. Her definition of revolution is worth citing in full: "Social revolutions are rapid, basic transformations of a society's state and class structures; and they are accompanied and in part carried through by class based revolts from below."[16] Because the definition contains within itself a causal proposition—namely, that the great changes she has in mind are brought about by class upheaval—Skocpol has built her theory into the definition. If we accept the validity of the latter, we are forced to accept the former. Inevitably, scholars who proceed on the basis of Skocpol's definition of revolution have little to do but illustrate what she already knows.[17]

Consider also the radically different ways in which Skocpol uses *revolution*. At times, the term connotes transformation or change; at other times, it is meant to stand for some notion of popular upheaval; at still other times, Skocpol suggests that revolutions and crises are the same, that revolutions are merely enormous problems and challenges.[18] We need look no further than her preface for ample illustrations of this confusion. Skocpol first refers to "revolutionary crises" on p. xi. Two sentences later she notes that "revolutions themselves are traced from the original outbreaks through to the consolidation of relatively stable and distinctively structured New Regimes" in the book.[19] Then consider the first two sentences of chapter 1: "Social revolutions have been rare but momentous occurrences in modern world history. From France in the 1790s to Vietnam in the mid-twentieth century, these revolutions have transformed state organizations, class structures, and *dominant ideologies*" (emphasis added).[20] One page later we learn that revolutions are "rapid, basic transformations of a society's state and class structures" *only* and that they are "set apart from other sorts of conflicts and transformative processes above all by the combination of two coincidences: the coincidence of societal structural change with class upheaval; and the coincidence of political with social transformation."[21]

Not only are we told that state structures are organizations—and not, like structures in general, relationships—but we also discover that revolutions can be crises, outbreaks, processes, occurrences with transformative consequences, transformations, and, last but not least, coincidences, which is to say, all of the above. So casual an approach to conceptual clarity surely will not do. We have no way to determine what Skocpol means by revolution and thus no way to evaluate whether her theory is sensible. Indeed, confronted with such a barrage of connotations, we can only conclude that revolution for Skocpol is merely a code word for a Very Big Thing.

In light of such exorbitant ambiguity, it is hardly surprising that *States and Social Revolutions* should suffer from conceptual vagueness—even though the set of referents to which her concept of social revolution applies is small, containing only the French, Chinese, and Russian cases. Once again, the very first page of the book reveals the problem in its most acute form. Skocpol says that the book focuses on "the French Revolution of 1787–1800, the Russian Revolution of 1917–1921, and the Chinese Revolution of 1911–1949." At the bottom of the page she notes that "revolutions themselves are traced from the original outbreaks through to the consolidation of relatively stable and distinctively structured New Regimes: the Napoleonic in France, the Stalinist in Russia, and the characteristically Sino-Communist (after the mid-1950s) in China."[22] Are we to conclude that the Russian Revolution ended in 1921 or sometime in the 1930s, when Stalinism established itself as a distinctive new regime? Did the Chinese Revolution end in 1949 or in the mid-1950s? Skocpol's emphasis on transformation suggests that the latter dates are appropriate. Her preference for revolution as upheaval suggests that the former dates better capture the reality. Either choice is fine, but to opt for both is inadmissible.

CAUSES AND COINCIDENCES

As I noted earlier, Skocpol explicitly suggests that revolution is a coincidence: upheavals and changes must and do go together during revolutions. Indeed, the going together of these phenomena is what marks a revolution. Such a mode of analysis must meet at least two challenges. The first is that the simultaneous occurrence of peasant upheavals and rapid, fundamental, and comprehensive change appears never to have taken place in history. Upheavals, after all, are frequent; rapid, fundamental, and comprehensive changes are, as Skocpol implies, rare. The number of such revolutionary changes that were also accompanied, from beginning to end, by peasant upheavals may be zero.

Moreover, common sense suggests that occurrences are relatively brief phenomena; upheavals—like revolts, uprisings, and the like—have distinct beginnings and ends, and they generally do not last for more than several months. Indeed, we would be correct to suspect that an upheaval purporting to last much longer—the Palestinian intifada was a case in point—is really a series of upheavals. In contrast to upheavals, revolutionary changes of class and state structures are not occurrences or events but outcomes of processes or of a series of events.[23] Although occurrences can take place during processes, they cannot logically be the points at which processes culminate in genuine change. No less problematic is that both upheavals and revolutionary changes cannot possibly begin at the same time, if only because Skocpol seems to believe that upheavals are among the causes of revolution. Skocpol's inability to set the chronological bounds of two of her revolutions illustrates this point. Even if we assume that upheavals took place in 1917–1921 in Russia and in 1911–1949 in China (can an upheaval last thirty-eight years?), they were obviously not simultaneous with the changes that culminated in the mid-1930s and the mid-1950s.

If finding any instances of the coincidence of upheavals with revolutionary changes is logically and empirically impossible, Skocpol's definition of revolution as coincidence presents her with a task that is, ipso facto, equally impossible. But even if we assume that such coincidences could be found, explaining them entails a project quite different from that which Skocpol embarks upon. The goal of such a theory should then be to explain not why outbreaks erupted or why change occurred at any particular time but why outbreaks and such fundamental change occurred simultaneously and not sequentially. To argue, as Skocpol does, that a "mutually reinforcing" influence exists between upheavals and change is not useful, because it assumes that the task at hand is to show how both elements cause or facilitate each other. But a coincidence perspective is not interested in the relationship between outbreaks and change; it is solely interested in the simultaneity of their occurrence.

We may state the problem in shorthand notation in the following manner. If U stands for upheaval, C for change, u for the cause of U, c for the cause of C, and z for the cause of the simultaneous occurrence of U and C ($U + C$), from a coincidence perspective Skocpol's task is to find the z that explains $U + C$, such that $z \neq u$ and $z \neq c$. From a sequential perspective Skocpol would have to find, say, the u that causes U, which in turn acts as the c that causes C. In other words, a coincidence approach may be summarized as follows: $z : U + C$, whereas a sequence approach looks like this: $u : U : C$. Finding z is an enormously difficult task, if only because we must initially assume that $z \neq u$. Eventually we may indeed determine that $z = u$, but to make such an assumption at the outset leads only to circularity.

Skocpol does not distinguish between these two approaches. Instead, by conflating them she can search for u and then claim that it is z, without ever having made an effort to discover z on its own terms. Naturally, this strategy only restates the question Skocpol claims to have answered. As a result, what we get from Skocpol is, as I have noted, not explanation—after all, we learn neither of u nor of z—but mere description, in other words, a narrative retelling of U and C. In this sense Skocpol's theory of social revolutions is a throwback to natural history—which also means that the third generation is really the first generation redux—not because structural theories are necessarily unviable but because conceptual incoherence produces historical narrative at best and nontheory at worst.[24]

REVOLUTIONARY THEORY

Skocpol's theoretical failings point to a larger, and far more important, question asked by Nikki Keddie: "Can revolutions be predicted?" Keddie's answer is no.[25] History consists, or so she claims, of contingencies and conjunctions that by their very nature cannot be captured by a theory in general and a predictive theory in particular. Goldstone answers yes, erroneously proffering his theory as proof thereof.[26] As I argue later, Keddie's answer is correct but for reasons involving not so much the nature of history as the limitations of revolutionary theory.

The question of predictability may be important to students of revolution, but, as Lenin fully appreciated, it is absolutely vital to makers of revolution.[27] Revolutionaries cannot just interpret the world, describe it, explore its intertextuality, or delight in its representations, imaginings, and the like, as such endeavors offer them no guidance in their enormous undertakings. *Verstehen* says nothing about when, how, and whether the revolutionary project can succeed or fail. Nor can revolutionaries merely argue that revolutions as a class are more likely to occur in certain circumstances, because such an inexact claim would have little utility for their immensely complicated labors in particular settings. As makers of revolution, revolutionaries must make predictions, because, given the complexity and difficulty of revolution as well as the dangers associated with failure, to do anything less would be foolhardy. Because a revolutionary prediction amounts to the claim that a particular revolution *must* come about as a result of certain causes, forces, or other circumstances, revolutionary theory—as the generalized theory explicitly formulated by individuals and groups committed to, and believing in the inevitability and desirability of, rapid, fundamental, and comprehensive change here and now—can but make extremely strong predictions about individual events. Were revolution a bet, it would have to be a sure bet, better by far than Pascal's wager.

Revolutionaries differ on what the prime mover of revolution is, just as they differ on what kind of revolution is imperative. Marxists insist that material forces in general, and capitalism in particular, must lead to revolution. Leninists and Nazis claim that only a revolutionary vanguard can do the trick.[28] Free-marketeers believe that the market has profoundly transformative powers. Some claim that only socialist revolution is genuinely revolutionary and that all other "revolutions" are actually counterrevolutionary.[29] Others turn the tables and call capitalist revolution authentic and socialist revolution inauthentic. We do not have to take sides in these debates. The important point is that the structure of these arguments is identical, that the claims are identical, and therefore that they can all be considered manifestations of a larger category, revolutionary theory (RT). In this sense expert revolutionaries are little different from experts on revolution. Revolutionaries have revolutionary theories, whereas scholars have theories of revolution, but the two are obviously similar. An iron-clad theory of revolution should be the best revolutionary theory possible, in that its capacity to explain and predict would translate into a capacity to implement or prevent.[30]

As a predictive enterprise, revolutionary theory aspires to grand episte-mological heights and deserves to be judged by the standards of its propo-nents' choosing. If so, revolutionary theory fails. It cannot, as I show shortly, claim to be historicist, and it falls far short of inductive and deductive pre-tensions. Except for blind faith, no other ground for claiming such strong pre-dictive powers exists. That faith can move mountains and motivate individu-als to accept enormous sacrifice and undertake grand projects goes without saying. That faith can also, under certain conditions, be an unalloyed good may also be true. I do not dispute the heroism or perhaps even necessity of saints. Whether faith alone can deliver on its *secular* promises, however, and whether nonbelievers should believe simply because believers say so—these are the views that I dispute.

HISTORICISM AND INDUCTION

If revolutionary theory grounds its predictive pretensions in its alleged dis-covery of the laws of history, it opens itself to Karl Popper's devastating cri-tique of historicism. As Popper sees it, historicists believe that history unfolds according to an intrinsic evolutionary logic, that this logic moves societies forward inexorably, and that it can be discovered. "But can there be a *law* of evolution?" asks Popper. His answer is worth citing at length:

> I believe that the answer to this question must be "No," and that the search for the law of the "unvarying order" in evolution cannot possibly fall within the scope of scientific method, whether in biology or in soci-ology. My reasons are very simple. The evolution of life on earth, or of human society, is a unique historical process. Such a process, we may as-sume, proceeds in accordance with all kinds of causal laws, for example, the laws of mechanics, of chemistry, of heredity and segregation, of natural selection, etc. Its description, however, is not a law, but only a singular historical statement. Universal laws make assertions concerning some unvarying order, as Huxley puts it, i.e. concerning all processes of a certain kind; and although there is no reason why the observation of one single instance should not incite us to formulate a universal law, nor why, if we are lucky, we should not even hit upon the truth, it is clear that any law, formulated in this or in any other way, must be *tested* by new instances before it can be taken seriously by science. But we cannot

hope to test a universal hypothesis nor to find a natural law acceptable to science if we are forever confined to the observation of one unique process. Nor can the observation of one unique process help us to foresee its future development.[31]

Popper's argument rests on the view that natural laws can be formulated only on the basis of extensive inductive experience—a point I pursue later—and subsequent testing. And we cannot repeat or test what is historically unique. In turn, Arthur Danto suggests that the very notion of an overarching historical truth is logically unsustainable:

Substantive philosophy of history is a misconceived activity, and rests upon a basic mistake. It is a mistake . . . to suppose that we can write the history of events before the events themselves have happened. . . . Historians describe some past events with reference to other events which are future to them, but past to the historian, while philosophers of history describe certain past events with reference to other events which are future both to these events and to the historian himself. And I wish to maintain that we cannot enjoy a cognitive standpoint which makes such an activity feasible.[32]

In other words, historians may and do interpret the past in terms of its future—both of which are in *their* past—but they have no way, as historians, to interpret their own past or present in terms of a future that has not yet materialized.

If revolutionaries retreat from such grand historicist claims, they might opt for grounding their predictive claims in induction. Here too however, RT's shortcomings are, as Popper has already suggested, equally egregious. Popper famously disputes the very possibility of making any kind of inductively grounded predictive claim; other philosophers of science disagree.[33] Regardless of who is right, both sides in the debate presuppose a large N for induction even to be an issue. The problem for revolutionary theory, however, is that the number of revolutions encountered in history, regardless of what definition one uses, is small. The great revolutions are arguably only three in number—France in 1789, Russia in 1917, and China after 1949. Using a broader definition conveniently couched in fuzzy terminology, Charles Tilly finds somewhere between thirty and fifty since the fifteenth century.[34] Whatever the number—three, fifty, or something in-between—it is far too small for us to claim that we know, on the basis of experience, that revolutions come about for certain reasons. And if we cannot plausibly claim to know this, we would be foolhardy to risk staking our future on what amounts to a mere hunch, not a sure bet.

DEDUCTIVE-NOMOLOGICAL APPROACHES

According to Carl Hempel, deductive-nomological (D-N) explanations have the following components: the *explanans*, consisting of a covering law of the "If $F(x)$, then $G(x)$" variety and a set of initial conditions, *a*, *b*, and *c*; and the *explanandum*, which results from deducing $G(y)$ from the covering law acting upon *y* under conditions *a*, *b*, and *c*. Deductive-nomological explanations thus claim to be able to derive some outcome, contained in the third component, invariably and inevitably from certain premises contained in the first and second components. In this sense, as Hempel and others have noted, to explain is to predict and to predict is to explain.[35]

My critique of revolutionary theory as a D-N project will not address the criticisms leveled at the Hempelian model. Suffice to say that, as Wesley Salmon has shown, massive criticism has been exercised, substantive parts of the model have withered under the attack, significant alternatives and/ or revisions have been proposed, and the field of philosophy of science is divided into a variety of schools, some supportive of modified Hempelian accounts and others, if not most, critical of the D-N model.[36] Clearly, if the D-N model is flawed, revolutionary theory must, as a D-N project, also be flawed.

Instead, I maintain that revolutionary theory does not have, and cannot have, a covering law to justify its explanatory claims.[37] The first—and weaker—part of my claim flows from the discussion of RT as an inductive enterprise. Familiarity with the scholarly literature on revolutions shows that no natural law of the "If $F(x)$, then $G(x)$" form exists, where $G(x)$ stands for revolution. To be sure, a variety of theories is available, as are even more hunches, suppositions, and collections of conventional wisdom and common sense. But none of these accounts, or all of them in their entirety, even approaches the status of a natural law. Indeed, the existence of so many competing and often contradictory accounts of revolution is sufficient proof that a covering law, even if it could exist, does not yet exist in the writings of revolutionaries and scholars studying revolution.

My second claim is far stronger, suggesting that a covering law concerning revolution could not exist.[38] If a law is a regular and stable conjunction of two objects or events, can there be a law involving revolution as one of the objects or events? To put the question in this manner is partially to answer it. The things that are conjoined in laws may or may not have to be empirically observable—the question of observability is one that we do not, fortunately, have to address—but they are supposed to be universally agreed-upon categories. Scientists no longer debate what atoms are, what energy is, what electricity and magnetism are, and so on. They may have, at some earlier time in the development of science, when none of these entities would have figured in laws anyway.

In contrast to these entities, revolution, as I have already demonstrated, is far more difficult to grasp. We can make a case for this definition or that one, but language itself, the etymology of the term, and the diversity of interests of scholars and practitioners will always produce conceptual pluralism, if not actual confusion.[39] But if scholars cannot, even in principle, agree on the conceptual boundaries and corresponding empirical referent of revolution, it follows that any hope of constructing a law involving revolution must fail. We might be able to construct lawlike contenders for each plausible definition of revolution, such as those suggested in chapter 1. It may be possible to argue that revolution as change is caused by X, revolution as upheaval by Y, and revolution as turmoil by Z. But even if such rare unanimity could be achieved, we would have succeeded in producing lawlike generalizations for three different entities or events and not for revolution per se. And that is because there is no such thing as revolution per se.

These same considerations also preclude the possibility of specifying the initial conditions of a revolutionary theory. After all, initial conditions cannot be pinned down until the explanandum is pinned down. But the impossibility of providing one, and only one, list of defining characteristics translates into the impossibility of producing a set of universally accepted criteria for settling problems of extension and intension. Even if scholars and revolutionaries could agree that revolution is rapid, fundamental, and comprehensive change, they would still disagree on what precisely those terms mean, where cutoff points should be located, and where boundaries should be drawn. How rapid is rapid? Who is to stipulate that five years is rapid and that six is not? Who is to stipulate that fundamentalness involves all the dimensions of a sphere of life and not just most, or perhaps even some? And finally, who is to stipulate that comprehensiveness must relate to politics, economy, society, and culture and not to some other combination? My suggestion was to append "more or less" to each of these boundary issues, but, although not useless, this solution clearly is partial.[40]

Even if we could somehow overcome this deficiency, we would still be in hot water. Because revolution involves an enormous systemic transformation, it necessarily entails change along a broad range of dimensions, some of which relate to the intended changes, whereas others do not. As a result, revolution is an undertaking that is pursued under constantly shifting initial conditions. But if initial conditions are indeterminate, a deductive theory of revolution—even assuming that a covering law existed—is impossible. Andreas Pickel and Helmut Wiesenthal make just this point in arguing for the impossibility of the "grand experiment" pursued by the Bonn authorities in the newly acquired eastern provinces of the former German Democratic Republic.[41]

THE STRUCTURE OF REVOLUTIONARY THEORY

But let us yet again assume otherwise—either that such a covering law and such initial conditions exist or that their existence is somehow unnecessary to the theoretical task at hand. In other words, let us, in the spirit of the revolutionary endeavor, leave these issues behind and look only at the actual theoretical claims that RT makes. Revolutionary theory insists that some factor X (inevitably, inexorably, inescapably) brings about R, where R stands for a particular revolution. We need not deal with the terms in parentheses, because these were the subject of the previous discussion. My task in this section is to examine the $X : R$ relationship in greater detail.

Let us also assume that the issue of extensional and intensional criteria and boundaries has been resolved satisfactorily. If so, revolution consists of at least three of four dimensions (society, culture, politics, economy), each of which possesses characteristics of varying degrees of fundamentalness, ranging from minimal (if it involves merely people) to maximal (if it involves structures or institutions). A revolutionary theory therefore argues that $X : R$ translates into $X : (A,B,C)$, where (A,B,C) stands for the cluster of comprehensive dimensions affected fundamentally. $X : (A,B,C)$ may mean one of two things, either $X : A : B : C$ or $X : A, X : B, X : C$. (The order of the variables is immaterial to the argument.) In the first instance, $X : A : B : C$, one covering law cannot account for a causal chain involving different combinations of causes and effects. If so, $X : A : B : C$ cannot hold, even if, as I assumed, the problem of covering law and initial conditions was assumed not to exist.

In the second instance, $X : A, X : B, X : C$, we are, in effect, in the presence of a "theory of everything," one purportedly capable of explaining *all of life*.[42] And life, I emphasize, is exactly what is at issue here, inasmuch as fundamental change in *A*, *B*, and *C* affects everything, that is to say, life. At this point two equally fundamental problems confront us. First, it is hard to imagine what the natural law covering a theory of everything could be. Indeed, one would expect the theory of everything to function as the covering law for the law supposedly covering it! And second, it is impossible to imagine what the initial conditions of such a theory could be, because they would necessarily have to be included in the explanandum, which is everything, and thus could not logically be separated from it.

GAMBLING LOSSES

If revolutionary theory cannot be predictive, theories of revolution must be equally deficient.[43] But this means that theories of revolution can at most be probabilistic in a very weak and inexact way, at most able to identify only the factor or factors that make possible and facilitate, but not determine, the occurrence of revolutionary change. Probabilistic social science theories cannot, in the manner of probabilistic natural science theories, pinpoint the degree of probability involved. All we can do is resort to that convenient phrase, "more or less."

As the search for *the* explanatory theory of revolution is illusory, revolutionaries—as well as scholars of revolution—would do well to heed Jürgen Habermas's proposition that "it is not the philosophers who can change the world" and to abandon their epistemological hubris.[44] "What is the best strategy for transforming a socialist economy into a market economy? The simple answer is," according to Pickel, "we do not know."[45] Because we have no reason whatsoever for accepting the claims of revolutionaries, be they of the self-styled or the malgré soi variety—they cannot, even in principle, deliver on their promises—the revolutionary option amounts to betting all of one's life chances on a miserable nag. A sliver of a chance of winning exists, but surely, in light of the magnitude of virtually certain loss, such a bet would be the height of folly, even for proletarians who own little more than their chains. If I am right, reformers, no matter how unimaginative and unspectacular, may *always* be preferable to revolutionaries—not because they are reformers and thus likely to be right but because they are not utopians and thus doomed to be wrong.

chapter 3. revolutionary losses

If revolutionary theory cannot predict revolution, if it cannot claim to have isolated successfully the causes or conditions that necessarily lead to revolution, revolutionary theory cannot be a useful guide to change. (It may of course serve other functions, such as mobilizing constituencies around a myth, maintaining the hegemony of the "ruling class," or sustaining cadre discipline, be it that of a movement, class, or society.[1]) If so, revolutionaries pursuing explicitly revolutionary policies are necessarily doomed to failure: that is, to the nonattainment of the intended change.

And yet we know that, although the revolutions desired and pursued by revolutionaries evidently are not possible, revolution clearly is—there are, after all, historical examples of rapid, fundamental, and comprehensive systemic change. How, then, can revolution, which does take place, ever occur? Revolution might be the result of a chance conjuncture of historical events that are utterly unrelated to the efforts of revolutionaries or, for that matter, of anybody else. In this sense revolutions would be like asteroids—exogenous intrusions that no theory could explain in terms of the system into which they suddenly crash. That revolutions frequently follow on the heels of war lends credence to this view.[2] Wars destroy, upend, and transform structures, institutions, policies, behaviors, and people. In so doing, wars effectively promote revolutionary change within a country, even though, from a neorealist theoretical perspective at least, they are the product of interactions taking place at the world system level.[3]

Second, that revolutionaries cannot bring about the consequences they intend does not mean that their efforts cannot result in rapid, fundamental, and comprehensive change—but of a different, unintended kind. We know from Anthony Giddens that people can and do affect structures, institutions, organizations, and cultures all the time, and we suspect that, if their resources are sufficiently large, they can bring about substantial, perhaps even revolutionary change as well.[4] But because the consequences of their revolutionary efforts will always be unpredictable, the revolution that does occur will not be the one they intended. Recall the poor Bolsheviks, who witnessed the transformation, rapidly, fundamentally, and comprehensively, of Russia, only to realize in 1921 that they were drowning in a sea of hostile peasantry.

It stands to reason that revolutionary attempts from above and from outside should be most likely to bring about genuinely revolutionary—albeit unintended—change, inasmuch as elite revolutionaries will have at their disposal the not insignificant resources of the state. Hitler, Ataturk, and Stalin significantly changed—and perhaps revolutionized—Germany, Turkey, and the USSR, even though they expressly failed to launch the new ages their programs had envisioned. Nazi Germany became egalitarian in spirit and not, as David Schoenbaum has pointed out, in reality; big business remained beyond the state's totalizing ambitions and control.[5] Although secular institutions undermined the power of the clergy in the 1920s, Kemalist Turkey fell under the influence of conservative classes by the 1930s.[6] The Soviet Union rapidly became, as Trotskyites used to call it, a "degenerate workers' state."[7]

Revolutions from outside, which involve the full-scale intrusion of one state into the affairs of another, should be even more likely to bring about rapid, fundamental, and comprehensive change, especially if war is involved. Nazi Germany thoroughly transformed the occupied territories in Eastern Europe but failed to produce a spacious lebensraum populated by slavishly obedient *Untermenschen* serving the herrenvolk. The USSR occupied the lands already devastated by the Nazis, quickly imposed communist structures, institutions, policies, behaviors, and personnel, but failed to create efficient, effective, and legitimate socialist societies within which the proletariat ruled.[8] Most significant perhaps is the inability even of democratic revolutionaries committed to such ostensibly natural goals as democracy and the market to implement their intended changes in eastern Germany. Helmut Kohl's effectively revolutionary stewardship failed to make the former German Democratic Republic into a modern, market-oriented democracy, despite West Germany's annexing the *Ostländer*, occupying them militarily, purging their elites, imposing its own legal system, and investing $100 to 150 billion annually after the *Wende* (change).[9] Indeed, Daniela Dahn nicely illustrates how, almost a decade after reunification, self-styled Ossis still confronted self-styled Wessis, and the *Ost*, although the product of genuinely revolutionary change, remained markedly different from, and not integrated into, the *West*.[10] Andreas Pickel is even harsher in his assessment: "Rapid and comprehensive reform has not created the conditions for self-sustained economic development, as had been expected. Instead, it has led to the collapse of the East German economy, 'freed' almost half the workforce, and created lasting structural damage."[11] All this may amount to revolution but, clearly, not to Kohl's intended revolution.

FAUX REVOLUTION

Although Western policy makers and scholars have consistently expressed a preferential option for what amounts to revolutionary change in the postcommunist states, their expectations have frequently rested on conceptual confusion. Revolutionary rhetoric notwithstanding, revolution from within has taken place in no formerly communist state, whereas attempted revolution has occurred only in Russia. Instead, postcommunist elites have generally pursued state consolidation and nation building, many have cultivated civil society, only some have transformed their economies, and few can be said to have established democratic regimes and rule of law.[12]

According to the definitions proposed in chapter 1, Poland, Hungary, the Czech Republic, Slovenia, and Estonia have not, contrary to conventional wisdom, experienced revolution but something akin to radical reform, transition, or transformation. Indeed, they could not have undergone revolution, because in 1989–1991 they already possessed many of the defining characteristics of noncommunist societies: coherent state apparatuses, competent elites, incipient civil societies, vibrant political cultures and national identities, and, most important, significant political contestation and protomarket behavior. These attributes of "normality" permitted them to confine "shock therapy" to a relatively narrow range of economic activities that were comfortably nested in more or less functioning institutional frameworks. The bangs that went off in most of these countries were therefore quite small, whereas the therapy that was applied was limited to a few malfunctioning features of otherwise not unhealthy organisms. In stark contrast, most post-Soviet states emerged from seventy years of communism with few, if any, institutions that characterize states, markets, civil societies, rule of law, democracy, and nationhood.[13] Constructing all these institutions simultaneously, and ex nihilo, would have required a systemic Big Bang of mind-boggling proportions. Anders Aslund's advice—"the paramount task of the new, noncommunist leadership was to build a democratic state as simply and quickly as possible"—betrays a fundamental underappreciation of this fundamental fact.[14] Building a "democratic state"—that is, building both a democracy and a state—cannot ever be accomplished "simply and quickly," especially in the virtually complete absence of democratic and state institutions.

Unlike Russia, Ukraine, Romania, Albania, and most Soviet successor states, therefore, the privileged east-central European countries did not have to undergo as much change in order to approximate rule-of-law states and democratic, market-oriented civil societies.[15] Whereas the former would have had to experience genuine revolution in order to attain these goals, the latter did not: in their case, lesser forms of change, even if called velvet revolutions, self-limiting revolutions, and the like, would have sufficed and did suffice. As Marshall Goldman puts it, "The purposeful attack on market institutions for over seventy years in most of the former Soviet Union meant that those countries began the transition process a full stage of development behind most of eastern Europe. A completely new institutional, legal, and competitive framework has to be reinvented before healthy growth can be expected."[16] Poland and its central European neighbors proved not that revolutionary change could work—if only self-interested policy makers acted with vision and courage—but, quite the contrary, that reform, transition, and transformation could succeed if they followed in the wake of a long series of protracted institutional reforms stretching back several decades.[17]

Marshall Tito adopted self-management and "market socialism" soon after Yugoslavia's break with the Soviet Union. The aftermath of the Croatian crisis of the early 1970s witnessed still greater economic and political devolution, of which Slovenia and Croatia were the longer-term beneficiaries. Poland enjoyed private agriculture since 1956 and a private service sector since the 1970s; it also had a societal counterhegemon in the Catholic Church and, after 1980–1981, in Solidarity. Hungary's Janos Kadar introduced a significant degree of political tolerance after the rebellion of 1956 and, equally important, a variety of market-oriented measures known as the New Economic Mechanism in 1968. Estonia—and, to a lesser degree, Latvia—served as a laboratory for Soviet experiments in economic liberalization since the 1960s while also enjoying significant exposure to noncommunist ideas via television and "vodka tourists" from Finland.[18]

Interestingly, the Czech Republic suggests that serious limits exist even to transformation in postcommunist circumstances. Although Czechoslovakia became one of the most repressive of east-central European satellites after the Prague Spring of 1968, Bohemia and Moravia retained significant elements of their prewar democratic political culture and possessed a host of sophisticated and Westernized political, economic, and cultural elites. Perhaps not too surprisingly, once the communist regime collapsed in 1989, the democratic opposition was able, almost too easily, to outmaneuver the old guard and push through what seemed to be the quintessence of the Czech nation's "European-ness"—laissez-faire market reforms à la Vaclav Klaus. By 1996–1997, however, it was evident that the Czech Republic was not quite as advanced as it had seemed. Privatization of large industry was minimal, insider trading and corruption were widespread, and the currency had weakened.[19] The Czech Republic's totalitarian past had caught up with it. In a partial vindication of Samuel Huntington's argument about institutionalization, Klaus's market reforms had outstripped the capacity of the system to sustain them.[20] In particular, the Czech state's lack of effective rule-of-law institutions appears to have ensured that, after leaping forward majestically, Klaus and his overly ambitious program would, like Icarus, fall.

LEGACIES AND TRAJECTORIES

The states of east-central Europe and the former Soviet Union have settled into two distinct and stable, if internally variegated, groups. The first consists of polities that are closest to democracy, civil society, rule of law, and a market economy. Most observers would agree that these include Poland, the Czech Republic, Hungary, Slovenia, Estonia, Latvia, Lithuania, and perhaps Slovakia. The second group consists of all the rest. Although this group is hardly homogeneous, most important for present purposes is that these countries share one key characteristic: they lag behind the first group.[21] Least advanced are Albania, Azerbaijan, Belarus, Kazakhstan, Tajikistan, Turkmenistan, and Uzbekistan. Somewhat more advanced are Armenia, Bulgaria, Croatia, Georgia, Kyrgyzstan, Macedonia, Moldova, Romania, Russia, and Ukraine.

Although Western observers generally blame indigenous policy makers for these differences, their criticism misses the larger point that, when clusters of states evince similar patterns of behavior, something other than policy incapacity must be at work. The missing link is institutional. The Soviet empire, of which most of these states were a part until 1989–1991, left them with a complex set of institutional legacies. Some combinations encouraged minor but significant change; others effectively precluded it; still others permitted but did not encourage change.

These institutional legacies are best captured by two concepts: totalitarianism and empire. The Soviet bloc had the dubious distinction of being the world's only totalitarian empire. The Communist Party of the Soviet Union

and the secret police, the KGB, reigned supreme in an all-encompassing totalitarian system that, where effective, permitted only pro-Soviet and pro-
Communist institutions to exist.[22] The public activities that characterize democracy, rule of law, civil society, and the market were taboo. In turn, the
imperial structure of the Soviet bloc privileged the party-state apparatus
housed in Moscow, ensured that the party-state elite was either Russian or
Russified, and deprived the non-Russian Soviet republics and the east-central
European satellites of sovereignty.

Where states stood in terms of the extent of totalitarianism and empire in
1989–1991 had a decisive impact on their subsequent reform trajectories. A
high degree of totalitarianism precluded the existence of democracy, civil society, rule of law, and the market economy. A low degree of totalitarianism
permitted discrete institutions or protoinstitutions to emerge. A high degree
of imperial rule, also known as "formal empire," precluded the existence of
full-fledged political institutions and elites in the colonies. A low degree of
"informal" imperial rule was premised on Moscow's collaboration with a local network of well-developed institutions and elites.[23] Maria Csanádi addresses these legacies in her discussion of the two types of the "party-state
system's power structure." System A, for which her prototype is the USSR,
evinced a "centralised structure with little structural feedback." System B, as
typified by Hungary, had a "relatively decentralized structure with dense
structural feedback."[24] She concludes:

> In contrast to system A, disintegration in system B comes about
> through the steady weakening of the cohesion that once characterised
> this system. . . . In system A, where the process of gradual disintegra-
> tion did not take place, at the time of the collapse interests, behaviour
> patterns and the social and property structures are much less differen-
> tiated, while state property rights are much more extensive, and cen-
> tralised economic power is much stronger. . . . There is also a greater
> time constraint on the formation of new political organisations in sys-
> tem A compared with system B. Because of the atomisation, and the
> poor bargaining capacity and willingness to compromise that stem
> from this, in the course of the transformation the new political and in-
> terest organisations will, for a considerable period, remain isolated and
> incapable of growth and cooperation.[25]

Various combinations of totalitarianism and empire had four broad consequences. The first is most obvious. Countries with some institutional elements

of democracy, civil society, rule of law, and a market economy had a head start on those without any such elements. Having less to build, they had less to do. The second reason is somewhat less obvious. Having made some progress toward these institutional goals, these countries did not have to start from scratch; instead, they could build on strengths and already-achieved successes and avoid altogether the devilishly complex question of where to start and which sequence of reform to pursue. Third, those countries enmeshed in informal empire possessed a nonsovereign form of statehood replete with a range of political institutions that, upon independence, could easily serve as the institutional base for reform in general and for the introduction of rule of law and democracy in particular. Fourth and last, informally ruled states also inherited experienced quasi-elites that had the expertise and perhaps the vision to promote reform. In sum, minimally imperial countries had the capacity to embark on reform, whereas minimally totalitarian ones had the capacity to respond to reform. Polities with both features—namely, the east-central European countries currently closest to democracy and the market—were thus most able to embark on and successfully introduce measured change, precisely because reform, transition, and transformation, and not revolution, were both possible and desirable. This was path dependence with a vengeance.

PRECONDITIONS AND SEQUENCES

For those formerly Soviet republics that were an integral, and thoroughly communized, part of the USSR since the 1920s, however, rapid, fundamental, and comprehensive change was impossible, because the structural legacy of the USSR's collapse effectively precluded the successful pursuit of revolutionary change. Because change had to take place in the absence of a state, civil society, rule of law, democracy, and the market, and because some desired institutional ends were necessary conditions of others, a logic of systemic change dictated the optimal sequence that elites should follow and *would* in all likelihood follow, if only to preserve their status as elites. Faute de mieux, protracted and sequential or simply evolutionary change—however unspectacular, dull, and unsatisfactory—was the only alternative.[26]

A sequentialist argument such as this presupposes that the desired ends of change be conceptualized as clusters of institutions and not as dispositions or groups of individuals. It views democracy as consisting not merely of self-styled democrats or the holding of "fair and free" elections but as a set of institutions involving the division and balance of governmental powers and a specified procedure for electing elites through popular participation; it views the market as a set of regularized procedures for exchanging capital, labor, and land and not as the prevalence of enterprising individuals[27]; it views rule of law as a set of predictable and transparent rules and regulations governing the internal workings of the state and its relations with society and the economy; and it views the state as the administrative and coercive apparatus that enforces laws and regulates economic relations. It follows from these conceptualizations that democracy and the market presuppose that rule of law specifies how powers should be divided and balanced, how elites should be elected and how people should participate, and how economic relations should be structured and conducted—and that rule of law presupposes the state.[28]

Not all ends are preconditions of others. States, as elaborate kinds of political organizations; nations, as collections of culturally related people; and civil societies, as sets of nonstate institutions situated between the political authorities and the individual do not require the prior existence of democracies, markets, and rule of law.[29] By not presupposing one another, states, civil societies, and nations were equally viable projects under post-Soviet conditions. Not surprisingly, those countries that were able, however partially, to escape the sequentialist logic were the objects of the massive intervention of external actors willing and able, like Bonn, to attempt revolution from outside, or of wars. Bosnia and Georgia, for instance, experienced rapid economic growth in 1996–1998 primarily because they survived devastating conflicts that flattened their institutional legacies and made both more receptive to reform.[30]

IMAGINING INSTITUTION BUILDING

Although the argument for the logical necessity of sequencing functions at a fairly high level of institutional agglomeration, a more focused analytical look at institutions also shows that the very notion of institutional change presupposes a variety of steps, or preconditions, that almost by definition can neither be built—as the language of "institution building" would have it— nor imposed. Imagine for the sake of simplicity a society with only two institutions, ABC and $DE(-F)$, where AB and DE denote either discursive or behavioral steps—it matters not which—in some procedure culminating in the institutional goals, C and $(-F)$. Thus, to attain C, one must engage first in A and then in B. Imagine now that this simple society must experience profound institutional change, such that XYC replaces ABC and GHF replaces $DE(-$

F). In the former instance, the goal remains the same, but the steps change. In the latter, both goal and steps change, and the goal is the opposite of that originally given.[31]

How can these two institutional changes come about? First, the shift from ABC to XYC and from DE(-F) to GHF presupposes, as a necessary condition, adequate knowledge of XY and GH on the one hand and of their institutional connection with C and F on the other. Second, such a shift would presumably be facilitated by the absence of an affective attachment to both AB and DE. Third, the shift requires as a necessary condition a fundamental value reorientation from (-F) to F. Finally, even if these three conditions are in place, we have no reason to expect a shift actually to occur unless XY works better than AB to produce C and GH works better than some alternative, PQ, to produce F. And "working better" cannot be proved theoretically; it has to be the case, manifestly and practically. This said, imagine how much more difficult such a shift would be if ABC were to be replaced with X(-F)C and not XYC. Under such conditions, F would have to replace (-F) as an institutional end point or goal (DE[-F] becoming GHF), whereas (-F) would have to be demoted from a goal to a mere step leading up to a goal (DE[-F] becoming X[-F]C).

If these abstract considerations more or less accurately represent what is involved in institutional change, I do not see how it is possible for such change to occur rapidly, comprehensively, and fundamentally. Knowledge dissemination takes time, as do affective disattachment, value reorientation, and working better. No less important, although shifting even two simple two-step institutions seems to be an incredibly complex undertaking, real societies consist of at least four clusters of many interrelated institutions (political, economic, social, and cultural)—and we have no reason to think that effective knowledge dissemination, affective disattachment, value reorientation, and working better will proceed in sync in a mutually reinforcing manner. The "market" and its incentives are no solution, because the market, as GHF, is precisely the institution that has to be introduced in the first place. Even vast amounts of coercion cannot really solve the problem. People may be forced to go through the motions, but unless coercion is sustained for several generations, going through the motions need not involve actual changes in knowledge, affect, and so on. "What we need," recommends Jürgen Habermas, "is a little more solidary practice, without which even intelligent activity remains without foundations and without effect. In turn, such practice requires reasonable institutions, rules, and communicative forms that do not overtax citizens morally, but promote the virtue of being oriented toward general well-being in small steps."[32] Only time, and the actual working better of *XYC* and *GHF*, can do the trick, imparting greater knowledge of alternative institutions and inducing cultural shifts regarding the normative desirability of existing procedures and goals. But time takes time, and only with the passage of time can institutional change occur—somewhat in the manner of David Laitin's notion of "tipping games."[33] As more people switch, the incentive to join increases, and one institution "tips" over into another.

These remarks are especially relevant if the institutional change concerns movement toward democracy as in the postcommunist states. Soviet-era elections, for instance, did involve an irreproachably democratic goal, but the elections nonetheless were not democratic, because the population did not reach that goal by means of an institutionally democratic process involving the dissemination of knowledge and the reorientation of cultural values. In other words, democratization presupposes some degree of confrontation, engagement, and debate—or deliberation—all of which combine to promote the institutional shift culminating in the tip toward democracy.

A comparison of the two largest, most similar, and arguably most Soviet post-Soviet states, Ukraine and Russia, illustrates why, if we value democracy, sequentialism was preferable to big-bangism. If capitalism is all that matters, Russia may have been "ahead" of Ukraine until the Russian economic meltdown of mid-1998 suggested that its putative lead was both fragile and marginal at best and illusory at worst.[34] But if deliberative institutions matter as much as the distribution of state assets, Russia appeared to be substantially "behind." Naturally, Russia received the applause of big-bangists for attempting revolution and giving priority to the market. Ukraine was perceived as hopelessly inert, the paragon of plodding sequentialism. Their respective images, however, and Russia's somewhat greater movement toward market relations, concealed a far more important—or, at the least, an equally important—reality, namely, that Ukraine had developed democratically, whereas Russia had experienced democratic retardation. Except for a revolutionary free-marketeer wedded to the belief that the market, the omnipotent X factor of revolutionary theory, is, always and everywhere, more important than anything else, Ukraine's slow-paced development of deliberative—and therefore protodemocratic—institutions could not have been entirely bad news.

INCHING ALONG IN UKRAINE

Although a sequentialist priority, state building proceeded slowly and fitfully in Ukraine, because its administrative agencies were woefully understaffed and underfunded, their functionaries were undertrained, and their relations with one another were undefined. Not surprisingly, the protostate was immediately seized by the nomenklatura, former Communist Party functionaries who retained their positions of central, regional, and local dominance.[35] By presiding over the state-controlled economy, they were able to pursue untrammeled rent seeking, acquire fortunes, and accelerate the economy's decline. Because the protostate lived off itself, it seemed easy to predict that such an organism could not be viable in the long, if not short, run.[36]

A closer look inside the Ukrainian protostate, however, revealed that, although it appeared to be monolithic on the outside, it was actually rent by severe divisions within. The "party of power" was anything but unified, because from the start the protostate was an arena of elite contestation. Elite factions based on regional loyalties, personal ties, functional roles, and generational differences were involved in a continual struggle for power, resources, and policy.[37] Had the system been stable, elite contestation might have resembled that found in Soviet times: policy goals, although not unimportant, would have taken a back seat to struggles over power and wealth. But because the economy was visibly collapsing and because the imperatives of state building were clear to all, policy had to figure in the forefront of elite infighting. Thus President Leonid Kuchma's adoption of a radical program in late 1994 was no great surprise in light of the policy-driven vicissitudes within the Ukrainian party of power. Inasmuch as Leonid Kravchuk, his predecessor, had stood for little or no economic reform, and inasmuch as the economy was indeed a mess, his opponents, whoever they might be, were highly likely to be advocates either of marketization or of centralization. By the same token, it was also no surprise that Kuchma's reforms proceeded unevenly at best, both because the weakness of the Ukrainian protostate undermined his ability to pursue excessively radical change and because the pervasiveness of elite contestation permitted Communist forces with a more centralized vision of economic change to mobilize in opposition.[38]

The central struggle within the arena of the protostate involved the president and the parliament, whose relationship was, in the absence of a workable constitution, institutionally undefined and therefore deadlocked. In Ukraine as elsewhere, the deadlock contributed to an incapacity to pursue radical reform measures. This failing was not fatal, however, as the imperatives of sequencing would have ruled out premature marketization anyway. And it was, paradoxically, even desirable, because deadlock contributed to the consolidation within the state arena of desperately fragile post-Soviet institutions, the executive and legislature, and of elite deliberative practices approximating a democratic culture.

Because institution building concerns the establishment of stable and regularized rules and procedures, deadlock can contribute to institutionalization in general and democratic institutionalization in particular when and where the rules of the game are undefined and unclear. Deadlock, after all, is a game of sorts, one that has to be played by certain rules, the central one being the recognition by both sides of the existence, if not quite legitimacy, of the other. Government deadlock, somewhat like a seemingly endless game of chess, is frustrating, but it also underscores that a game is being played, that rules are being learned, and that both sides recognize the indispensability of each other to the very act of playing the game within a defined setting, the arena of the state. Deadlock forced Ukraine's elites to engage one another in a continual give-and-take, an iterative game of tit-for-tat, that, although a far cry from Habermas's notion of self-conscious rational deliberation in some rarified public sphere, increasingly acquired the defining characteristics thereof.[39] And it was deadlock that produced the Constitution of 1996, a founding document that, as the product of multiple competing interests, succeeded in accommodating all of them democratically, by creating more or less balanced executive, legislative, and judicial branches of government.

The parliamentary elections of 1994 and 1998, and the smooth transfer of presidential power from Kravchuk to Kuchma in 1994, also testified to the growth of real, if far from sturdy, deliberative institutions within the Ukrainian protostate. In particular, the March 1998 elections marked an important step forward in the institutionalization of Ukraine's nascent electoral, party, and legislative systems.[40] The introduction of a mixed parliamentary system, in which half the seats were assigned to, respectively, candidates elected in single-mandate districts and those parties receiving at least 4 percent of the total vote, promoted party consolidation—while also permitting the well-organized Communists deservedly to increase their share of seats. But the mere fact that parties on the left, right, and center campaigned once again and again played by the rules outweighed the relative gains of the Communist Party and its allies.[41] Even if the parliament's obstreperous relationship with the presidency were to continue and thereby block economic reform, political reform would have made impressive, if thoroughly unspectacular, gains. Doomed to playing a game of deliberation, neither reformers nor antireformers could easily extricate themselves from the evolving protodemocratic frameworks.

LEAPING FORWARD IN RUSSIA

In contrast to Ukraine, Russia inherited a more or less coherent, bureaucrat-ically defined central state but one afflicted with two Soviet-era deforma-tions. First, the bureaucracies that ran central ministries were too large for, and too mismatched with, scaled-down postimperial, post-totalitarian pur-poses. And second, the two institutions that stood out within the panoply of state agencies inherited from the Soviet period were the still-powerful secret police and army, which were assured a disproportionately influential position in the state by virtue of the comparative weakness and disorganization of other political institutions.[42] Small wonder that bloated bureaucracies and two of the USSR's most reactionary institutions had a vested interest in re-sisting change in general and the kind of change that threatened to bring about their demise in particular.

To borrow an image from Antonio Gramsci: Russia's central state appara-tus resembled a fortress surrounded by an elaborate system of defenses and situated within a post-totalitarian environment of institutional disarray and in-traelite infighting similar to that in other republics. As in Ukraine, post-totali-tarian chaos generated a variety of elite struggles based on region, function, personality, and policy. And, as in Ukraine, the manifest imperative of stem-ming economic collapse and state decay meant that policy would figure in elite contestations in important ways. But the postimperial, post-totalitarian nature of the Russian state and the prominence within it of the "structures of force" set the state on a collision course with elites committed to introducing radical economic change while political democratization and the transforma-tion of social and cultural institutions were underway. In effect, Russia's would-be reformers embarked on revolution, albeit unwittingly, by—in the notation I used in the introduction—adding A to (B,C) in the false belief that economic shock therapy could somehow be bracketed from the ongoing processes of change in the society as a whole.

The Ukrainian protostate could serve as an arena of elite struggle because it lacked an identity and structure of its own; the Russian state figured as one of the contestants in the struggle between conservatives and radicals. Be-cause Russia's revolutionaries were too weak to storm the state, their great leap forward necessarily fell short. Yegor Gaidar's pursuit of economic shock therapy encountered massive bureaucratic resistance and had to be aban-doned but not before it embroiled President Boris Yeltsin in a self-defeating struggle with the main source of governmental resistance to radical eco-nomic change—the parliament. Yeltsin prevailed, but, exhausted by the failed assault, he signaled retreat from revolution by appointing Viktor Chernomyrdin as prime minister in 1994 and by purging the remaining radicals in the course of 1995–1996.

Yeltsin's victory was Pyrrhic, undermining the democratic aspirations of the great leap.[43] Although parties multiplied, countless public opinion polls were taken, and elections were held, the institutional *conditio sine qua non* of democracy—a division and balance of governmental powers—had been dealt a potentially fatal blow in 1993.[44] By destroying the Parliament as an institution and establishing a presidency with virtually unlimited powers enshrined in a constitution tailored to his own needs, President Yeltsin accomplished exactly the opposite of what deadlock had achieved in Ukraine. Yeltsin upset the delicate balance between executive and legislature, nullified the emerging rules of the game, and promoted nondemocratic institutions.

The presidential elections of 1996 illustrated the nondeliberative nature of what passed for democracy in Russia. The vigor with which the media participated in the political process was impressive. But the forging by Yeltsin's political machine of a de facto alliance with the press and the economic magnates led by Boris Berezovsky testified to the marginalization of public rules, regulations, and procedures, even if of the incipiently deliberative kind as in Ukraine. Indeed, Yeltsin's style of governance—hiring, firing, and rehiring officials seemingly at whim while heeding the advice of dubious advisers, such as his bodyguard Aleksandr Korzhakov and his daughter, Tatiana—was indicative of the paucity of institutional forms of public deliberation.[45]

An all-powerful presidency was subversive of democracy directly, by negating the division and balance of powers, and indirectly, by setting back interelite deliberation in the public sphere.[46] Once the presidential apparatus was set apart from and against other state agencies, self-preservation, and not coordination or cooperation, became the bureaucratic leitmotif, resulting, as in Soviet times, in resource hoarding and personnel growth. The upshot was the consolidation of individual agencies and the fragmentation of the state as a whole. "The institution of government," writes Leslie Dienes, "bears little resemblance to that in Western states and has almost no collective responsibility. It is composed of competing yet interpenetrating elite cartels, effectualizing their interest through institutional intrigue and with no clear accountability."[47] With multiple sovereignty characterizing the state, deliberation became a chimera. Each organization might have been able to implement regularized internal procedures, but interagency rules could not take hold in what Vladimir Shlapentokh aptly calls an "early feudal" setting of competing duchies and princedoms.[48]

NETWORKS, NOT BLUEPRINTS

My approach to the question of postcommunist change has centered on the theoretical unviability of the revolutionary project and the preferability of any other, nonrevolutionary alternative. My point is not that sequencing works well—nothing really does or can in postcommunist, and especially post-Soviet, circumstances—but that sequencing works less badly than big-bangism and that it is also far less costly. Sequencing is a small bet with potentially modest payoffs, whereas big-bangism is a big bet with probably enormous losses. As my comparison of Ukraine and Russia suggested, however, another, more positive side to nonrevolutionary approaches exists. David Stark and Laszlo Bruszt consider the complexity of institution building and conclude that "sustained competitiveness depends on the ability to recombine resources adaptively: Strategies of innovation are strategies that recognize the complex and changing interdependencies of assets and actors." Thus, they claim, very much in the spirit of my argument:

> Transformative politics builds on this departure from design as blueprint. But in addition to using the indicators of economic processes (level of inflation, wage rates, export performance, and the like), it recognizes that the longer-term viability of a reform program depends on such noneconomic factors as levels and forms of public support, business confidence, voting behavior, and the like. The institutions of extended accountability provide this critical feedback. Through deliberative associations, politicians and the public alike recalibrate the parameters of change. . . . Goals do not dictate means, for it is only in pursuing our goals that we discover the full meaning of the initial idea and, through this learning about the implications of our goals, recalibrate both the instruments of vision and the practical tools for a further stage of experimentation. Transformative politics is experimental—not because society is the subject of a grand fixed design but because deliberations educate the educator, they transform the transformer.[49]

Transformative politics, or nonrevolutionary politics in my terminology, permits policy makers to make mistakes and to learn from mistakes, as institutions are built, rebuilt, calibrated, and recalibrated. Such an approach to change does not reify only one set of (probably not identifiable) initial conditions and it does not fetishize goals. Instead, this approach eschews the immodest "high modernism" dissected by James Scott, embraces the modest experimentalism associated with Karl Popper's "piecemeal social engineering," and, in promoting deliberative networks, promotes institutionalization, democratization, and perhaps effective and sustainable change.[50] The price paid by the Russian people was tragically high, but the severity of Russia's economic crisis in 1998–1999 may at least have provided powerful empirical support for the argument that, in light of the possible incompatibility of rapid democratization and rapid marketization, inching along politically *and* economically, à la Ukraine, was preferable to leaping forward politically and economically, à la Russia.[51] As Dienes puts it, "The Russian experience to date seems to show that the shock wave nature of market pressure made it harder, not easier, to lay the long-term foundations of a normal, law-governed, market economy."[52]

II. NATIONS

chapter 4. national inventions

According to Eric Hobsbawm, Benedict Anderson, and the "constructivist" school they inspired, national identity, like the nation claiming it, is invented or imagined.[1] Hobsbawm suggests that invention is the "attempt to structure at least some parts of social life . . . as unchanging and invariant"; the scope of invention "includes both 'traditions' actually invented, constructed and formally instituted and those emerging in a less easily traceable manner within a brief and dateable period."[2] Anderson claims that the nation is *"imagined* because the members of even the smallest nation will never know most of their fellow-members, meet them, or even hear of them, yet in the minds of each lives the image of their communion."[3]

Hobsbawm's definition is confused and confusing. Some reflection shows that construction, institution, emergence, and structuring are different concepts. Construction and structuring imply conscious activity of a directed and innovative kind; emergence suggests unwilled occurrences; and institution connotes an interaction between individual and mass human behavior. Anderson does better by arguing that imagination involves not just an image but an image of a nonexistent thing, the *communion* of the members of the nation. But he too leaves us without a clear sense of what imagination entails.

A closer look at invention and imagination might start with dictionary definitions: to imagine is "to form a mental image of (something not present)" and to invent is "to devise by thinking: fabricate," "to produce (as something useful) for the first time through the use of the imagination or of ingenious thinking and experiment."[4] Regardless of what they denote, inventing and imagining clearly connote a bringing into being of something previously absent. But what and how? Consider the act of invention. Whatever its form and whatever the context, invention—or, more precisely, the inventor performing it—transforms the materials at hand into something qualitatively different. The invented entity is novel, neither an agglomeration of previously given materials and therefore merely the sum of its parts, nor something hidden in these materials, as if it were waiting for the inventor to set it free. Thus a hammer is neither a piece of wood and a piece of metal nor the external manifestation of the "hammerness" they embody but a thing that, although consisting of wood and metal, represents an ontological reality different from theirs.

Imagination—or, again, the imaginer—works in the same way, juxtaposing or combining elements in novel ways that produce qualitatively new entities that would otherwise be nonexistent. I do not imagine the horse outside my window or the horns on the bull in my barn. But I do imagine a being that represents an amalgam of both—a unicorn. Likewise, I do not imagine the homeless in New York City—after all, I see them every day—but I might imagine a city without any poverty at all. I imagine Utopia, Schlaraffenland, and many other such *imaginary* situations, just as I imagine similarly nonexistent entities, such as phoenixes, trolls, and fairies, although I can see their component parts—wings, fangs, and wands—in everyday life.

Both invention and imagination presuppose preexisting building blocks on the one hand and their combination and subsequent transformation by inventors or imaginers into a novel end-product on the other.[5] We cannot invent or imagine ex nihilo. That is "creation," and we would do well to recall that as sacrosanct an authority as God decidedly did not claim to invent or imagine the world. Nor do we invent or imagine already existing things. That is "remembrance." Nor, finally, can invention or imagination occur without conscious inventors and imaginers. It is not enough for images passively to "live," as Anderson puts it, in people's minds. Imagination, like invention, requires *active* imaginers and inventors—that is, elites. In sum, invention and imagination have at least three defining characteristics: building blocks, conscious human agency, and novelty. If any characteristic is absent, invention or imagination cannot be said to have taken place.

UNPACKING IDENTITY

If traditions are *not* invented and if communities are *not* imagined in such a precise manner, invention and imagination are, at best, only metaphors. If constructivism does *not* argue that elites create national identity consciously, if the nationalists of whom Ernest Gellner writes as the "historic agents" of nationalism "know not what they do," we are left with a supremely trivial conclusion.[6] Because "men make their own history," as they obviously must for history to be more than the recording of natural events, everything in history is in some sense "made"—constructed—by men and women. Constructivism, then, *must* argue that national identity can arise only if elites, as the active imaginers, inventors, and constructors who figure in Miroslav Hroch's narrative, consciously take preexisting building blocks and transform them into national identity. So long as national elites are self-consciously acting as inventors and imaginers, it matters not whether they are rich or poor, powerful or powerless, with or without status and influence, and so on.[7]

Rather more interesting than the elites themselves is what they do. As self-styled inventors and imaginers, they act on the preexisting materials or building blocks of national identity. What these building blocks are depends on what national identity is or, more precisely, on how it is defined—and the definition, as we know, may not logically entail either a confirmation or a refutation of constructivism's claims. Defining national identity as a *set of beliefs* meets this requirement. As such a set, which may or may not be rooted in various psychological states of mind, national identity consists of *propositions* about life, statements of the "This is that" variety.[8] Identity construction is, then, a form of belief construction, and a nation is a group of people who hold certain propositions about themselves to be true. Constructivists must therefore claim that national elites consciously attempt to inculcate a population with a set of beliefs, each of the form $A' = B'$, $A'' = B''$ . . . $A^n = B^n$. As John Searle tells us, these propositions need not actually *be* true: they need not correspond to empirical reality and therefore qualify as facts.[9] By the same token, we have no reason to think, a priori, that they must be false or that, should they be false, national propositions would be all that different from most run-of-the-mill nonnational propositions.

One logical consequence of defining national identity as a system of propositions is that the entity we call a nation need not call itself that. The term may be absent from the language of the people concerned—the Inuit are a case in point—and even if the term were present, it might have a thoroughly different meaning from ours. For instance, Americans use the word *nation*—as in "this nation's capital"—to mean *country*.[10] Thus it must be possible for nations to have existed before the word nation or the doctrine of nationalism entered politics and the social science discourse. To suppose otherwise is either to conflate the etymology of the word nation with the origins of the phenomenon, as Liah Greenfeld does, or to reduce the phenomenon to a word or words, or a "stance," as Rogers Brubaker does.[11] In either case, the implicit—and unwarranted—assumption is that language constitutes all of reality.

NATIONAL IDENTITY AND LIFEWORLD

If national identity consists of knowledge claims, the preexisting materials from which the building blocks that constitute national identity are drawn must also consist of knowledge claims. What can this largest possible set of building blocks be and where does it come from? It could be a mere agglomeration of randomly aligned elements, or it could form a coherent collection of knowledge claims. If it is the former, it is unclear just how our inventors and imaginers could have happened to stumble upon just these building blocks and not others and just how and why, having stumbled upon them, they should have decided that they were suitable for building national identity. Randomness, serendipity, and whim might be at work here, but if they are, the case for conscious invention and imagination by self-conscious inventors and imaginers looks weak indeed. How, after all, could potential inventors buffeted by the winds of random knowledge claims ever decide to invent anything, not to mention invent something as recondite as national identity? Indeed, how could they even claim to know anything, be it about the world, themselves, or knowledge in general?

If, alternatively, this set of knowledge claims is coherent, I suggest it makes sense to call it a "lifeworld," the intersubjectively held knowledge claims—some true, some false—that a group, *any* group, presumably takes for granted and that enable its members to communicate with one another.[12] Although national identity refers to a particular way in which people see themselves, lifeworld refers to the ontological and epistemological claims they share in order to contemplate seeing themselves in a particular way, say, as having or as not having an identity.[13] Thus to ask about the origins of national identity is not to ask about the origins of lifeworlds. We expect lifeworlds to exist, perhaps as a result of some inner need on the part of men and women to deal with the existential frailty of the human condition, to give shape to shapelessness in an effort to overcome, as Peter Berger and Thomas Luckmann put it, "the night side" of reality.[14] The search for meaning may therefore be immanent in the human condition; national identity, at least according to nonprimordialist assumptions, obviously is not.

We can express the relationship between national identity and lifeworld, where N stands for national identity proposition and L for lifeworld proposition, as shown in figure 4.1. For the sake of simplicity, I have represented each N as a novel amalgam of only two different L's. Of course, no reason exists for N propositions to consist only of separate L pairs or for there to be fewer

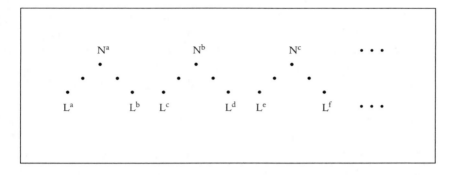

FIGURE 4.1
National and Lifeworld Propositions

N propositions than L propositions. These contrivances notwithstanding, the figure suggests important conclusions.

First, and most obviously, would-be inventors and imaginers invent and imagine under severe constraints. They may and do combine L propositions in novel ways to produce N, but they are confined to drawing on L and only on L. They cannot invent and imagine just anything that might, from the viewpoint of some outside observer, be theoretically possible to invent or imagine. Second, inventors and imaginers are constrained by more than just the field of L. Although N propositions could be constructed so as to contradict individual L propositions, the "nation" intended to entertain contradictory propositions is unlikely to be able to maintain such a balancing act for any meaningful length of time. We therefore expect the set of N propositions to be consistent with the set of L propositions, at least over time. By the same token, N propositions should, also over time, be equally consistent with one another. Third, the elites transforming L propositions into N propositions must be intimately familiar with the lifeworld. If they were not, they would be incapable of identifying its propositions and combining them in noncontradictory ways. But if the elites are firmly ensconced in the lifeworld, how could they, and why should they, invent or imagine N? Prenational elites have no reason even to suspect that L propositions could produce distinctly national N propositions. And even if they did, it is unclear why they should care. Inventions are useful things, but elites cannot know that N is useful before nations exist. Circularity seems to be unavoidable. Fourth, even if elites could create N, how and why do these propositions come to be accepted by the target audience? We have no reason to think that people at large share elite preferences; if they did, elites would be irrelevant to national identity formation. If, alternatively, the people are assumed to be indifferent to or ignorant of elite preferences, no reason exists to expect them to accept the veracity of propositions that represent novel additions to already functioning lifeworlds. Of course, elites might force these ideas on the masses, but coercion decidedly is not construction.

In sum, there appears to be no logically persuasive reason for national identity formation to occur as a result of conscious elite activity. Without introducing exogenous conditions into the argument, we cannot explain why elites should invent N or why masses should accept N. If nations or a discourse of nationalism are assumed to exist, we might be able to provide nonnational elites with a motive to invent their own N propositions and nonnational masses with a reason to believe them, but this solution is, of course, merely a restatement of the problem.

THE IRRELEVANCE OF ELITES

While accepting the logic of constructivism, the analysis revealed that the centerpiece of that approach—the proposition that national identity is constructed by elites acting in a self-consciously constructivist manner—is at best highly problematic. It will be worth our while to pursue this point by examining whether all instances of the construction of N really require conscious elites. If even some N propositions can and do emerge without elites, it logically follows that elites are not a necessary condition of their emergence.

What kind of truth claims can qualify as national propositions? Highly abstract philosophical statements that require the creative intervention of intellectuals obviously fit the bill. So too do elite- or state-initiated national holidays, political programs, and the like. More likely than not, however, national propositions will also take the form of the myths, traditions, rites, and rituals that Hobsbawm conveniently defines as mere "custom."[15] Clearly, if national propositions can legitimately encompass customary truth claims, the view of national identity as only an elite construct is manifestly false.

Orally transmitted myths, such as epics, poems, and songs, are collective undertakings as much as they are the creations of a Homer or the preserve of only the actual storytellers. Their collective telling and retelling—and the listening to their telling and retelling—translate into a continual process of textual creation and recreation within which authors and readers are more or less equally implicated.[16] The following passage, narrated by the young Muslim protagonist of Kurban Said's remarkable novel, *Ali and Nino*, illustrates this point:

> It really was amazing, what wonderful liars these people were. There is no story they would not invent to glorify their country. Only yesterday a fat Armenian tried to tell me that the Christian Maras Church in Shusha was five thousand years old. "Don't tell such tall stories," I told him. "The Christian Faith is not yet two thousand years old. They can't have built a Christian church before Christianity was even thought of." The fat man was very hurt and said reproachfully: "You are, of course, an educated man. But let an old man tell you: The Christian Faith may be only two thousand years old in other countries. But to us, the people of Karabagh, the Saviour showed the light three thousand years before the others. That's how it is." Five minutes later the same man went on to tell me without batting an eyelid that the French General Murat had been an Armenian from Shusha. He had gone to France as a child to make Karabagh's name famous there as well. Even when I was just on the way to Shusha the driver of my coach pointed at the little stone bridge we were about to cross and said proudly: "This bridge was built by Alexander the Great when he went forth to immortal victories in Persia!" "1897" was chiseled in big figures on the parapet. I pointed this out to the coachman, but he only waved his hand: "Och, sir, the Russians put that in later, because they were jealous of our glory!"[17]

Like national myths, national traditions can emerge without elites. Some customary ways of doing things appear to be rooted in their functionality within a given material context, and what is functional—such as cattle grazing in a flatland or wine growing on a mountainside—then "becomes," for reasons that anthropologists may be better equipped to answer, natural, meaningful, symbolically inevitable, and profoundly national without the necessary intervention of elites.[18] Other ways of doing things may appear to be, and may indeed be, materially dysfunctional but can make perfect sense within a cultural matrix that well-nigh demands such traditions for the sake of internal consistency and coherence. Human sacrifice may seem to be an odd way of overcoming droughts or economic distress, until it is recognized that appeasing angry gods who brought about the calamity requires especially precious offerings. Ritual sacrifice may logically be deduced from a worldview that assumes that emotional deities run the world and are wont to wreak havoc upon it.

Finally, some rites—such as church rites—may be dated to the creative intervention of a St. Basil, but we should beware of falling into the genetic fallacy by assuming that Basil the Great is the cause of the continued maintenance of currently existing rites among, say, Orthodox Serbs or Uniate Slovaks. He may have institutionalized the rites, but he cannot be held responsible for the existence of the institution. Who or what, then, is? Religious elites foster rites, but so do churchgoers who partake of the rituals. But—and I know this verges on circularity—so does the institution. Patterned behavior assumes a life of its own, independent of the volition of the individuals caught in its tentacles. Put another way, institutions involve people in predetermined relations that, in turn, determine the overall pattern of their behavior.[19]

In short, national propositions can easily exist without elites. And if elites are not a necessary condition of national identity formation, their being or not being conscious of identity construction is a moot issue. Equally important, these examples suggest that even generalized popular consciousness of construction may not be necessary for construction to occur. Many established elites, the office holders, construct identity simply by "doing their job," by "mindlessly" following the rules, patterns, habits, and procedures prescribed by institutions. By the same logic, ordinary people may also have an incremental impact on national identity formation. We do not suppose that the development of agriculture or art required premeditated invention; so too it should be possible for national "self-awareness," although admittedly different from agriculture and art, to be generated "unconsciously," by the force of numerous cumulative acts with unintended consequences. It strains the imagination to think that the enormously complicated social institutions involved in Searle's dissection of the seemingly straightforward act of ordering beer at a cafe could be the result of willfully made choices, of conscious, goal-directed activity aimed at creating the cultural practice of ordering-beer-at-a-cafe.[20] That some choices were made along the way is probably, and trivially, true, but to state this fact without specifying how they were necessary or sufficient to the emergence of beer-drinking-in-cafes is not very interesting. And if making the case for decisive choice in such a setting is difficult, it is all the more problematic in an infinitely more complex context such as nation formation, where F. A. von Hayek's remarks surely apply:

> Though our civilization is the result of a cumulation of individual
> knowledge, it is not by the explicit or conscious combination of all this
> knowledge in any individual brain, but by its embodiment in symbols

which we use without understanding them, in habits and institutions, tools and concepts, that man in society is constantly able to profit from a body of knowledge neither he nor any other man completely possesses. Many of the greatest things man has achieved are the result not of consciously directed thought, and still less the product of a deliberately coordinated effort of many individuals, but of a process in which the individual plays a part he can never fully understand.[21]

NATIONAL PROPOSITIONS

Let us now look more closely at national propositions and nations. Rather than filling the notion of nation with positive content, and thereby suggesting that nations have essences, I propose—in the spirit of Anthony Smith and Fredrik Barth—that national identity be seen as a coherent package of propositions relating to historicity and boundaries. Historicity provides a nation with a place in the flow of time, whereas boundaries grant it present-day distinctiveness.[22] Note that it is both empirically and logically unnecessary for historicity to be understood only in terms of the past. National historicity can also be defined, and frequently has been defined, in terms of the *future*. Otto Bauer, for instance, like many of his Austro-Marxist colleagues, saw the nation as the apogee of the historical development of classes.[23] Yaroslav Hrytsak has shown that nineteenth-century Ukrainian socialists-turned-nationalists rarely referred to the glorious history of the Ukrainian nation, preferring instead to concentrate on its glorious future.[24]

The view that national identity necessarily involves some sense of the past—and, even more so, some distorted sense of the past—is thus false. Tradition need not be invented or imagined, not just because—as I have suggested—inventors and imaginers may be irrelevant but also because imagining and invention need not involve tradition. Historical place can be projected forward or backward into time; it can also be found in the present. That historians generally focus on the historical distortions and glorifications in which nationalists engage may have far less to do with reality or with theory and rather more with the fact that historians study the past and thus may be professionally inclined to treat it with special reverence.

At the very least, therefore, nations are groups of people who believe in two things: that their group, as a group, has a place in history, and that their group differs from other existing groups in ways other than historicity.[25] If a national identity must consist of both sets of propositions, it can do so if and only if they fit together in a single propositional package. If propositional sets are at odds with each other, then, as I argued earlier, the protonation will be unable to sustain both for any meaningful length of time. Sooner or later one set will have to be abandoned or modified. Another defining characteristic of national identity must therefore be the logical *compatibility* or *complementarity* of propositions regarding a nation's historicity on the one hand and its boundaries on the other. A nation, then, exists, or comes into being, when people sharing a lifeworld believe in a set of logically complementary propositions regarding historicity and otherness.

Consider the following example. Contemporary Ukrainians generally trace their origins as a nation to the state of Kievan Rus,' founded about one thousand years ago. They also define themselves in contrast to their quintessential version of "the other," the Russians. Both propositional sets complement each other perfectly. By claiming Rus' and Kiev for themselves, Ukrainians challenge the prevailing Russian originary myth and exclude the Russian other from their past and from their present. By differentiating themselves from the Russians, they perforce reject the Russian rejection of Ukrainian historicity and thereby claim historical legitimacy for themselves. Inasmuch as these two complementary propositional sets exist in contemporary Ukraine and are believed by some of its inhabitants, they make of their believers a nation even if, as is indeed the case, many "Ukrainians" might dispute their nationhood or prefer the term *narod* (people) to *natsiia* (nation).[26]

Seen in this light, the distinction between civic and ethnic nationalism—or, more precisely, national identity—appears at best confused.[27] Because all nations stake out claims to a place in history and to certain boundaries, all national identities are exclusionary. Even the *Verfassungspatriotismus* (constitutional patriotism) propagated by German intellectuals can appeal only to German-language speakers enjoying a certain kind of historicized relationship with a well-nigh deified *Grundgesetz* (basic law).[28] More important, the quality of being more or less exclusionary or inclusionary has nothing to do with whether a putative ethnicity underlies the putative nation, because there is— from this point of view and thus contrary to Smith—no meaningful difference between an ethnic group (or ethnie) and a nation.[29] Both entities accept propositions about their place in history and both draw boundaries. Even if we conclude that nations are merely ethnic groups writ large or modern-day ethnic groups, we still posit a fundamental continuity that overrides whatever differences may emerge in the course of time. Thus all nations are ethnic nations, inasmuch as ethnicity and nationhood are conceptually synonymous.

ISOLATING NATIONALISM

What, then, is nationalism? As Konstantin Symmons-Symonolewicz rightly points out, most definitions of nationalism fall into one of three semantic fields: nationalism as ideology, as social movement, or as group conscious- ness—or, to use somewhat different terms, as ideas, collective action, or cul- ture.[30] Nationalism cannot be defined as some pair of these, because any pair- ing ineluctably conveys causality. John Breuilly, for instance, argues that "the term 'nationalism' is used to refer to political movements seeking or exercis- ing state power and justifying such actions with nationalist arguments."[31] For Breuilly nationalism evidently is both action and ideology, and—worse still— the ideology implicitly causes the action. Symmons-Symonolewicz's defini- tion is no better: "Nationalism is the active solidarity of a larger human col- lectivity which shares a common culture, or a common fund of significant experiences and interests, conceives of itself as a nation, and strives for politi- cal unity and self-government."[32] Having purposely decided to include "all three basic meanings of nationalism" in his own, Symmons-Symonolewicz manages only to produce an unwieldy synthesis of causes and effects. Simi- larly, Michael Hechter argues that nationalism is "collective action designed to render the boundaries of the nation congruent with those of its governance unit."[33] Hechter's oversight is especially surprising, inasmuch as the rational choice perspective he uses must presuppose a distinction between ideas, val- ues, and norms on the one hand and behavior on the other, if only because the central puzzle of rational choice theorizing—the problem of collective ac- tion and free riding—is puzzling only if one assumes that ideological goals do not automatically translate into, or go with, the appropriate behavior.[34]

Faute de mieux, I place nationalism within the semantic field of ideology, ideas, or, more generally, belief systems. The problem with treating nation- alism as collective action is that nothing is intrinsically nationalist about the behavior in which people who call themselves nationalists engage. Collective actions, like social movements, are the coordinated activities of groups. A fas- cist collective action differs in no way, as a collective action, from a Commu- nist, Catholic, or nationalist collective action. Crowds of demonstrators, un- derground cells, strikes, mobs, clubs, petition drives, and so on are just that and nothing more, and as such they can be appropriated by any group and in- fused with any meaning. Even agitation and propaganda are not the proper- ty of any one ideology or movement, because it is not the act of agitation or propaganda but its content that imparts a certain ideological overtone to the collective action.

Nationalism as culture, cultural identity, group consciousness, or ethnic solidarity is an even worse choice, because it is so completely useless. To be aware of one's subjective and objective ethnic markers (language, color, religion, customs, etc.) surely cannot be nationalism; to love one's nation, to be proud of it, to swear loyalty to it—none of this can be nationalism, because otherwise everything involving culture or nationality must be nationalism. All these forms of communal sentiment are universally held today, and to reduce nationalism to any one of them is to convert all human beings into nationalists. Here the problem is the exact opposite of what we encountered in the preceding paragraph: nationalism as collective action seems to have no referents, whereas nationalism as culture seems to have everything as a referent.

If nationalism is neither action nor culture, all we are left with is belief system. That is, nationalism must be a specific type of belief, idea, doctrine, or ideology. As Mark Hagopian usefully suggests, nationalism may be conceived of as an "ideal"—"a broad symbol that entails values and goals that make it worthy of notice and acceptance"—and not an ideology, which attempts to follow its "own logic" and reach a "level of coherence that constitutes a system." Because the "very vagueness of the ideal prevents its developing an accompanying doctrine that follows a certain logic and displays a high level of coherence," nationalism "is sometimes on the right; it is sometimes in the center; it is sometimes on the left."[35]

Nationalism is not just any ideal, however, but a distinctly political ideal: that is, it posits certain political ends and highlights certain optimal political relationships. Nationalism, obviously, is about nations, but it is about much more than that as well. Nationalism connects nations with the "essence" of the political—states—and claims that all nations should have their own political organizations in control of administration and coercion in some geographic space or, as Hechter puts it, that the "boundaries of the nation" be "congruent with those of its governance unit." Nationalism is a political ideal that views statehood as the optimal form of political existence for each nation, or, in Gellner's words, "a political principle, which holds that the political and the national unit should be congruent."[36] Nationalists are men and women who share or promote this belief—whether willfully or not—and a nationalist collective action is a collective action that is premised on or approaches such a goal. Nationalists can therefore call themselves "nationalists" or they can call themselves something else, say, patriots, democrats, populists, and so on. Because nationalist activity is logically premised on the absence of a state for the entire nation or part thereof, once the context changes and a state exists, the collective or other actions that transpire within its jurisdiction, even if labeled nationalist by their initiators, are better conceptualized as the everyday politics of states.

This definition of nationalism suggests why nationalism can be so pervasive and coexist with a variety of other political doctrines and behaviors, including communism. Except in some teleological sense concerning ultimate greatest goods, the nationalist commitment to a nation's statehood is quite compatible with ideologies that give priority to social classes.[37] This is so conceptually (we can always define, say, the Third Estate as the nation) and, far more important, practically: unless we define class relations as a zero-sum game, it is perfectly possible for all classes to benefit, even if unequally, from a nation's statehood. All that nationalism innately opposes are doctrines that explicitly deny the existence of nations and the possibility of states. In the twentieth century, however, such doctrines have been virtually nonexistent. Several hundred years ago, of course, conditions were different and one can easily understand why nationalism could but have had a revolutionary impact on then-prevalent notions of political legitimacy and social order.

NATIONALISM BEFORE NATIONALISM

It is tempting to argue that nationalism as a belief system could have emerged—and did emerge—only in modern times. Elie Kedourie, for instance, traces the origins of nationalism to a variety of intellectual currents in the eighteenth century, in particular to Immanuel Kant's notions of will and self-determination.[38] Carlton Hayes and Hobsbawm view nationalism as the historical product of the French Revolution and industrialization.[39] Smith sees its origins in the crisis of an intelligentsia confronted by the demise of religion and the challenge of the "scientific state."[40] Gellner traces its roots and ascribes its persistence to a complex interaction among industrialization, modernization, education, high culture, and competition.[41] Finally, Greenfeld sees nationalism as the product of a unique conjuncture in seventeenth-century England and explains its subsequent spread as a function of its appeal to intellectuals undergoing crisis and suffering from *ressentiment*.[42]

Although all these explanations are correct to locate the origins of the self-styled ideal of nationalism in the eighteenth and nineteenth centuries, I wish to emphasize that there is nothing necessarily modern about a belief positing a relationship between groups of people sharing certain kinds of complementary propositions and a certain type of political organization. The self-styled ideal called nationalism may be and is modern, of course, but the concept, like any concept, can, as the introduction argued, exist whenever its defining characteristics can be identified as a cluster, even if the modern term appended to it is absent. It should therefore be just as possible to find instances of unself-styled nationalism in prenationalist times as it is possible to find nationalism among modern-day movements that sincerely reject the nationalist label (such as the non-Russian popular fronts in "support of perestroika").[43] Nationalism, like the nation, exists whenever and wherever its defining characteristics exist. A priori, we cannot claim that nationalism must be modern, even if, as is indeed the case, the self-styled ideal called nationalism is modern. There can, thus, be nations before nationalism and, more shockingly, even *nationalism* before nationalism.[44]

chapter 5. national weaknesses

Primordialism appears to have come upon bad times. The "view of the nation as constructed or invented" is, as Geoff Eley and Ronald Suny put it, "currently dominant."[1] "Primordialist theory," claims David Laitin, is "theoretically discredited."[2] Even a scholar as skeptical of constructivism as John Armstrong concurs: "Like nearly all social scientists discussing nationalism, this study [sic] rejects the naive 'primordial' assumption that any specific nation has existed immemorially. Like all other social constructs, nationalism has been 'imagined' and 'invented'."[3]

Ironically, by presupposing a binary opposition between two monolithic theories, one bad, the other good, reports of primordialism's death and constructivism's triumph are as misleading as they are anticonstructivist in spirit. Contrary to the impression conveyed by the conventional wisdom, however, primordialism and constructivism are not theoretical monoliths but variegated sets of related theoretical approaches. Only as monoliths must primordialism involve undifferentiated notions of immutability, objectiveness, timelessness, and naturalness, and constructivism, its polar opposite, must involve similarly undifferentiated notions of mutability, subjectiveness, temporal boundedness, and artificiality. Once we appreciate that, as in all instances of concept formation, defining characteristics may be loosened, we see immediately that these properties can come together in various ways and to varying degrees, thereby producing a variety of semantically related types.[4]

To be sure, primordial approaches to the nation differ from constructivist approaches along three dimensions. First, with respect to how nations are caused, all primordialisms contend that they are not purposefully constructed—or not necessarily constructed—by self-conscious nation builders. Second, with respect to where nations are located in time, all primordialisms countenance the possibility that nations could have emerged before what

Ernest Gellner calls the "age of nationalism"—a period that began sometime between the English Revolution of 1688 and the French Revolution of 1789 and that continues to this day—and may exist, or even emerge, in the future.[5] Third, with respect to the properties of nations, all primordialisms argue that, because they are not easily susceptible to elite manipulation, they are more or less stable. In contrast, all constructivisms argue that nations are constructed, invented, or imagined in the age of nationalism by constructors, inventors, or imaginers. As I show shortly, these important commonalities conceal differences that are no less important.

If approaches to the nation are termed the *family,* primordialism and constructivism are its *genera,* and the extreme, strong, and weak variants of each are the *species.*[6] Table 5.1 illustrates the differences between and among the species, which naturally are ideal types.[7]

In both genera, the assumptions are loosened as we proceed to the right—from the extreme to the weak types. The extreme variants thus make the most radical, and arguably the most uncompromising, claims about the nation. The weak types make the least radical claims within their genera. The strong types are positioned somewhere in-between. Because all the stronger types subsume the claims of the weaker ones, criticism of a weaker species also applies to the stronger variants, whereas the reverse need not be true. Drawing on well-known texts that more or less approximate the ideal types, the sections that follow discuss first the stronger variants of both types and

Primordialism		
EXTREME	STRONG	WEAK
Cause	Immanent	Conjunctural	Indeterminate
Time	Transcendent	Historical	Recurrent
Properties	Immutable	Permanent	Conceptual

Constructivism		
EXTREME	STRONG	WEAK
Cause	Discourse	Elites	Human Activity
Time	Ahistorical	Contemporary	Modern
Properties	Discursive	Malleable	Constructable

TABLE 5.1

Approaches to the Nation

then their weak alternatives, saving what to my mind is the least unpersuasive, weak primordialism, for last.

EXTREME PRIMORDIALISM

According to extreme primordialism, nations are temporally transcendent human communities with immutable properties immanent in life itself. Extending from the distant past, through the present, and into the distant future, nations effectively are outside history. As unchangeable ontological realities, such entities are "caused" by nothing less than existence itself. Nationalists, such as the "fat Armenian" of Kurban Said's novel, frequently imagine their nations in such terms. "Nature has set limits to the desires of other men, but not to those of the Greeks," Benjamin of Lesvos observed. "The Greeks have not been subject in the past nor are they now subject to the laws of nature."[8] Variants of extreme primordialism, frequently in the guise of the "ancient hatreds thesis" (or, in Brendan O'Leary's colorful terminology, "Dark Gods theory"), are also entrenched among journalists and policy makers.[9] In this reading the recent wars in Bosnia-Hercegovina and Nagorno-Karabakh are struggles between existentially hostile nations, Africans possess a mystical property called "négritude," and the "American spirit" is invincible, indefatigable, and democratic.[10]

Elements of extreme primordialism may be found among scholars as well. A formerly popular variant, termed *naturality theory* by O'Leary and *perennialism* by Anthony Smith, "postulates an unchanging essence of the nation beneath different forms. Hence, each form adds a new layer of meaning and colour to the underlying principle of the nation."[11] Harold Isaacs argues that ethnic identity ineluctably derives from the culture into which an individual— *every* individual—is born.[12] Practitioners of Jewish studies still display a pronounced tendency to treat Jews as a group whose "Jewishness" has remained unchanged since biblical times. Because Jew haters are presumed to be motivated by the same irrational fears since time immemorial, the ancient hatreds thesis finds its apotheosis: with both sides locked in a uniquely implacable struggle, everything about that struggle, and especially the Holocaust as its culmination, must be a priori unique.[13] Significant strands within black studies attribute similar characteristics to Africans and their oppressors.[14] Last but not least, psychological theories of national identity, such as those of Donald Horowitz and Pierre van den Berghe, approximate extreme primordialism by ultimately deriving national identity from evolutionary processes intrinsic to human beings, thereby removing the nation from history, rooting its existence in life itself, and endowing it with natural properties.[15]

The most recent—and probably most celebrated—of scholars writing in this mode is Samuel Huntington, who takes extreme primordialism to new heights by effectively attributing its characteristics to human communities that are even larger and more complex than mere nations. For all practical purposes Huntington's civilizations, like Lesvos's Greeks, stand outside history, appear to have no identifiable cause, and do not change. The following potpourri of passages makes the point nicely:

> Human history is the history of civilizations. It is impossible to think of the development of humanity in any other terms. . . . Civilization and culture both refer to the overall way of life of a people, and a civilization is a culture writ large. . . . Civilizations are comprehensive. . . . A civilization is thus the highest cultural grouping of people and the broadest level of cultural identity people have short of that which distinguishes humans from other species. It is defined both by common objective elements, such as language, history, religion, customs, institutions, and by the subjective self-identification of people. . . . Civilizations have no clear-cut boundaries and no precise beginnings and endings. . . . Civilizations are mortal but also very long-lived; they evolve, adapt, and are the most enduring of human associations.[16]

Huntington's critics have correctly noted that his civilizations are reifications that serve policy makers poorly.[17] Rather more important for our purposes is that his analysis, almost as pure a version of extreme primordialism as one can imagine, is unsustainable on conceptual and theoretical grounds. First, even those social sciences that model themselves least on the natural sciences are inconceivable without clearly bounded concepts, variables, factors, and the like. Extreme primordialism rejects the very notion of boundedness, both temporally and causally: its categories—be they nations or civilizations—are, as it were, everywhere. "Civilizations have no clear-cut boundaries," says Huntington, "and no precise beginnings and endings." Second, every social science theory presupposes some initial conditions that delimit its range and utility. Extreme primordialism amounts to a theory of everything that rejects any limitations on its explanatory pretensions. According to Huntington, all "human history is the history of civilizations." Third, social science, like science in general, countenances laws and lawlike statements of greater or lesser robustness but only after prolonged batteries of tests, observations, and experiments fail to invalidate hypotheses, hunches, and theories. Extreme primordialism, in contrast, makes a priori lawlike claims. "It is impossible," claims Huntington, "to think of the development of humanity in any other terms."

The sophisticated theories of Horowitz and van den Berghe suggest that, as tinkering at the margins is no option for a holistic enterprise that rejects boundedness, extreme primordialism can be salvaged only if it is abandoned as a social scientific enterprise and rooted in the natural sciences. One may doubt the feasibility of explaining nations and civilizations in terms of physical and psychological traits—such a move attempts to bridge what may be unbridgeable, the gap between physical reality and social reality—but one would be hard-pressed to dispute the scientific legitimacy of biology and evolutionary psychology and thus the attractiveness of such an undertaking.[18]

STRONG PRIMORDIALISM

According to strong primordialism, nations are human communities that, as the product of some conjunction of historical forces, possess not immutable but merely permanent properties. Such views resonate with nationalist ideologies that eschew the mystifications of extreme primordialism, with weaker variants of the ancient hatreds thesis and with scholarly approaches premised on the importance of political culture, either on its terms or as it relates to national identity. Because political culture involves a deeply, perhaps even structurally, rooted set of beliefs, attitudes, norms, and significations, it makes sense to locate its origins in some long-past conjunction of historical forces and to assume that it changes so slowly as to be almost permanent.[19] As such, a distinctly national political culture—or, to use a currently unfashionable term, *national character*—is virtually indistinguishable from strong primordialism's notion of the nation.

Strong primordialism is rather more widespread than we might have imagined. Liah Greenfeld traces nationalism in England, France, Germany, Russia, and the United States to historical developments before, during, and after the emergence of nationalism as an ideology while also claiming that nations retain their birthmarks for years, perhaps even centuries, thereafter.[20] Rogers Brubaker roots contemporary French and German cultural attitudes to nationhood and citizenship in formative periods two hundred or more years ago and concludes that, given the continued strength of these attitudes, extending citizenship to Germany's minority populations is highly unlikely today.[21] Anthony Smith claims that nations and nationhood are products of complex historical processes and that stable myths or mythomoteurs are at the core of national identities.[22] Finally, despite his constructivist reputation and use of constructivist terminology, Benedict Anderson actually proffers a fairly strong primordialist account of nation formation that demonstrates how particular historical conjunctions produce highly stable identities.[23]

What Huntington is to extreme primordialism, however, Daniel Goldhagen is to strong primordialism. Indeed, by ascribing to Germans, as a well-nigh immutable and stable collectivity, a well-nigh immutable and stable characteristic, Goldhagen's claim that Germans were imbued with an exterminationist anti-Semitism that necessarily impelled them to kill Jews comes dangerously close to Huntington's version of primordialism. Goldhagen sidesteps the charge of immutability by historicizing German anti-Semitism and explicitly asserting that it is only permanent:

1. The existence of antisemitism and the content of antisemitic charges against Jews must be understood as an expression of the non-Jewish culture. . . .
2. Antisemitism has been a permanent feature of Christian civilization (certainly after the beginning of the Crusades), even into the twentieth century.
3. The widely differing degree of antisemitic expression at different moments in a bounded historical time (of, say, twenty to fifty years) in a particular society is not the result of antisemitism appearing and disappearing . . . but of a generally constant antisemitism becoming more or less manifest.[24]

Because Goldhagen's many critics may have demolished his book's historical pretensions, my comments focus on its weakest theoretical link.[25] The claim of permanence is untenable for three reasons. First, strong primordialism cannot maintain that something that emerged historically could become immune to history and acquire permanence. Historical variation and temporal constants do not sit well together: if a historical conjunction could produce a nation or a national trait, a subsequent conjunction should be able to "unproduce" it. Second, the claim of permanence rests on the genetic fallacy—the erroneous assumption that the origins of something constitute its essence.[26] For Greenfeld, Brubaker, and Goldhagen, Germans are doomed to remain what they became several hundred years ago, when they emerged as the nation they supposedly still are today.[27] Third, although it is hard to grasp how something permanent can emerge from contingent historical processes that contravene permanence, it is just as difficult to understand how a permanent cultural attribute can be compatible with "the widely differing degree" of its behavioral "expression." In this case, historical constants and temporal variation do not sit well together. Brubaker's strong primordialism can only be baffled by the intensity of Germany's current debate over nationality and citizenship; Goldhagen's language—with "constant" things "becoming more or less manifest"—lapses into semantic *non*sense and mysticism. Wittingly or not, Goldhagen finally confronts the implications of his tortured logic in an appendix, where he casually negates his entire thesis by asserting that "Germany's political culture has obviously changed in the fifty [n.b. point 3] years since the end of World War II . . . its antisemitic component has diminished enormously and is, by and large, changed in character."[28]

STRONG CONSTRUCTIVISM

Strong constructivism maintains that the nation is a malleable human community with properties that were created, invented, or imagined by self-styled nationalist elites pursuing conscious, goal-oriented action in nationalist—that is to say, modern—times. Like any theory stressing the efficacy and indispensability of elites, strong constructivism is perfectly compatible with most nationalist ideologies. Ironically if unsurprisingly, most self-styled constructivist scholars (who, like Eley and Suny, are usually critical of nationalism) are also adherents of strong constructivism, perhaps because, as an activist program, it can work both for and against nationalism.

Eley and Suny provide a neat summary of the strong constructivist stance:

If politics is the ground upon which the category of the nation was first proposed, culture was the terrain where it was elaborated, and in this sense nationality is best conceived as a complex, uneven, and unpredictable process, forged from an interaction of cultural coalescence and specific political intervention, which cannot be reduced to static criteria of language, territory, ethnicity, or culture.[29]

The process is not quite as unpredictable as Eley and Suny claim, however, as they also note that creative political action is required to transform a segmented and dis-united population into a coherent nationality, and though potential communities of this kind may clearly precede such interventions (so that they are rarely interventions into a vacuum), the interventions re-main responsible for combining the materials into a larger collectivity.[30]

Clearly, because nation formation is impossible without elites inclined to form nations, elites are a necessary condition of the "process" of "nationality." For Eric Hobsbawm, also a strong constructivist, they are a sufficient condition: nations "are, in my view, dual phenomena, constructed essentially from above, but which cannot be understood unless also analysed from below."[31]

Even if we grant—as we know from chapter 4 that we should not—that elites are necessary to nation formation, strong constructivism still suffers from two flaws. First, despite the critical emphasis it places on elites, strong constructivism cannot explain where nationalist elites come from. Greenfeld, for instance, as a historically minded strong primordialist, can: a variety of historical forces transform nonnationalist elites suffering from *ressentiment* into nationalists.[32] The argument may or may not persuade her critics, but it is consistent with its premises. In contrast, if strong constructivism assumes nationalist elites are in place, it begs the question of why and how the mov-ing spirit of the theory got there. However, if strong constructivism does not make such an assumption, it has to explain why and how nonnationalist elites could ever make the leap of consciousness toward a hitherto unimagined and unimaginable nationalism in general and their uninvented nationalisms in particular (a problem I discussed in chapter 4). The obvious solution would be for strong constructivism to attempt to explain elites historically. But to do so undermines strong constructivism's antiprimordialist logic for the simple reason that historical explanations of nationalist elites may not, without our lapsing into circularity, be confined to the age of nationalism. Although a na-tionalist elite may have found its voice only at that time—"A modern nation-ality," Eley and Suny insist, "is only possible within the modern (roughly post-American Revolution) discourse of nationalism"—the reasons for its emergence, the circumstances that made it possible, and the conditions that made its message resonate predate the age of nationalism.[33] But the further back in history that strong constructivism goes—as it must in order to ac-count for nationalist elites and thereby salvage itself—the more it comes to resemble strong primordialism.

The second flaw flows from the first. Because strong constructivism is completely dependent for its coherence on the elites it cannot explain, they

can only assume overwhelming explanatory power as necessary and/or sufficient conditions of nation formation.[34] If follows that, if elites can create nations, they should also be able to pull off, as most strong constructivists
would indeed grant, the far less complicated task of whipping them up into
a nationalist frenzy. But if such omnipotent and prescient elites can create nations *and* whip them up, they must be no less capable of "whipping down"
nations and, indeed, of "un-creating" them. Consistency demands that, if
elites are assumed to be capable of inventing, imagining, and whipping up at
time *t*, in the face of presumably recalcitrant culture, institutions, preferences, and norms, they must be assumed no less able to reconstruct or deconstruct their creations at time $t + n$. Having led us to expect something—
reconstruction and deconstruction—that just does not seem to occur, strong
constructivism cannot then claim that, once created, nations somehow assume a life of their own, perhaps for institutional reasons. If elite capacity
suddenly, and inexplicably, vanishes, and elites become helpless before their
own creations, that essentially sacrifices elites on the altar of social institutions and culture. But if institutions and culture matter at time $t + n$, why
should they not matter equally at time *t*? By the same token, although the
"age of nationalism" may, as I argue in chapter 6, promote whipping up, it
cannot, as a facilitating condition, serve as an insurmountable obstacle to
whipping down, especially for such impressively endowed elites.

Strong constructivism cannot escape this conundrum by assuming that
"potential communities," protonations, ethnic groups, or ethnie are already
in place, as if it were waiting for more modestly empowered elites to uncov-
er or galvanize them. A strong constructivist could not possibly know that
some actually existing community is, *really*, potentially a specific—still nonexistent, still unimagined—nation. And should potential nationness be knowable, the problem of nation formation would merely be transposed to a period before the age of nationalism, confounding strong constructivism once
again. Either way, the language of "potential community" makes sense only
in a primordialist context.

EXTREME CONSTRUCTIVISM

Extreme constructivism makes the bold and simple claim that, although nationalism as a discourse is ontologically real, nations, being contemporary
discursive constructs, are only words. As such, the word *nation* is an empty
signifier, lacking an empirical referent and having no real place in history. Na-

tionalists obviously would reject such a view, whereas postmodernists generally would embrace it.

The later Brubaker argues for an extreme constructivism par excellence:

> To argue against the realist and substantialist way of thinking about nations is not to dispute the reality of nationhood. It is rather to reconceptualize that reality. It is to decouple the study of nationhood and nationness from the study of nations as substantial entities, collectivities, or communities. It is to focus on nationness as a conceptual variable, to adopt J. P. Nettl's phrase, not on nations as real collectivities. It is to treat nation not as substance but as institutionalized form; not as collectivity but as practical category; not as entity but as contingent event. Only in this way can we capture the reality of nationhood and the real power of nationalism without invoking in our theories the very "political fiction" of "the nation" whose potency in practice we wish to explain.[35]

One immediate consequence of Brubaker's insistence that the nation be thought of as "conceptual variable," "institutionalized form," "practical category," and "contingent event" is that, despite the liberal use of metaphors, he cannot—unavoidably, I suspect—develop a straightforward definition of his own. Variables, forms, categories, and events can be everything and they can be nothing. Lacking semantically useful equivalents of nation, "nationalizing state," and "national minority," Brubaker perforce opts for continued use of the conventional terms, even though he appreciates that their connotations are radically different from, and indeed subversive of, his intended meanings.[36]

More substantive objections flow from these semantic failings. First, how is it possible for mere terms to have such "real power"? If this power resides in the variables, forms, and categories per se, they must, as I pointed out in the introduction, be exceptionally powerful reifications, on the order of the Other and Discourse. If this power resides outside the terms—that is, if it is in the hands of their users—we are back to the problem of superelites, discussed in the previous section. Second, even if we concede Brubaker's antisubstantialist claim about the nation, logically it would have to be extended to every other signifier used by scholars. Indeed, *not* to extend this claim would be to privilege the nation in a decidedly anticonstructivist manner. Although the nonexistence of nations as substantialist entities may not strike us as an utterly implausible proposition, pursuing this view to its logical conclusion should. The argument that everything is words reduces even science, and its claims about atoms and molecules, to just another discourse. Such a radical skepticism may ultimately be irrefutable on epistemological grounds—Sokal's hoax shows that it can lead to profound intellectual embarrassment—but it does spell the end of scholarship, in the process reducing extreme constructivism itself to a postmodernist discourse no different from, although perhaps politically more retrograde than, other, even nationalist, discourses.[37] If science falls, extreme constructivism crashes and burns.

WEAK CONSTRUCTIVISM

Weak constructivism makes a simple claim—that nations are substantialist human constructs that emerge, and can only emerge, in modern times—in other words, the age of nationalism. Human activity, human endeavors, and human struggles interact with the discursive, cultural, and institutional context of the age of nationalism to produce human communities called nations. Because inventive nationalist elites need not be involved in this process, weak primordialism, although compatible with nationalism, is unlikely to attract any but the most fainthearted of nationalists, those with little confidence in their political abilities or in the fatedness of their nations. In contrast, weak constructivism almost intrinsically appeals to historians, whose disciplinary inclinations fully endorse its precepts—that men and women "make their own history" and that historical phenomena should be understood contextually.[38]

Ernest Gellner's highly depersonalized account of "what *really* happens" approximates the weak primordialist position:

> The cultures it [nationalism] claims to defend and revive are often its own inventions, or are modified out of all recognition. Nonetheless the nationalist principle as such, as distinct from each of its specific forms, and from the individually distinctive nonsense which it may preach, has very very deep roots in our shared current condition, is not at all contingent, and will not easily be denied. . . .
>
> Nationalism is, essentially, the general imposition of a high culture on society, where previously low cultures had taken up the lives of the majority, and in some cases of the totality, of the population. It means that generalized diffusion of a school-mediated, academy-supervised idiom, codified for the requirements of reasonably precise bureaucratic and technological communication. It is the establishment of an anonymous, impersonal society, with mutually substitutable atomized

individuals, held together above all by a shared culture of this kind, in place of a previous complex structure of local groups.[39]

As I argue in chapter 6, many of Gellner's individual points may be construed as perfectly valid facilitating conditions of nations and nationalism. By the same token, and when viewed through the theoretical lens implicit in the approaches to the nation delineated in this chapter, weak constructivism's claims also seem eminently acceptable. Indeed, I submit that the first half of weak constructivism—that nations are human constructs—is even true. Unfortunately, this proposition is interesting only as a counterpoint to the preposterous claims of extreme primordialism. For if *everything* beyond the materially real world of atoms and molecules is a human construction, weak constructivism's claims are commonplace.[48] To point out that nations are humanly constructed may therefore be true—and I hasten to add that even strong primordialism would not necessarily dispute every instance of this claim—but it is as true as the larger statement that *all* nonmolecular, nonatomic reality is constructed, in other words, that culture is a reality and that nations are cultural artifacts.

The second half of weak constructivism's claims—that, as Zygmunt Bauman succinctly puts it, "modern nations are products of nationalism, and can be defined only as such"—is simply wrong.[41] Although all constructivisms assume that nations cannot emerge without nationalism, we have no reason to think that this assumption must be true, unless nations are defined a priori as modern entities that only nationalist elites can construct in nationalist times. If, alternatively, nations are definitionally divorced from nationalism and nationalist elites—as I recommended in chapter 4—it is just as possible for all three to be causally unrelated as to be causally related. In insisting, therefore, that nations, as conceptually organized clusters of properties, cannot exist in the absence of the nationalist word nation, constructivists—weak, strong, and extreme—treat an empirical (or synthetic) question as if it were definitional (or analytic) and thereby stumble into circularity.

WEAK PRIMORDIALISM

Both more and less ambitious than weak constructivism, weak primordialism is a conceptualist enterprise that insists that nations are human collectivities that, as collections of conceptually delineated and thus stable properties, emerge whenever those defining characteristics come together. As such, nations are ontologically real groups of people who share ontologically real features that, in principle, could coalesce at any time—recently, several decades or centuries ago, or in the distant past—and in any place—Serbia, Rome, or Sparta. Because these claims make nations simultaneously substantialist and less than fully substantial, nationalists should neither violently object to, nor be effusive about, them.

Weak primordialism is thus both very ambitious *and* very modest. Unlike all other variants of primordialism and all variants of constructivism, weak primordialism says that nations are always and everywhere possible, because we have no reason to believe that the defining characteristics of nations—when specified independently of the terminological categories produced by nationalists and the age of nationalism—can coalesce, or must coalesce, only during that historical period. Unless we endow the nation with properties A, B, and C that derive from, and make sense only in terms of, the language and logic of nationalism—which not only places the tools of scholarship in the hands of nationalists but, to repeat, is also a circular maneuver—it is impossible to claim, a priori, that A, B, and C cannot emerge and coalesce at any other time or in any other place.

At the same time, the claim that the properties of nations are determined conceptually and are always possible historically prevents weak primordialism from proffering a grand theory of the nation. With so much variation built into its very foundations, weak primordialism cannot, even in principle, aspire to anything like a covering law. Gellner, in sharp contrast, does have such an aspiration (even if expressed in self-contradictory fashion): "It is not denied that the agrarian world occasionally threw up units which may have resembled a modern national state; only that the agrarian world *could* occasionally do so, whilst the modern world is *bound* to do so in most cases."[42] The alternative to grandiosity, however, is neither contradiction (what is "bound" to happen cannot do so only "in most cases") nor mere description. Although weak primordialism, unlike Gellner, is necessarily silent about the sufficient condition(s) of nation formation, its conceptual core enables it to isolate some of the necessary and facilitating conditions thereof. As I suggested in the introduction, the defining characteristics of the nation, A, B, and C, could also qualify as the necessary conditions of nation formation: depending on the theory at hand, the nation (A,B,C) could not be formed in the absence of A, B, and/or C. In turn, conditions that promote the emergence of A, B, and C would qualify as facilitating. As a result, we expect "clusters" of nations to emerge when and where the conditions promoting their emergence are most in evidence. Thus, although the stronger constructivisms consider nationalist elites, nationalist discourses, and industrial society to be necessary and/or sufficient for the emergence of nations, weak primordialism demotes them to facilitating status and thereby explains why nations have clustered to such a large degree in modern times. By the same token—and other things being equal—weak primordialism would expect such clustering to diminish if, say, nationalist discourses wither away and postindustrial society takes hold.

The combination of theoretical self-restraint and open-endedness enables weak primordialism to propose an irenic alternative to primordialism's claim that nations are virtually timeless and to constructivism's claim that they are fleetingly contemporary. Instead, weak primordialism can simply assert that, inasmuch as nations emerge whenever A, B, and C coalesce, they also cease to exist whenever some of or all its defining characteristics disappear. Nations may therefore exist for very brief periods or for vast stretches of time, in the past, in the present, or in the future. Nothing intrinsic to A, B, and C favors any particular time span in any particular period and thus privileges the stronger variants of either primordialism or constructivism. Weak primordialism resolves their disagreement by refusing to acknowledge its validity. In so doing, moreover, weak primordialism can also meet the challenge posed by evolutionary psychology without necessarily having to acknowledge its exclusive theoretical validity.

UPS AND DOWNS

With strengths and weaknesses on both sides of the divide, primordialism in general and weak primordialism in particular should be perfectly capable of holding their own in any intellectual competition with constructivism. Extreme primordialism is no less preposterous than extreme constructivism, and strong primordialism is no less flawed than strong constructivism, whereas weak primordialism is only slightly less modest than weak constructivism. Primordialism's "discredited" theoretical status cannot therefore be a function of its inherent weaknesses. Instead, it may be a victim of two related developments. First, primordialism has become an academically unacceptable term—but not, I emphasize, *concept*—one reminiscent in this regard of totalitarianism and its disreputable status in the scholarly world of the 1970s and 1980s.[43] Why terms come in and out of academic fashion may have to do with the fact that most concepts are, as William Connolly puts it, "essentially contested" and hence subject to political calculations.[44]

Second, primordialism may be academically unfashionable as a result of the cyclical nature of social science theorizing. Once again, we need not inquire into the reasons to recognize that theories, like concepts, come and go and then reappear with almost predictable regularity. After the state was brought "back in," systems theorizing fell into disuse; with the rise of the "new institutionalism," systems theorizing is back in everything but name. For a while, rational choice silenced its competitors; they may now be on the verge of mounting a counterattack.[45] Such recurrent "paradigm shifts" do not necessarily preclude the growth of knowledge, but they do suggest that, as with fashionable concepts, epistemological robustness is far from the only factor involved in deciding the fate, or popularity, of theories. These considerations lead to the conclusion that, although the language and logic of postmodernism are currently in style, sooner or later it too will lose its place in the sun. At that point, primordialism may very well make a comeback.

Should this happen with the next turn of the theoretical cycle, however, constructivism will probably be supplanted by the primordialisms found in the worlds of journalism and policy making and practiced by such influential authors as Huntington and Goldhagen. After all, what may be most significant about the "Goldhagen phenomenon" is that, by resonating so loudly with both popular prejudices about Germans and the assumptions of the age of nationalism, his book appears to have attained enormous popularity precisely because of, and not despite, its strong primordialist methodology.[46] If so, the stronger primordialisms' possible theoretical primacy would be a double tragedy, because they could marginalize alternative approaches in the manner of all dominant theoretical paradigms while reaffirming the language and logic of the worst kind of nationalism.

chapter 6. national strengths

Nations exist wherever and whenever compatible propositions regarding historicity and boundaries exist within the belief set of some group of people. Complementarity, like spontaneous combustion, may come about serendipitously. But inasmuch as we expect national (N) propositions to be, over time, as consistent with one another as with lifeworld (L) propositions, the mostly unpremeditated process by which N propositions emerge in all likelihood tends "naturally" toward national identity formation. If N' and N'' are consistent with each other and with L, N''' will have to emerge and take root in a propositional setting that is defined by N', N'', and L and the web of logical consistency they create. As a result, a self-propelling dynamic may be built into propositional construction, one that pushes N propositions toward complementarity. This said, facilitating conditions are not sufficient conditions, and actually attaining complementarity is an entirely different matter, one that is not a logically necessary consequence of this presumed dynamic.

What, then, is? I do not know. More important, I *cannot* know. As I argued in chapters 4 and 5, however, I do claim to know that national identity can come about as a result of elites *and* nonelites, acting and speaking as nationalists *and* as nonnationalists. I also claim to know that no grounds exist for arguing that national identity formation could not have taken place before, say, 1789. The ancient Israelites, whose national belief system provided them with a distinct place in time and space, were as much of a nation as most contemporary nations. The Romans, especially during the republic, appear to have fit the definitional requirements as well. So too did the Byzantine Greeks, whose myths provided them with origins and whose distaste for "barbarians" testified to their refined sense of "the other."[1] Finally, I claim to know why nations have been far more common in recent centuries than in the distant past. Several "modern" conditions facilitate national identity formation—sec-

ularism, modernization, the market, the state, democracy, and nationalism—
and these deserve a closer look.

PROMOTING NATIONS

As a set of ideas regarding the worldly rootedness of humanity and its ability to determine its destiny according to this-worldly needs, secularism promotes, as well as translates into, a concern with historicity. Associated with
the Enlightenment and the rise of science, secularism replaces theistic accounts of the world with self-consciously historical ones that view the past
not as the prologue to a divine future but as the key to the present. Accordingly, to understand better where we are and who we are, we want also to understand where we—as nations, states, groups, races, and so on—came from
and where we are going.[2] Anthony Smith thus ascribes the emergence of national identity among nineteenth-century European elites to the crisis of an
intelligentsia confronted with the rise of secularism in a religious world.[3] The
Entzauberung of the world appears also to have facilitated the growth of secular religions. Human rights—and perhaps psychoanalysis with its mystical
ids, egos, and superegos—may be one such contemporary substitute for the
divine. More powerful a traditional ersatz is the nation, or, until recently,
class. Whatever its existential significance, the fervor with which nationalists
and communists have dedicated themselves to their causes—manifested in
their willingness to sacrifice their lives for the higher goal of an abstract ideal—has often resembled that of religious devotees.

Second, such related phenomena as urbanization, communications, print
capitalism, mass literacy, and industrialization—perhaps best subsumed under
the catchall label of "modernization"—bring disparate peoples together, compel them to interact and communicate with one another, and thereby enhance
awareness of otherness and perhaps the creation of boundaries.[4] Modernization also explains why the communities sharing a national identity would have
been, in general, substantially smaller in the past than in the present. Although
we know that people can attain a sense of groupness and share in its propositions by means of the actions of a charismatic warrior, priestly caste, barbar-
ian invader, itinerant bards and poets, or, even, themselves, obvious physical
limits exist to how many people can be brought together under an overarching identity in ancient or premodern times. In contrast, modernization increases exponentially the number of people that national identity can encompass and who can "imagine" themselves as a nation.[5]

Third, the market forces people and peoples to compete with one another for material goods and opportunities, and where competition exists, we are sure to find winners and losers, even if only in relative terms. Under conditions such as these, "ethnic markers" can conveniently be imputed with a symbolic salience that permits both winners and losers to form boundaries and mobilize.[6] What is more, the market has a differential impact on regions, rewarding efficient ones and penalizing inefficient ones. As Michael Hechter has argued, the market's accentuation of regional differences can help create national differences, thereby generating the drive toward independence as the only perceived solution to the inequities of capitalist relations.[7] By logical extension, market conditions can affect states in no less uneven a manner: although comparative advantage and free trade is supposed, ceteris paribus, to benefit all states, the stubborn reality of "path-dependent" institutional development tends to makes things unequal and thereby sully the expectations of pristine theories.

Fourth is the state. By its very existence a territorially defined state "imposes," though not in any remotely constructivist sense, physical unity—that is, both territorial and conceptual boundaries—on a population. A modern bureaucratic state goes even further and imposes administrative unity on some territorially bounded population. If complex, such a population might, as Ernest Gellner proposes, interact more easily and efficiently if united in a belief system endowing it with an overarching identity.[8] Where a complex population exists within a unified political-spatial setting, such as that which the state defines, a national identity functions to overcome the cleavages dividing the population and to provide it with the ability to communicate and act more effectively, to live more meaningfully. At the very least, shared beliefs facilitate cooperation by reducing, if not eliminating, the "free-rider" problem and associated transaction costs.[9] The resulting identification of the nation with the state also contributes to historicist inquiries hoping to root the latter, and hence also the former, in a historical past or glorious future connoting naturalness and legitimacy.

Fifth, democracy promotes national identity.[10] Democratic regimes are self-styled popular regimes; they derive their legitimacy from the people and from their activity on behalf of the people. The American Declaration of Independence, in its insistence on government by, for, and of the people, is thus a quintessentially nationalist document. Naturally, the people can be a multicultural, even a multinational, association, yet it is likely that a democratic regime, in its appeals to the people, will either emphasize the national characteristics of that people (if they are culturally homogeneous) or will attempt to create more or less homogeneous characteristics (if the people are cultur-ally heterogeneous). Because legitimacy requires that a strong connection be established between government and "the" people, the logic of the situation demands that a people, or people in general, be transformed into a collectiv-ity deserving of the definite article.[11]

Finally, as constructivists of all stripes insist, the modern ideal known as nationalism explicitly argues for the complementarity of the two proposi-tional sets constituting national identity and proposes that the existential needs of nations demand their conjunction with states. As a self-styled ide-al that matches both the term and concept of the nation with the term and concept of the state, nationalism—and in particular its consolidation as a modern zeitgeist—clearly facilitates nation formation by making the case explicitly for nation-statehood as the most legitimate modern form of polit-ical existence.

These six conditions may explain why nations have multiplied with modernity; if so, they also suggest that nations are likely to be with us for a long time to come. On the one hand, we have no reason to think that the propositional sets constituting national identity should disappear anytime soon. On the other hand, the conditions facilitating their existence do not seem to be, contrary to the claims of postmodernists and globalizers, on the verge of extinction. Thus secularism seems here to stay, even if, as I suspect, religion—and not just of the fundamentalist variety—has been prematurely relegated to the ash heap of history. Modernization will, if anything, acquire even greater salience in the foreseeable future. Capitalism is, or so its avatars tell us, the wave of the future, and, for better or for worse, they seem to be right. Even if their claims are grossly exaggerated, there is no disputing that market forces have the upper hand, at least at this point in time, in much of the world. Democracy too is surely here to stay. Rather more controversial is the future of the state and of nationalism. As I argue in this chapter, howev-er, despite the popularity of claims that the state and nationalism are passé, they are anything but.

PROMOTING STATES

With respect to the state, it may be useful to remind ourselves that it is thriv-ing in precisely those countries that claim to be on the verge of having out-grown it—the developed industrial democracies of the so-called West. Gov-ernment expenditures as a percentage of gross national product have increased almost everywhere in the last hundred years, despite vigorous neo-conservative efforts to roll back the state in recent decades.[12] As the *Economist* points out:

> At the beginning of this century government spending in today's industrial countries accounted for less than one-tenth of national income. Last year [1996], in the same countries, the government's share of output was roughly half. Decade by decade, the change in the government's share of the economy moved in one direction only: up. During war it went up; during peace it went up. Between 1920 and the mid-1930s, years of greatly diminished trade and international economic contact, it went up. Between 1960 and 1980, as global trade and finance expanded, it went up. Between 1980 and 1990, as this breeze of globalisation became a strong wind, it went up again. Between 1990 and 1996, as the wind became a gale, it went up some more.[13]

No less important, from 1960 to 1985 the growth of the civil service significantly outstripped the growth of the labor force in a whole range of developed countries: 70 percent compared with 5 percent in Germany, 37.5 percent compared with 17.5 percent in France, 42.5 percent compared with 12.5 percent in the United Kingdom, 65 percent compared with 5 percent in Italy, 70 percent compared with 2.5 percent in Austria, 57.5 percent compared with 15 percent in Belgium, 127.5 percent compared with 23.75 percent in Denmark, 110 percent compared with 17.5 percent in Finland, 42.5 percent compared with 32.5 percent in the Netherlands, 117.5 percent compared with 20 percent in Sweden, and 75 percent compared with 17.5 percent in Switzerland.[14]

The state's share of the workforce continues to remain high.[15] The frenzied efforts made by European governments to meet the Maastricht criteria for joining the European Monetary Union (EMU) may have restrained the state, but the widespread preference given to one-time measures and accounting tricks suggests that at best it is much too early to suppose that a secular diminution in the state's size and importance is underway. Given these indicators, Stephen Krasner is surely justified in claiming that not only has there been "no challenge to juridical sovereignty" but a historically informed comparison of states and state sovereignty since the emergence of the Westphalian system shows that "state control has actually increased over the long term: de facto sovereignty has been strengthened rather than weakened. Contemporary developed States exercise greater and probably far greater de facto sovereignty than either their historical European ancestors or contemporary developing States."[16]

The state's continued strength, vitality, and durability appear to be due to at least three factors: the market, the international system, and globalization. Although many governments have shifted some state functions to the market in recent years, it is equally true that countervailing pressures are pushing the state to assert itself. Even if the market is the most efficient form of economic organization today, it does not seem to be able, on its own, to guarantee the just distribution of the social product, be it in the form of public services, social safety nets, or, as Ulrich Beck points out, even of something as rudimentary as employment.[17] Short of the realization of utopian socialist visions of the self-rule of autonomous workers—or of utopian economist visions of frictionless capitalist societies—the state will continue to be most responsible for the fair division of the social surplus and for the creation of conditions under which citizens will be best able to pursue what they universally consider to be their rights. Even in Beck's vision of socially engaged labor performed for the good of civil society, renumeration, whether it be in money or in-kind, can be guaranteed only if some entity raises the resources and/or ensures their fair distribution.[18] Unless reified beyond recognition, civil society cannot perform either function because it has none of the coherence, executive authority, or directive capacity of the state. This last point suggests that markets may be most apt to promote states under conditions of democracy, when some degree of popular empowerment and a broad acceptance of notions of entitlement are likely, as Dennis Quinn and John Woolley note, to push political elites to reduce the risks and stabilize the returns associated with market volatility by means of state intervention.[19]

Indeed, the market arguably presupposes the state. As I noted in chapter 3, markets are unthinkable without the institutional underpinnings of rule of law, and rule of law is unthinkable without the state.[20] Efficient markets require efficient states, whereas inefficient and/or abysmally weak states virtually preclude the existence or emergence of genuine market relations. Although the seemingly inexorable spread of the market may not presuppose the prior creation or consolidation of states—a functionalist argument such as this would not be persuasive—it is hard to imagine how such a momentum can be sustained unless efforts to establish both rule of law and effective states are taken, especially by capitalists themselves. Whether they can overcome the limitations of their "class interests" both brings to mind an earlier neo-Marxist literature on the "relative autonomy" of the state and suggests why states still play a uniquely important role in preventing excessive capital concentration and thus in preserving both competition and the market.[21] Note, finally, that the case for the state becomes much stronger if we alter our initial assumption regarding the unparalleled economic efficiency of the market. If and when recessions strike, economies melt down, and bubbles burst, the state will once again reemerge as insurer of last resort—in all likelihood because, as neo-Marxists used to claim, the capitalists will insist on its intervention.[22]

The division of the world into states also privileges the state, so much so that the Carnegie Commission on Preventing Deadly Conflict—as liberal internationalist a group as one can imagine—recommends that such strife can best be prevented by and through existing states and not, as one would expect, by the United Nations acting on its own.[23] State elites support states, perhaps because they have some normative interest in doing so, perhaps because their stability, security, and prosperity depend on it. Inasmuch as the international system of states is a system of interconnected parts, the stability of that system rests in part at least on the stability of the states that comprise it.[24] Not surprisingly, the United States was unwilling to countenance the collapse of its cold war enemy, the "evil empire," until the August 1991 coup attempt in Moscow and the subsequent declarations of independence by the non-Russian republics created a fait accompli and doomed the Soviet Union. Washington was no less reluctant to dismember Iraq—despite talk of Saddam Hussein's being another Hitler—in the aftermath of the Gulf War. The 1997–1998 financial crisis in Asia also demonstrated the lengths to which international actors and great powers will go in order to prop up failing states.

Hendrik Spruyt suggests a more subtle reason for the state's continued indispensability to the international system:

> Political entrepreneurs and social groups had good reason to prefer a system of sovereign states: such units created some measure of regularity and predictability in both their domestic economies and in international relations. The principle of territorially delimited authority, which was sovereign within those borders, delineated what was to be "domestic" and what "international." . . . Despite the much-lamented existence of sovereign territoriality, it is in fact a method of structuring international relations that makes interaction more predictable and organized.[25]

In other words, states are a useful organizing principle, an analytical device for ordering relations, as it were, "within" and "without." Not surprisingly,

Ian Clark concludes that "overall, it is difficult to detect any major restructuring of the operative principles of international politics." His counterfactual is persuasive: "To put it in its simplest terms, a Talleyrand or Metternich reincarnated at the present time would have little difficulty in mastering the rules of the international political game."[26] Those rules may be under fire, but they are unlikely to disappear altogether, so long as no contenders demonstrate superior utility. The claim that the distinction between inside and outside, internal and external, is artificial, although true, both misses the point—after all, all analytical distinctions are artificial constructs—and, by ultimately asserting only that everything is everything, offers no alternative for structuring international relations in a "more predictable and organized" fashion.

Seen in this light, international organizations appear as one of the central props of states. International as well as regional organizations use states as their organizing principle, while enshrining their integrity, inviolability, and sovereignty in founding acts that transform these notions into international norms that may be violated only if some overriding security threat can plausibly be identified.[27] Arguably, this is why more or less stable interstate relations could emerge so quickly between and among the Soviet successor states. In contrast to many polities that arose from the ruins of the Habsburg, Hohenzollern, and Ottoman empires, the post-Soviet republics were immediately drawn into a stable international system whose key players—the United Nations, the International Monetary Fund, the Organization for Security and Cooperation in Europe, and the World Bank—could successfully imbue these republics with the external attributes of "stateness" that befit bona fide international actors.[28]

Last, globalization—defined here provisionally (I return to this theme in chapter 9) as the acceleration and multiplication of political, economic, social, and cultural forces that transcend or transgress nation-state boundaries—undermines *and* promotes states. There is no denying that the transnational movement of capital diminishes or constrains state sovereignty and, as the 1998–1999 worldwide financial crisis showed, can even affect state stability.[29] The emergence of cross-border megafirms with capital assets that far outstrip most state budgets and with the capacity to pick and choose their locations on the basis of lowest possible taxation rates is also a challenge to state sovereignty, state viability—and, as Charles Lindblom argued many years ago, democracy.[30] By the same token, economic globalization and some of what it supposedly entails—in particular, the viability of smaller units of political and economic organization—can also promote state formation in regions that, from a more traditional Weberian point of view, might have been incapable, or have been deemed incapable, of sustaining statelike institutions because of their size, geographic isolation, and the like.[31] Small wonder that, as James Rosenau states, "the number of sovereign states grew tenfold between 1800 and 1985, with most of the growth occurring during the current, relatively brief period [1945–1985] of turbulence in world politics."[32]

The growing number of small states on the one hand and the economic success of certain small states on the other suggests that state proliferation and globalization may go together. The states of the future may be weaker and more brittle than the states of the past, and they may no longer run the entire show internationally. Indeed, according to Wolfgang Mommsen, "the traditional idea of a world of sovereign, self-reliant nation states claiming the right to assert themselves and pursue their essential national interests by taking recourse to force, against their own nationals or against other nations, appears to be on the way out."[33] Although this possibility may be a cause for concern for mainstream International Relations theory, it will not subvert the state—at least not just yet.[34] Quite the contrary, weakened states may even become the objects of greater loyalty and adulation, partly because they will be the sole barriers between citizens and global capital volatility and partly because firms may be intrinsically less capable of generating the affective equivalents of patriotism and nationalism.

WESTERN EUROPEAN EXCEPTIONALISM?

An obvious objection comes to mind. Does not the ongoing process of European integration suggest that the sovereign state is really on the way out? In answering this question, we may for starters want to distinguish between rhetoric and reality. Eurorhetoric suggests that Europe is inexorably headed toward unification, that wars have finally come to an end, and that the millennium, indeed the end of history, is around the corner. We would not be too remiss in greeting such grandiose claims, surely not the first to herald the end of strife and the coming of paradise, skeptically. The euphoria of 1989 disappeared within a mere year. The buzz word of the 1970s and 1980s was *Eurosclerosis,* and not *Eurooptimism,* and all slogans—like proletarian internationalism, *die Neue Ordnung,* and the new world order—appear to have a limited life span. We would also do well to remember that, even if it is unquestionable that the state is about to be superseded in Europe, the implications of that demise are limited. If Western Europeans no longer need the state, that is no reason to think that other peoples can also dispense with it. And even if advanced industrial democracies no longer need the state, all manner of other societies may still need it. The future of Western Europe may turn out to be the future of the world, but the null hypothesis should be that it is merely the future of Western Europe.

Although skepticism may not be an inappropriate way of placing this question in clearer focus, the question still deserves an answer. Inasmuch as the cornerstone of the argument for the growing irrelevance of the state is the EMU, we would do well to examine it, and its likely impact on European states, somewhat more closely. Additional grounds for skepticism quickly appear. First, the success of EMU is by no means assured, and the verdict will not be in until some time after the year 2002, when the euro will have become Europe's sole currency. If critics are right to argue that the euro's introduction will, in the absence of far-reaching economic and political reforms, only exacerbate already intolerably high levels of unemployment and intensify social dissatisfaction, the new currency could also have the unintended consequence of strengthening, or even generating, political forces committed to greater state control over economic and other matters.[35] A host of far-right parties is already in place to make the case for "self-determination" in the face of the tyranny of faceless European Union (EU) bureaucrats and, far worse, indifferent central bankers. Jörg Haider's Freedom Party in Austria, Gianfranco Fini's National Alliance in Italy, and Jean-Marie Le Pen's National Front in France have dominated the headlines, but they have counterparts in Belgium, Denmark, the Czech Republic, the Netherlands, and Germany. And the argument for blaming the European Central Bank for Europe's woes will not be entirely far-fetched, because the interest rates it sets will perforce be too high for some countries and too low for others, compelling governments to cope with exogenously induced difficulties that could encourage them to politicize the EU's monetary policy and thereby produce a "soft" euro.[36] If so, cautions Maurice Obstfeld, such a currency "would undermine the gains that EU members have made in reducing inflation." And, conceivably, "if the EU countries that do not initially enter EMU prosper relative to those that have joined, EMU could fall apart."[37] Or perhaps not. Either way, EMU is in for some rough sailing in the years ahead.

Second, even if the euro does not exacerbate political divisions, the decision of the United Kingdom, Denmark, Greece, and Sweden to stay out of the EMU, at least for some time—together with the creation by the "ins" of a consultative mechanism consisting of finance ministers that will exclude the "outs" from its central deliberations—means that the European Union's future institutional development will be bifurcated and thus un-likely to promote common political institutions that could supersede all states. De jure bifurcation will rest atop de facto bifurcation, because the EMU countries already consist of a hard core with reasonably sound econ-omies—Germany, France, Austria, and the Benelux countries—and the rest, spearheaded by Italy.

Third, the possibility of the European Union's expansion—and the finan-cial, organizational, and administrative difficulties that membership, or even the pursuit of membership, by Poland, Hungary, the Czech Republic, Esto-nia, Slovenia, and perhaps Cyprus will impose on the EU—will produce still a third group of states least affected by Europe's centripetal forces. A Europe of many speeds and concentric circles may be a perfectly viable and laudable project, but it will not promote short-term political unification. The inclusion of the east-central European states will, as the EU's *Agenda 2000* recognizes, vastly complicate an already unwieldy decision-making mechanism by rais-ing most pointedly the question of majority voting versus unanimous voting versus weighted voting.[38]

Fourth, it is not at all clear that an increasingly self-confident Germany—especially one ruled by anyone less fanatically committed to Europe than Helmut Kohl—will continue to sacrifice its perceived national interests to pan-European goals and therefore fail to provoke the fears of its neighbors, especially France.[39] Alternatively, if we grant that the Frenco-German rela-tionship is likely to remain stable and strong, it becomes even harder to imag-ine how both states could transfer so much sovereignty to EU institutions as to empower significantly their smaller and weaker neighbors. The continued dominance by the Security Council of so ostensibly egalitarian an organiza-tion as the United Nations suggests that, even in the best of circumstances, genuine limits exist to what the strong will surrender to the weak. Far more likely than the *sliianie* of Germany and France, to use the unificationist ter-minology of Soviet propaganda, is that they will dominate a self-styled union that in reality will be a loose confederation of sovereign states.

Fifth, if, as seems likely, growing European integration promotes the resurgence of regions in general and self-determinationist movements in par-ticular—Padania may be less of a joke than a trendsetter—it is all but certain that a pro-state backlash will eventually occur, one concerned with main-taining existing institutions, boundaries, and national identities. Individual states may, like Italy, Spain, and the United Kingdom, either toy with or ac-tually introduce federalist schemes, but these too will be premised on states as the units within which federalism functions. Some multinational states may voluntarily fragment along the lines of Czechoslovakia, but, as Ottawa's tenacious defense of Canada suggests, the Czech-Slovak divorce may have been a special instance of the delayed collapse of Leninist multinational states and not a harbinger of things to come within democratic settings.[40] And even if it is, successful secessionists are unlikely to settle for anything less than states of their own.

Finally, despite the manifest absence of a security threat and thus of a genuine raison d'être for NATO, Europe's states are committed to retaining, and expanding, the North Atlantic Treaty Organization. The statist spirit of NATO clearly contravenes the unificationist spirit of the EMU and the EU, because NATO consists of states—not economies—and "its" armed forces are simply the armed forces of its member states.[41] Not surprisingly perhaps, the discussion of NATO expansion revealed just how much French and German elites—the future core of united Europe, mind you—were still concerned with the balance of power between their countries. Indeed, French insistence on Romania's inclusion in NATO seems to have been largely motivated by the desire to balance Germany and its dependencies—Poland, Hungary, and the Czech Republic—with a French ally.[42]

In sum, declarations of European unity and the death of European states are still premature. There is no reason to believe that in Europe, as within the international system, states will not continue to thrive, albeit in different, perhaps weaker forms. As Krasner reminds us, "The survival of de jure sovereignty for more than 400 years in an environment of radically changing technologies, military capabilities, actors, and power distributions could only have occurred if the specific components of de facto sovereignty were malleable."[43] That the states of the twenty-first century may be less like the states of the nineteenth heralds the end of the state only if we reify nineteenth-century stateness and term it the apogee of the state.

PROMOTING NATIONALISM

What, then, are the prospects for nationalism? My answer is that they are quite good. As I suggested earlier, good reasons exist for thinking that nations and states will be with us for a long time to come. Because nations and states are two of nationalism's defining characteristics, their continued existence bodes well for nationalism. Moreover, nationalism already exists, enjoying widespread popularity as a discourse, ideology, or ideal among large segments of the world's population. The task before us now is to determine what might promote nationalism by making plausible its central claim, that states are good for nations. As I show next, four such factors exist: elites, the international system, human rights, and democracy. In brief, because the nation and the state are the dominant organizing principles, the first social and the second political, of the contemporary world, the continued striving of national elites for their own states is all but inevitable in an international system that pays homage to nation-states, human rights, and democracy.

I start with what I hope is the more or less uncontroversial "observation statement" that elites are ubiquitous.[44] Even if they are not inherent in all forms of social organization, conditions of modernity seem virtually to guarantee that ethnic majorities and minorities will possess elites. The spread of education, urbanization, and industrialization may or may not attenuate ethnic differences, as modernization theory at one time suggested, but they clearly produce strata that are socially mobilized, technically trained, and cognitively equipped to mobilize their nations for the advancement of their and/or their nations' interests—should reason to do so exist.

The international system provides one such powerful reason by legitimating the nation-state in and through such institutions as the United Nations, the International Monetary Fund, the World Bank, and so on. Nation-statehood is, as John Breuilly suggests, a ticket to the promotion of elite ambitions and the acquisition of international largesse.[45] Junkets to Davos and luncheons at the White House are not available to nonstate elites without national constituencies. What is good for a national elite need not be equally good for the nation, of course, but because the elite usually defines the nation's interests in terms of its own, the attractiveness of nationalism as an ideological rationale is only enhanced. Although the international system has also encroached on state sovereignty, perhaps producing a state not quite up to nationalist standards, even a weaker state rests on, and presupposes, the continued legitimation of the nation-state principle—and not of some alternative.

Inasmuch as the discourse of human rights exerts a hegemonic influence on contemporary thinking—dictators in particular feel impelled to proclaim themselves their solemn defenders—modern elites may have no choice but to appropriate the language of rights in general and of self-determination in particular. Human rights hegemony does not suffice to propel national elites onto the path of nationalism, but it greatly facilitates such a move. Human rights literally invite elites to assert themselves; moreover, they provide elites with a universal language and with irrefutable arguments, so much so that opposition to human rights demands must also be couched in the language of human rights. Ironically, official elites are thereby forced to pay homage to a principle that the universal implementation of which, by privileging the sovereign individual or the sovereign group over the sovereign state, would lead to the destabilization of the international system and to the internal delegitimation of their rule.[46]

Also pushing national elites toward the pursuit of states for their nations is democracy.[47] Political freedom, party competition, voting, and the like permit, encourage, and compel elites to pursue their interests in the most efficient manner, and that often means using nations as vehicles of self-promotion. Conditions of freedom remove whatever political obstacles to the pursuit of nationalism may have existed. Parliamentary competition accentuates the "groupness" of groups and thus provides elites with ready-made vehicles for their ambitions. The imperative of popular legitimation forces elites to identify with the supposed repository of sovereignty and in this manner to support the nation. National elites in democratic settings are therefore likely both to express nationalist sentiments and actually to translate their beliefs into the pursuit of some form of self-government.

Whither nationalism? As far into the future as the nation and the state, I suspect, and that may be quite far. After all, nationalism is not some atavistic premodern phenomenon that is slated to disappear with the growing modernization of the world. To the contrary, many trappings of modern life promote nations, states, and thus nation-states. Robert H. Jackson and Alan James are, I believe, quite correct to argue:

> Nowadays no less than previously the population of the world is divided into separate, independent States each with their own identities, territories, and symbols which mark them off from one another. The vast majority of people still owe their allegiance to the independent countries to which they belong. . . . National identity and self-determination show no sign of receding. . . . The independent political entities referred to as 'States' have their own governments organized according to their own political enlightenment and ideologies. And the governments decide their own policies, make their own decisions, and carry them out—for the most part—with their own agents, agencies, and resources. There is nothing to indicate that in the foreseeable future such entities will not continue to be the preferred and predominant form of political organization just as they are today and have been in previous centuries. Present indications are—if anything—that the desire and de-

mand for independent statehood will remain strong, so that, as multi-
ethnic States come under pressure from secessionists of one kind or another, independent States will perhaps continue to proliferate as they
have done throughout most of the present century.[48]

We can, in sum, expect nationalism to grow in intensity as modern states become even more modern and unmodern states embark on the road to
modernity. Besides huffing and puffing, postmodernists and globalizers can
do little about this. The former's rejection of grand narratives and inherent
inability to propose an alternative organizing principle and the latter's incan-
tation of globalization and globalism amount to an abdication before modernity. If only because the field is bereft of conceptual contenders, modernity
can only continue to breed nationalism.

III. EMPIRES

chapter 7. imperial structures

Tycoons build empires, conquerors dream of empire, oppressed peoples rebel against empires. Empire brings to mind Andrew Carnegie and William Randolph Hearst, Cecil Rhodes and Hernando Cortez, Frantz Fanon and Albert Memmi, Alexander the Great and Augustus Caesar. We imagine Xenophon's *Anabasis*, *The Song of Roland*, and Rudyard Kipling's stories. The cornucopia of images suggests that *empire* is an empty signifier. If so, it may be more useful, as Mark Beissinger recommends, to shift our inquiry from the concept to its manifold representations.

But this maneuver fails. Ironically, Beissinger's injunction that "empire must be understood not as a thing, but as a set of practices that give rise to perceptions and claims that the polity represents a fundamentally alien rule, an 'other'," amounts to a definition that, as a definition, belies his claim that the perceptions and claims of others are all that really matters.[1] Moreover, Beissinger's definition is just as much of an imposition on reality as those of other scholars and, like all definitions, is open to evaluation in terms of vagueness, ambiguity, and consistency. Suffice to say that a "set of practices" with certain alienating consequences is an unusually vague and ambiguous notion that, while doing little to pinpoint empire, does incorporate a causal proposition in the definition.

With so many signifiers bearing down upon us, perhaps it would help to turn to history or, more precisely, to historians for definitional guidance? *Jein*: yes and no. It is of course trivially true that historical knowledge about self-styled empires is indispensable to conceptualizing empires. But even history falls silent, if we appreciate that empires in name are not all there is to empire. For if we may call the Union of Soviet Socialist Republics an empire, even though its leaders vigorously rejected the label, we should be equally entitled to go against the terminological preferences of self-styled emperors and insist that their realms really may *not* have been empires.[2] The so-called

Central African Empire of Emperor Jean-Bedel Bokassa is a case in point. We rightly dismiss Bokassa's claims as absurd because they do not correspond to the image of empire we already have in mind.

What is true of our contemporaries, such as Bokassa, must by logical extension also be true of our historical predecessors. With them as with him, we must ask whether their language and their appellations, be they self-consciously imperial or not, correspond to our understanding of empire. If they do, it just so happens that we all agree. If they do not, our preferences must take priority over theirs, not so much because we know better or are wiser but because we are the ones doing the writing and, for better or for worse, the theorizing. Conceptual imperialism creates empire.

APPROACHING EMPIRE

A closer look at several definitions may help us get a better grasp on empire. Michael Doyle suggests that "empire . . . is a relationship, formal or informal, in which one state controls the effective political sovereignty of another political society."[3] George Lichtheim defines empire as the "relationship of a hegemonial state to peoples or nations under its control."[4] S. N. Eisenstadt notes that "the basic center-periphery relations that developed in the tsarist empire were characterized—in common with those of many other historical empires—by the differentiation, specification and crystallization of centers in general and of political centers in particular, as autonomous, structurally and symbolically distinct entities."[5] David Lake suggests that "in empire, one partner cedes substantial rights of residual control directly to the other; in this way, the two polities are melded together in a political relationship in which one partner controls the other."[6] Geir Lundestad states that "empire simply means a hierarchical system of political relationships with one power being much stronger than any other."[7] Finally, Alexander Wendt and Daniel Friedheim claim that "informal empires are structures of transnational political authority that combine an egalitarian principle of de jure sovereignty with a hierarchical principle of de facto control."[8]

Their terminological differences notwithstanding, these six definitions agree that empire is much more than a set of practices. Indeed, in addition to involving some kind of "alien rule," empire appears to entail a special kind of relationship between at least two entities. Surely, one such entity must be "nonnative" and the other "native."[9] And, just as surely, the relationship between the two must be one of domination. In an empire, there-fore, a nonnative entity dominates a native entity. Because the empires with which we are concerned belong, above all, in the realm of politics, the non-native entity must at a minimum exercise *political* dominance. If so, we must be in the presence of, simply, the imperial state, by which I mean some version of Weber's notion of a political organization with a monop-oly of violence and a ruling elite. Of course, we also expect the nonnative entity to exercise some degree of *economic* dominance, perhaps as a func-tion of its political dominance, perhaps independently thereof. Whatever the case, two analytically distinct forms of domination, one political and one economic, raise the possibility that the core elite may be "bifurcated," consisting of two subelites. That possibility in turn suggests that the rela-tionship between these two subelites cannot be assumed to be harmonious, especially in capitalist empires.[10]

What can we now say about the native entity, the "political society" whose "effective political sovereignty" is controlled, and the kind of control exerted by the dominant elite over the subordinate natives? That political society can-not be just any inchoate population, because a mere collection of people is not quite the coherent entity we are looking for. Nor can that political soci-ety be a full-fledged state, because the resulting relationship would amount to "hegemony," or one independent entity's domination of the foreign rela-tions of another independent entity.[11] Native entities can be more than sim-ple social agglomerations and less than full-fledged polities if their elites are "nonpolitically political" natives in just the way Doyle's terminology sug-gests. As elites they must be in charge of local affairs, but as dominated na-tive elites they must only govern or, more exactly, administer the native enti-ties. In an empire, therefore, native elites are deprived of their political authority without losing their social status. They are, as it were, suspended in midair, serving both as objects of central policies of domination and as sub-jects in their administration and execution. In short, native elites are nonsov-ereign elites.

Inasmuch as an empire minimally involves a sovereign state's domination of a native society and its nonsovereign elite, we expect both to be housed in territorially distinct regions inhabited by culturally distinct populations—the nonnatives and the natives—who share physically real or merely imagined characteristics and are different, with respect to these characteristics, from other populations in other regions.[12] The region housing the nonnative state may then be termed, in accordance with common usage, the *core* (or *metro-*

pole), whereas the native regions are the *periphery*.[13] Although the number of peripheral regions must, as I presently explain, be at least two, the more important point for the time being is that their combined populations and territories not be "ridiculously" smaller than those of the core. However open to interpretation, such a limiting condition would still permit us, should we be so inclined, to call Moscow's relations with Chechnya or Washington's relations with Puerto Rico "imperial," without forcing us to conclude that giant Russia and tiny Chechnya or the United States and Puerto Rico therefore form empires.[14]

Note, finally, that my emphasis on the relationship between two entities says nothing at all about the political arrangements within, or regime type of, those entities. We often assume that empires must be dictatorships, both within the core and the periphery, because the relationship between the core and the periphery is often dictatorial. But there obviously is no reason that should be so. One democracy can dominate, even dictate to, another democracy (or democratically organized "political society"): nothing about the concept of democracy precludes such an eventuality. And we also know, empirically, that many empires have had democratic cores—those of the British, French, and Americans are cases in point—as well as democratic, or more or less democratic, peripheries, such as India and the Philippines.

IMPERIAL STRUCTURE

Let us now look more closely at the relations that bind core elites to peripheral elites. Naturally enough, we expect core elites to run the agencies, organizations, and institutions of the imperial state and peripheral elites to administer their peripheral outposts. We therefore expect core elites, like all state elites, to craft foreign and defense policy, control the armed forces, regulate the economy, maintain law and order, extract resources, pass legislation, and delineate borders. In turn, we expect peripheral elites, like all regional elites in all states, to implement core policies.[15] But note that the division of labor between core elite and peripheral elites in empires is little different from that between central elite and regional elites in all states. And although the relationship between core elite and peripheral elites is unequal, premised on the dominance of the former and the subservience of the latter, that too is no different from center-periphery relations in many hierarchically organized multinational states.

Our inability to draw a neat line between colonial elites and regional elites points to a more serious problem—that the distinction between the core state and its peripheral outposts is, in the final analysis, an unpersuasive terminological contrivance, one that Ronald Suny appreciates in calling empires "composite" states.[16] Our problem is simple. We cannot house peripheral elites in states of their own, because that would preclude an imperial relationship. But neither can we simply incorporate them functionally into imperial states, because that too precludes an imperial relationship. Nor can we, finally, deprive the peripheral elites of any political status whatsoever.

How, then, do we construct a boundary between nonempire and empire? I suggested earlier that an empire must consist of at least two peripheral regions. Indeed, Bruce Parrott defines empire as a "dominant society's control of the effective sovereignty of two or more subordinate societies that are substantially concentrated in particular regions or homelands within the empire."[17] We can now see why. So long as a core elite has only one peripheral unit to dominate, we can never establish a definitional boundary. Once at least two such units exist, however, we can go beyond the functional division of responsibilities between core elite and peripheral elites and focus on their relationships.

Consider figure 7.1. The core state and elite (C) occupy the center and dominate the peripheral entities (P). Far more important, however, the figure also shows that empires have a peculiar structure. Core-periphery relations resemble an incomplete wheel, with a hub and spokes but no rim.[18] The most striking aspect of such a structure is not the hub and spokes, which we expect to find in just about every political system, but the absence of a rim— or, to use less metaphorical language, of relations between and among the peripheral units. This "rimlessness" extricates us from the conceptual cul de sac we have just entered. The core state can keep its outposts and the peripheral elites may be functionally indistinguishable from merely regional elites, but, with the addition of structure, empire is transformed into a peculiar kind of polity, one that is, as we expect, both quite similar to, as well as substantially different from, run-of-the-mill hierarchical multinational states. Although his "structural theory of imperialism" is, to my mind, a misnomer, Johan Galtung gets the structure of empire exactly right: "There are four rules defining this particular interaction structure:

1. Interaction between Center and Periphery is vertical.
2. Interaction between Periphery and Periphery is missing.

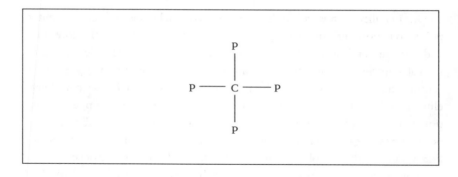

FIGURE 7.1
The Structure of Empire

3. Multilateral interaction involving all three is missing.
4. Interaction with the outside world is monopolized by the Center, with two implications:
    a. Periphery interaction with other Center nations is missing.
    b. Center as well as Periphery interaction with Periphery nations belonging to other Center nations is missing.[19]

IMPERIAL BUTS

Naturally, a few qualifications are in order. Inasmuch as everything is connected to everything else, keeping the peripheries of even the most hierarchically organized empire completely separate is impossible. By the absence of a rim, therefore, I mean only that no "significant" relations between peripheries can exist without the intermediation of the core. In nonimperial systems, in contrast, we expect the relations between and among regions to be more or less independent of each other, and we expect them to be significant. In an empire, therefore, political consultations, military cooperation, and security arrangements between and among peripheries will take place only, or largely, on the initiative and under the direction of the core. Metropoles that command peripheries to interact significantly would in essence be withdrawing from empire.

Equally important is that the core serve as a hub for significant economic relations (a requirement that raises the intriguing possibility of, as I had earlier intimated, the political and economic structures' not being fully in sync). That is, interperiphery exchanges of resources should also take place, largely if not exclusively via the core. The resources that course along imperial channels may comprise money, goods, information, and/or personnel; the kind, or mix, of resources that flow in an empire will be a function of the imperial economy at any given time. Ancient empires are likely to have seen flows of material goods; modern empires would have witnessed shifts toward financial flows and information. As the physical channels through which resources flow, the transportation networks of empires (roads, railroads, and sea, air, and information links) generally reflect this structure, even if imperfectly.[20] In contrast, with a greater number of horizontal linkages in nonempires, all roads, whether highways or information highways, should not, and do not, lead to Rome.

In the overseas empires of the British, French, Dutch, Americans, Spanish, and Portuguese, for instance, goods and people were transported from the hinterlands of colonies to their coasts, where they were loaded onto ships that brought them to the metropoles, which in turn provided the colonies with manufactured goods. Tsarist Russia's railroad system had St. Petersburg and Moscow as its hub. In Austria-Hungary roads, railroads, and telegraphs centered on Vienna and to a lesser degree on Budapest and Prague—as we would expect in a severely "decayed" empire.[21] The Soviet transportation network had Moscow as its reference point, so much so that even in the late 1980s it was most convenient to travel between different republics via the Soviet capital. Many centuries earlier goods, people, and information traveled along roads and sea routes to and from Rome and Constantinople. A future empire would in all likelihood be the hub of worldwide information, communication, and financial flows.

The Soviet Union was the quintessence of an imperially structured polity, because the rigid centralization of the Communist Party guaranteed that virtually all significant political and economic channels would link the core and the periphery but not the periphery with the periphery. The economic structure was just as centralized, with the all-union State Planning Committee developing exact input and output measures for all Soviet republics and, in essence, decreeing that flows of resources should be centralized as well.[22] In addition, core political and economic elites were, for all practical purposes, one and the same. With so highly centralized an imperial structure, interregional ties were unavoidably minimal. Symptomatically, when such powerful non-Russian bosses as Volodymyr Shcherbytsky of Ukraine, Sharaf Rashidov of Uzbekistan, and Dinmukhamed Kunaev of Kazakstan sought autonomy from the center, they rarely pursued relations with one another.[23]

The structure of U.S. rule in Central America also was, for much of the nineteenth and twentieth centuries, hublike and thus imperial in everything but name. Nicaragua, El Salvador, Honduras, Guatemala, Cuba, Haiti, Panama, and Puerto Rico were overwhelmingly dependent on the United States politically and economically; their elites were, like all colonial elites, little more than "nonpolitically political" local satraps.[24] Unlike the Soviet empire, however, which placed political and economic control in the hands of one elite, the party nomenklatura centered in Moscow, the U.S. empire witnessed a formal separation of powers, between a political elite centered in Washington and an economic elite in possession of vast capital resources.[25] Whether the former was, as Marxists used to argue, merely the handmaiden of the latter should not obscure the larger point, that they closely cooperated with respect to maintaining hublike relations of dominance in regard to the colonies. Those relations varied, of course, ranging from formal rule involving outright military involvement to more benign forms of informal governance and reaching their imperial apex in the period of "dollar diplomacy" during the first three decades of the twentieth century. But even thereafter, despite Franklin Delano Roosevelt's "good neighborliness" and John F. Kennedy's Alliance for Progress, the structure of domination remained mostly imperial, even though the terminology used—except of course by the Latin American left—was exactly the opposite.[26]

STRUCTURED SYSTEMS

Thinking of empires as hublike arrangements between cores and peripheries is another way of proposing that empires may be better conceptualized not as states per se but as systems.[27] Like all political systems, empires consist of distinct units—the core state and the peripheral societies. Second, these units are not just randomly collected elements but constituent parts of a coherent imperial whole. Just as no empire can exist without core states and peripheral societies, the characteristics of each are defined in relation to the other: core states presuppose peripheral societies and core elite status presupposes peripheral elite status and vice versa. Third, these units occupy specific places within the empire. The elites of core states must be situated in a distinct core, and the elites of peripheral societies must be situated in distinct peripheries. Fourth, the relations between core state and peripheral societies are structured in a way that defines the system as a whole. Core elites rule; peripheral elites govern. The core elite is dominant; the peripheral elites are subordinate. The absence of significant relations between peripheral elites completes the picture.

The most important theoretical implication of systems analysis is that change in any one part of the system necessarily affects all others. Indeed, Robert Jervis argues that, because other things can never be held constant in systems, it is in principle impossible to claim, in the straightforward social scientific fashion to which we are all accustomed, that A causes B, or that if A, then B.[28] If more or less linear cause-and-effect relationships are necessarily absent from systems, however, systems are, as Jervis implicitly recognizes, of little use to social scientists with just such concerns on their minds. Perhaps unwilling to plunge into the murky world of infinite intertextuality and representational richness, Jervis does concede that certain relations are more obviously central than others—if only because not all elements of a system could be *equally* affected by some change.[29]

Jonathan Culler makes just this criticism of Ferdinand de Saussure's insistence that all the elements comprising a linguistic system are equally important to its overall coherence: "If the word *mutton* were dropped from English certain local modifications would ensue: the value of *sheep* would change radically; *beef, pork, veal*, etc. would become slightly more anomalous with the disappearance of one member of their paradigm class; . . . but vast areas of the language would not be affected in discernible ways." Culler's conclusion is of relevance to us as well: "The example of linguistics need not lead one to expect the complete solidarity of every system. Relations are important for what they can explain: meaningful contrasts and permitted or forbidden combinations."[30]

The problem of boundless intertextuality disappears once we recognize that, although ponds, rain forests, tribes, markets, empires, and polities can all have systemic characteristics, systems, like all other concepts, are no more ontologically given than states or regimes. We can theorize systemically—if we find such an approach to be intelligible and useful—or we can theorize nonsystemically if we do not. That everything may be connected to everything else may therefore be true, but it is trivially and obviously so, because the very point of conceptual thinking is to distinguish between things, to draw boundaries, and to assert priorities. As a result, although all the parts of a system may "really" be hopelessly interconnected, nothing should stop us from claiming that some interconnections are more equal than others and that these more salient relationships give the system the property of *structure*.[31] For this reason David Easton's work on political systems can argue that systemic inputs into the black box of government do indeed result in systemic outputs or policies.[32] Precisely because systems may be conceptualized, not as formless blobs but as sets of structured parts—even if systemic variables *A* through *Z* seem to be connected in a complex web of mind-boggling permutations and combinations—we can still claim that *A* is most directly related to *B*, *G*, *M*, and *Z*. Like systems, structures are socially real conceptual constructions, but, I emphasize, they are *our* constructions.

EXCEPTIONS AND ANOMALIES

What distinguishes empires from centralized multinational political systems, therefore, is structure. The nonnative state's elite located in the core coordinates, supervises, and protects the peripheral native societies, which, in ideal-typical terms, interact with one another only via the core. Empires, then, are structurally centralized political systems within which core states and elites dominate peripheral societies, serve as intermediaries for their significant interactions, and channel resource flows from the periphery to the core and back to the periphery.

As structured systems, empires need not have emperors, ideologies, and exploitative relationships to be empires; by the same token, nonempires may have these features without being empires. Robert Wesson disagrees:

> But however much may be copied from one empire by another, their essential alikeness in varied climates, cultures, and economic conditions probably owes more to the logic of single rule over tremendous areas and multitudes. The overgreat state resting primarily on force practically requires, as symbol of authority and final arbiter, a single and all-powerful ruler, whose person is elevated far above ordinary mortals. To govern, there must be a large corps of professional administrators in a pyramid beneath the throne. Checked only by its self-restraint or incapacity, the imperial state feels free to interfere with the economy, to take wealth to its own uses, and to tax mercilessly. Finding criticism inconvenient, it inevitably checks free expression; on the other hand, it finds it advantageous to propagate a suitable religion or ideology. And the autocrat will surely have a huge court, overflowing with ornaments, pleasures, toadies, and parasites.[33]

Like Wesson, we almost naturally expect highly centralized polities such as empires to be ruled by monarchs, emperors, or dictators. Nor are we surprised that they, like all polities, develop legitimating ideologies. Nor, finally, is it unusual for dominant elites to exploit peripheries economically. Wesson has a point, but we can easily accommodate his concerns by claiming that self-styled emperors, imperial ideologies, and economic exploitation are potential consequences and thus associated characteristics of empire.[34] Decoupling these characteristics from the definition also makes empirical sense, because we know that the Roman Empire developed some of its peripheries economically, that the Habsburg and Ottoman realms were relatively benign, that the Soviet Union appears to have produced economic disaster for everybody concerned, that the French, British, and U.S. empires had democratic institutions in their respective cores, and that the Soviet ideology explicitly legitimated communism and not empire.

Meeting Wesson's objections does not mean that my definition of empire can be perfectly "instantiated." The degree of cultural distinctiveness, like the degree of coordination, supervision, and control, has always varied, and all real empires have only approximated the definitional ideal type. The Ottomans of Constantinople, Rumelia, and Anatolia shared Islam with most peripheral elites; ethnic Germans formed a sizable portion of tsarist Russia's ruling elite; Caracalla extended Roman citizenship to all the empire's free subjects in 212 A.D.; all elites shared a Soviet Russian culture in Leonid Brezhnev's USSR, whereas republican elites enjoyed a fair degree of genuine autonomy; the Mughal empire rested on local governance by Rajput chieftains and on direct military rule.[35] If these qualifications are valid, it must also be the case that parts of empires may be definitionally imperial, whereas others may not, and that the same territory, with the same core state, may or may not be termed an empire at various times in history, regardless of what it is officially called and how it emerged. That the physical space is the same and that some sort of political entity occupies it need not mean that that entity cannot have different defining characteristics at different times. Accordingly, it would be illogical to call Byzantium an empire on the eve of Constantinople's seizure by the Ottomans in 1453 or to fail to recognize that, although Moscow's relationship with Eastern Europe was no less imperial than its relationship with the non-Russian republics, the former differed from the latter in significant ways. Empires can therefore flow in and out of history—which, as chapter 8 argues, has important implications for our ability to theorize about empires.

IMPERIAL TYPES

In order better to accommodate the diversity of imperial experiences we would do well to distinguish between types of empires. Because the defining characteristic of greatest relevance to us is structure, it makes sense to make structural variation central to an imperial typology. One obvious structural feature is the "length" of spokes. Some empires are territorially concentrated, whereas others, consisting of far-flung, perhaps overseas possessions, are not. That is, the imperial wheel can be small and have short spokes, or large and have long spokes; more likely than not, of course, the wheel, having both long and short spokes, will not be a circle. A second, equally obvious feature is the number of spokes—that is, of core-periphery relationships. That number can range anywhere from two to N, where N is some number less than the total number of potential peripheries in the world at any time. Empires with few short spokes are *dense* and those with many long spokes are *loose*.[36] And, of course, many others are in-between.

We can also differentiate empires according to the degree of control exerted by core elites over peripheral elites. Peripheral elites with least autonomy may be said to be implicated in a "formal" empire; as Wendt and Friedheim suggest, those elites with more substantial amounts—for instance, Judaea under King Herod, the many principalities within the Raj, Nicaragua under the Somozas, Haiti under the Duvaliers, and the USSR's east-central European satellites—belong in "informal" empires.[37] In formally ruled empires the core elite appoints and dismisses the peripheral elites, sets the entire (external and internal) policy agenda, and determines all domestic policies. In an informally ruled empire the core elite influences the appointment and dismissal of peripheral elites, sets the external policy agenda, shapes the internal agenda, and determines external policies while only influencing domestic policies. In a hegemonic relationship, meanwhile, the dominant polity has little or no voice over the appointment and dismissal of elites and over internal agendas and policies. At most, it determines the external policy agenda and influences external policies. Because all these sentences should be qualified by adding "more or less," we can easily imagine further classificatory subdivisions, such as vassal states, client states, and the like.[38] We can combine both dimensions—territorial density and type of authority—to produce the matrix that appears in figure 7.2.

Although different empires—or different parts of empires—may represent different types, we also know that the same empire may, over time, fit into any or all of these quadrants. Indeed, other things being equal, we expect the rise and fall of empires to proceed around the figure, from quadrant IV, through quadrants I and II, to quadrant III. We "naturally" expect young empires to have formally ruled dense territorial holdings. Assuming that empires continue to grow, we expect them to acquire more loosely arranged

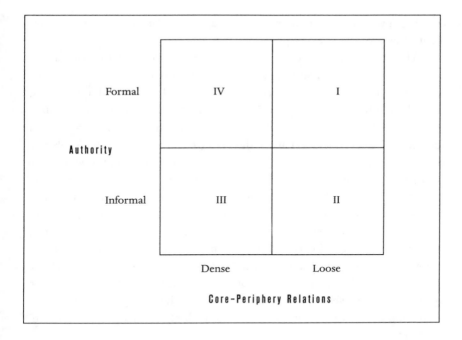

FIGURE 7.2
Types of Empires

territories. In time, should they begin to decline, we expect the core's authority to decline and, finally, its holdings to shrink as well. As Rein Taagepera has shown, the parabola-like pattern of rise, persistence, and fall of many empires more or less confirms this hypothesized relationship between authority and holdings.[39]

And yet, because "other things being equal" and "more or less" are the operative phrases here, we can, as the introduction suggested, always construct a variety of conceptually coherent stories that fit the facts the stories are supposed to fit. That empires appear to have a "natural history" is one such not unpersuasive story.[40] Equally persuasive ones could, in principle at least, start the narrative in quadrants I, II, or III and proceed forward or backward, up, down, or sideways. That we imagine empires as beginning at the beginning and ending at the end makes sense, of course, but no reason exists, a priori, for empires to rise and fall in just this fashion. The Eastern Roman Empire, for instance, emerged full formed as a coherent imperial structure.[41] Indeed, if we countenance—as I believe we should—the theoretical reality of exogenous forces, it is perfectly possible to imagine empires as being "pushed off" the matrix entirely, as a result of the functional equivalent of asteroids and earthquakes.[42]

Such shocks obviously can and do occur in the world of the natural sciences, and we have no reason to suppose that they dare not raise their heads in the world of the social sciences. Any number of theoretical approaches, from the methodologically individualist to the structural, can accommodate them, even if at the cost of sullying their pristine beauty. Agency-oriented theories can treat shocks as part of the background conditions that enable or constrain actors. For voluntarists, for instance, crises represent a window of opportunity.[43] Structural theories generally interpret shocks as triggers or accelerators that intensify inherent systemic contradictions and thereby break the camel's back. From the nonvoluntarist perspective, shocks—to mix my metaphors—finally push the system over the edge.[44] The ability of theories to adapt so resourcefully to recalcitrant data should not surprise us. But that is both some consolation and absolutely no consolation. In the final analysis, the mere possibility of such highly contingent contingencies underlines once again—as if that were, by now, still necessary—the tentativeness of all our theorizing in general and about the rise and fall of such large entities as empires in particular.

chapter 8. imperial trajectories

At the core of much of the theoretical literature on empire is a glaring flaw: the conflation of empire with imperialism. It should be obvious that empire refers to a *kind* of polity, that imperialism denotes a set of policies, and that polities and policies are different things. Once the concepts of imperialism and empire are recognized as being distinct, it necessarily follows that the presumed connection between imperialism and empire has to be established, not assumed. And establishing it will, as we shall see, not be easy.

Even more obvious is that, as I emphasized in the introduction, it is inadmissible to define an entity, be it empire or anything else, in terms of its cause or effect and not on its own terms—as John Strachey does by calling empire "any successful attempt to conquer and subjugate a people with the intention of ruling them for an indefinite period."[1] To smuggle an explanation, imperialism, into the definition of the concept, empire, is to engage in sleight of hand and in effect to pass off a theory as a definition. That would be sufficient cause for concern, even if defining empire in terms of imperialism did not have three other baleful consequences. The first is to reinforce the untenable view that empire formation necessarily presupposes imperial, if not imperialist, intent. The second is arbitrarily to give priority to imperialism and thus to exclude from consideration nonimperialist forms of imperial rise and fall. The third is to blur the distinction between integration and imperialism and thus between state building and empire formation.

RESTATING THE PROBLEM

An excellent reason for not thinking that empires are the product of imperialist choice is semantic. Most theorists concerned with empire grapple with the reasons for or consequences of what is, at root, a very simple proposition, namely, that states choose (or do not choose) empire. The language is usually more opaque—David Lake claims that it is "the desire to reduce the potential for opportunism by their partners that drives states toward empire"— but after a suitable translation is undertaken, the gist is the same.[2] Although such a proposition is demonstrably false in light of the manifold ways in which empires can be formed analytically—a point I return to shortly—and have formed historically, far more damning theoretically is that such a sentence is of dubious semantic and thus ultimately explanatory usefulness.

The first problem concerns the subject—*states*. Despite any number of as-if devices one might adopt, Weberian political organizations with a monopoly of violence and the like obviously cannot "make choices."[3] If states can and do make choices, it is only because they are, in reality, not states but states*men* or states*women*. This semantic maneuver might be a harmless form of shorthand were it not for the ancillary assumption—already encountered in Theda Skocpol's discussion of the Janus-faced state—that when states(men) decide to go to war or to make peace, the Weberian states automatically follow. Such an assumption might hold for some absolute monarchs and iron chancellors, but it is patently false in all other settings, and false assumptions do matter, as we know. Yale Ferguson and Richard Mansbach put it well:

A further distortion of the state-centric model is that states have been anthropomorphized, that is seen and treated analytically as unified actors. In fact, the most substantial of states are almost always divided in their actual behavior, rent by political factions, bureaucratic in-fighting, and interest-group politics. Many other states, of course, hardly function at all. It is important to remember that the state is almost never *itself* an actor in global politics. We can perhaps speak meaningfully about France's position on a particular issue at an EU summit, although the government official articulating it may not be accurately reflecting divided opinions at home. The truth of the matter is that all "state" policies, if they can even be identified, can be traced back to non-state sources. If we want to know where policies came from and whether they are likely to change, we shall have to trace them back to individuals and groups within the state, as well as pressures emanating from outside.[4]

The second problem concerns the predicate—*choose empire*. Although it may be true that statesmen can desire empire—after all, intentional imperialism is one of many ways for empires to emerge—it makes little sense to claim that they "choose" empire or any of its subsequent trajectories, such as persistence, collapse, or decay.[5] In the vast majority of cases of empire formation, no logically or empirically identifiable "point" exists at which such a choice could be contemplated and, least of all, made.[6] Elites could choose to buy or steal or marry into ready-made empires—precisely those instances of empire formation that choice-centered accounts ignore—but they surely do not choose empire when and if they choose to attack a state. Choosing to attack may be to choose imperialism, but unless we conflate empire with imperialism and thereby commit an even more egregious methodological error, that too is not to choose empire.

Finally, even if we grant that elites can choose empire, it strains the imagination to think that they would choose collapse, which is tantamount to collective suicide, or could choose persistence or decay. Because the latter usually take place over hundreds of years, during which time millions of choices are made, it would be as unhelpful to suggest that any one choice was decisive as it would be useless to claim that millions of choices mean that choice matters. To be sure, strategic withdrawal does entail choice, but the choice generally is not to resist, not to fight, not to expend resources. All these individual choices may strike us as the choice to abandon empire; in reality, they are, at most, choices not to stem imperial decline.

If the proposition that states choose empire is questionable semantically, the task before us shifts from explaining why such entities do or do not make such choices to the semantically more meaningful enterprise of accounting, in nonchoice terms, for the emergence and decline of empires as structured systems involving core states and their elites and peripheral societies and their elites in the kinds of hierarchical relationships discussed in chapter 7.

HOW EMPIRES ARISE

The three defining characteristics of empire—a distinct core elite and distinct peripheral elites; relations of dominance between the core elite and the peripheral elites; and a hublike structure to these relations—suggest a simple procedure for identifying how, but not *why*, empires rise and fall. Because these three defining characteristics "make" an empire, we can confidently assert that an empire has emerged whenever they come together in some time and place. And whenever a system with these three characteristics loses any or all of them, we can just as confidently claim that an empire has disappeared. As I argued in the introduction, there is no reason that, logically, defining characteristics cannot come together or fall away simultaneously—in which case utterly new systems may be said to have emerged or disappeared. There is also no reason that only one or two of these characteristics cannot appear or disappear for the systems possessing them to gain or lose the definitional status of empire.

Consider the implications of these observations. We generally assume that empires come into existence only as a result of the expansion of core control to some potential periphery. The conventional wisdom is obviously right to believe that a core elite can engage in straightforward imperialism and extend its influence into territories with already existing distinct elites via military campaigns, wars, and subsequent conquest. History is rife with examples of just this sort of military expansionism and of the empires to which it frequently gave rise. Time and again, Roman legions outclassed their opponents in battle, pushing the republic's boundaries far beyond Italy. Jingiz Khan's horsemen annihilated their sedentary opponents; European soldiers carved up Africa and Asia; Americans dismembered the Spanish Empire.[7]

But military conquest is not the only way in which the defining characteristics of empire can appear as a cluster. Empires can also arise if distinct elites (the first defining characteristic) emerge within a hierarchical and hub-like political setting and thereby transform mere regions into a core and a periphery. Johan Galtung's structural theory of imperialism suggests as much, leading Michael Doyle to call this conclusion an "unintended but significant irony."[8] Contrary to the opinion of Doyle, whose interactionist theory of empire formation precludes the possibility of empire-from-within, the unwarranted assumption that only imperialism can go together with empire forces us to embrace Galtung's irony. Indeed, the USSR illustrates how an empire can emerge when a dictatorial state promotes distinct peripheral elites and populations. In creating the Union of Soviet Socialist Republics, the Bolsheviks transformed revolutionary Russia's simple dictatorship over its newly acquired territories into a complex web of de facto imperial relationships premised on non-Russian administration of symbolically sovereign republics inhabited by distinct non-Russian populations.[9]

Second, there is no reason that, logically, relations of dominance must emerge only as a result of military expansion. "Ready-made" peripheries can be bought or otherwise acquired, perhaps by thievery, guile, or stealth. Geir Lundestad even speaks of "empire by invitation."[10] The Dutch bought Manhattan from the natives; the Habsburgs seized Bosnia in 1908 in clear violation of the resolutions of the Congress of Berlin; Prussia, Austria, and Russia agreed to partition Poland and then did just that. Stalin and Churchill are said to have divided east-central Europe on the back of an envelope.[11] The historical record offers just as many examples of dynastic unions between powerful and weak monarchs that led to the incorporation of the latters' realms on imperial terms. The emergence of the Polish-Lithuanian Rzecz Pospolita and the rise of the Habsburg empire are two such cases. Queen Jadwiga's union with Grand Duke Jogaila in 1386 pushed Lithuania down the slippery slope of dynastic union, incorporation, and empire. And although Robert Kann is quite right to say that "to trace the rise of the Habsburg empire to the marriage policy of the dynasty is a patent oversimplification of history," it is undeniable that that policy did contribute significantly to Habsburg expansion and consolidation of power.[12]

A change in regime can also move a polity in an imperial direction. Consider post-Soviet Russia. As an ethnoterritorial federation, Russia has culturally distinct administrative units—the non-Russian republics—populated by distinct populations and run by distinct elites. As products of centralized Soviet political-economic rule, their relations with Moscow are still far stronger than their relations with one another. Inasmuch as Moscow's relationship with these units is, at the time of this writing, pseudodemocratic at best and chaotic at worst, it cannot be deemed imperial. But that could change. Should democratization be abandoned, de facto if not de jure, and should Moscow's relations with the provinces then become dictatorial, the Russian Federation will have become, and rightly be deemed, an empire.[13]

Athens' relations with the city-states united in the Delian League provide an historical example of this possibility. At first, in the aftermath of the league's creation in 478–477 B.C., Athens exercised what Thucydides called a "hegemony over autonomous allies who participated in common synods."[14] As the Athenians increasingly became involved in war, first with Persia and later with Sparta, and then crushed rebellions by league members Naxos and Thasos, they turned, as Donald Kagan writes, "to ever harsher means to assure their control of the league. In the process they converted it into an empire."[15]

Third, empire formation can also take place if, with the first and second defining characteristics already in place—in other words, distinct elites and hierarchical core-periphery relations—the structure of core-periphery relations becomes hublike and thus imperial. Once again, the Soviets provide us with a good example. In the decades following World War II, the USSR's relations with Eastern Europe acquired just this structure, as Moscow forged bilateral political ties with its satellites and attempted to coordinate their economic activity via the Council for Mutual Economic Assistance. As a result, the Soviet bloc, although hardly uniform with respect to the authority exercised and the density of its spokes, became an empire only years after the Red Army's occupation of Eastern Europe and the subsequent communist takeovers had occurred.[16]

HOW EMPIRES FALL

Not surprisingly, the fall of empires can mirror the rise of empires. First on the list is the termination of relations of dominance as a result of cataclysms, wars, and national liberation struggles, which can produce long-term processes of decline, as in the case of the Byzantines and the Ottomans; rapid and comprehensive collapse, as was true of the Romanovs and the Habsburgs; or some combination of the two, as happened with the Roman Empire.[17] By the same token, empires can end as a result of strategic withdrawal, perhaps in response to wars, cataclysms, and liberation struggles, perhaps as a result of sober calculations of the costs of empire. The French were forced to withdraw after experiencing defeat in Vietnam and crushing a costly insurrection in Algeria. The British, after withdrawing from India, methodically continued their retreat from the rest of their holdings.[18]

Second, if peripheral or core elites lose their distinctiveness, empires cease to exist as a result of "integration." Alexander the Great's lieutenants adopted regional identities; Varangian marauders became Rus' princes; Mongol invaders were transformed into Chinese elites.[19] As with the silent emergence of empires, such internal realignments can occur as the result of economic development, demographic movement, and the subsequent intermixing and assimilation of cultural groups.[20] The actions of core elites—such as forcible assimilation, population resettlement, and ethnic cleansing—can also play, and historically have played, a major role in promoting, in effect if not in intent, the transformation of imperial peripheries into mere regions of dictatorial or nondictatorial multinational states. The Armenian genocide of 1915 is one example, a product, as Ronald Suny persuasively argues, of the nationalizing tendencies unleashed by the Ottoman elite's turn toward a Turkish national identity.[21] In destroying native elites and societies and thereby reducing them to insignificance, Americans unwittingly forestalled the possibility of nineteenth-century America's acquiring imperial features.[22] The creation of national states in Western Europe would also be inexplicable without reference to equally brutal actions aimed at eradicating core-periphery distinctions.[23]

Dynastic divorces and family squabbles can also end a hierarchical relationship. Andrei Bogoliubsky of Suzdal sacked the "mother of Rus' cities,"
Kiev, in 1169, while the Habsburgs' Spanish line went its own way after the
middle of the seventeenth century.[24] Although it seems improbable for an entire empire to be sold, parts surely can, as indeed they have: the French dis-
posed of Louisiana in 1803 and the Russians of Alaska in 1867; similarly, the
United States "leased" the Panama Canal Zone, whereas Great Britain acquired Hong Kong by treaty from the Manchus. Finally, just as a change of
regime can make an empire, so too can it break an empire. After 1947, when
it was transformed into several *départements* of France, Algeria formally
ceased being an imperial holding. Likewise, although I prefer to characterize
Vienna's post-1867 relations with Budapest as an example of informal imperial rule, one could legitimately claim that a qualitative change had taken place
after the *Ausgleich* and that, with Budapest's acquisition of approximate political parity, the late Habsburg realm was imperial in Cisleithania and, as
Franz Joseph's secondary title suggests, merely royal in Transleithania.[25]

Third, it is also possible for the domination of peripheral elites by the core
elite to continue while the hublike structure of core-periphery relations dissipates. Austria-Hungary arguably was heading in just this direction in the
early twentieth century, because rapid economic growth in most of the provinces, and especially in Budapest, led to the development of horizontal inter-
peripheral ties and the progressive decline of Vienna as the imperial hub.[26]
Communist China, in the wake of Deng Xiaoping's economic reforms, effectively permitted the emergence of capitalist economic relations that, while
leaving Beijing's imperial control over native Xinjiang and Tibet unchanged,
significantly advanced the economic and political autonomy and intercon-
nectedness of all the provinces.[27] The dense economic relations between
Guangdong and Fujian provinces and Hong Kong and Taiwan were eloquent
testimony to this point. Similarly, the Central American holdings of the United States became increasingly integrated into world markets in the aftermath
of World War II, while Central American left-wing elites sought, with varying degrees of success, to join the socialist system of states.[28]

Showing how empires rise and fall—by means of military conflict and the
many other moves suggested—cannot explain their emergence and decline,
but it does underscore the magnitude of the explanatory task and suggest the
kinds of theoretical questions that should be asked and can be answered. It is
safe to say that a nontrivial theory of imperial emergence and decline, one
that fully explains all possible patterns, will be, at best, immensely difficult to
formulate. And indeed, as I have already argued, a universal theory is in prin-

ciple impossible. Inasmuch as the explananda involved are radically different, the explanatory task, whether probabilistic or not, either requires very different covering laws or implies very different causes or combinations of necessary and sufficient conditions. A theory of everything would also be equivalent to a philosophy of history along the lines of Arnold Toynbee and Oswald Spengler, which, as Arthur Danto has shown, is impossible.[29]

STATE BUILDING AND INTEGRATION

The third consequence of conflating empire with imperialism concerns the distinction between state building and empire formation, understood here conventionally, and narrowly, as involving only the expansion and consolidation of political power.[30] Two difficulties, one semantic, the other theoretical, confront us. First, if every successful imperialist undertaking can only result in empire, empires and multinational states (which is to say, *all* states) are identical entities—and we should, for the sake of parsimony and clarity, probably abandon one term. Because the state is analytically indispensable to much social science, empire would be the more likely candidate for the conceptual ash heap.[31] Such a denouement would impoverish us, however, inasmuch as—or so chapter 7 tried to show—a valid and important difference exists between states as states and empires as something more than mere states.

Second, if the imperialism of states ineluctably results in empire, states as states could never become larger than their "original" preimperial size. But instead of a world of many large empires and many tiny states, we usually find some empires, more large states, and many small states. The puzzle disappears once we recognize that, although imperialism may result in empire, it can just as easily result in the annexation of territories, the assimilation of populations, and the integration of distinct elites—that is, in state growth. State building in France and North America is a case in point. The French kings expanded their authority over the feudal lords; Louis XIV consolidated it; after 1789, first the revolutionaries and then Napoleon perfected central rule, setting the framework for the subsequent transformation of "peasants into Frenchmen."[32] The United States expanded westward in a variety of distinctly imperial ways. But by eliminating local Spanish and Indian elites, extending U.S. military, legal, and administrative organizations into the acquired territories, and populating them with nonnative settlers, Americans built a state and not an empire.[33]

In sum, by collapsing empires into imperialism, we either collapse all empires into states semantically or prohibit the conceptual existence of polities larger than statelets and smaller than empires. Neither alternative is appealing and both transgress common sense. If, alternatively, empire and imperialism do not always have to go together, states and empires can—mirabile dictu—reemerge as legitimate analytical categories. The problem then shifts to isolating the conditions under which imperialism is likely to result in state growth, or integration, on the one hand and in empire, or nonintegration, on the other. In other words, we are in the presence of necessary and facilitating conditions with limited causal implications.

I submit that integration will be easier, and thus more likely, if the core and the periphery are territorially contiguous: proximity translates into fewer expenditures of resources, lower transaction costs, and simpler military planning. Integration also presupposes, as a necessary condition, that the relative power of the core elite be overwhelming in comparison to that of the peripheral elites: such an imbalance of power would enable the former either to annihilate the latter or to incorporate them or both. Because only especially strong states can pull off integration in general and the integration of neighboring territories in particular, integration should be most likely to occur relatively early in a polity's expansionary life—in quadrant IV of figure 7.2—when the core is flush with victory, the state is ascendant, and international threats are presumably minimal.[34]

Nonintegration—and thus empire—is both possible and likely only if the core elite cannot fully extend its administrative network into newly acquired territories, establish infrastructural linkages, and, most important, dispense with, emasculate, and/or afford to remove the local elites. Two conditions facilitate nonintegration. Geographic distance is an objective obstacle to the full-scale integration of territories, elites, and populations: the farther the holdings, the less the control. Imperial size is another obstacle, because we expect relative core power—and therefore core capacity to integrate—to decline with the number of annexed territories. Robert Gilpin and David Lake demonstrate how the accumulation of territorial assets involves a variety of significant costs that, at some point, may prove to be greater than the benefits accruing from expansion.[35] As resources are expended on expansion and the size of the core state grows, the amount of resources that have to be devoted to security, law and order, war making, and so on will increase at, in all likelihood, a faster rate than the income derived from territorial acquisition. Although the state need not go into decline as a result, its capacity for continued integration will necessarily diminish.[36] In a word, the greater the holdings, the less the control.

IMPERIAL OVERREACH

State building is likely when imperialism succeeds, whereas empire formation is probable not when imperialism succeeds but when integration cannot.
The more a core state expands; the more territory its elite buys, annexes,
steals, or integrates in some fashion; the more continued expansion is likely
to result in nonintegration and thus in a series of bilateral relations of domination between the core elite and distinct peripheral elites—in other words,
in empire. Imanuel Geiss makes a similar point:

> As expansion proceeded from the imperial centre to the periphery,
> from the imperial core to "distant provinces," power and its application
> diffused over the distance. . . . The greatest concentration of power is
> to be found in the imperial core, its capital city. . . . The capital is sur-
> rounded or protected by provinces of the imperial nation. . . . Further
> away live relatives, cousins adopted as equals. . . . At even greater dis-
> tance from the capital, but still within the reach of its military power,
> are the outer provinces. They were conquered, annexed and brought
> under direct rule in early stages of expansion. . . . Further towards the
> periphery we find two kinds of areas under diminishing indirect rule—
> vassal and client states. For conquered peoples, vassaldom was the
> mildest form of alien rule. . . . Furthest away from the centre, client
> states bordered on virtual independence or near-sovereignty.[37]

Thus expansionist states must first acquire and integrate peripheries and
only then, after biting off more than they can chew, do they develop imperial relations with acquired territories. In other words, empires are the direct
consequence of imperial overreach. Small states must first become larger
states before they can, in turn, become small and then large empires. After a
core, C, integrates territories a and b and thereby acquires regional great-
power status, every additional territorial acquisition will, if not integrated
into the polity, be placed in a dyadic relationship with the existing state. As a
result, the political and economic relations of each newly acquired periphery,
P, will be focused on C. With the addition of every new P to the system, C's
relations with the lot will begin to resemble a wheel without a rim, as in figure 8.1.

That empire and overextension actually go together would be an utterly
unremarkable observation, except that most empires are unusually durable
polities capable of persisting for many centuries. From Lake's choice-centered

Phase 1	Phase 2	Phase 3
Core	Integrated State	Empire
C	$a = C = b$	$P - [a = C = b] - P$

FIGURE 8.1

Phases of Imperial Growth

point of view, the costs of empire "rise with the degree of relational hierarchy, deterring states from imperialism."[38] Those costs may rise, but just how and why this should deter states*men* and states*women* is unclear. First, how could imperial elites estimate the true costs of empire? The thrill of the hunt may blind them to mundane accounting procedures. Nor do I see how, given the impossibility of measuring exactly all the consequences of something, such an accounting could work, except in an ex post facto theoretical manner.[39] Second, and more important, these costs evidently become prohibitive *only after* states expand at least as much as those of the Romans, Habsburgs, Ottomans, Byzantines, and Romanovs. It may therefore be true that too much imperial overreach will ultimately do empires in, but to put the matter in such terms is to see the marginal relevance of such a claim. If overreach gets empires into trouble after several hundred years of plenitude, surely it cannot be all that alarming.

Seen in this light, overextension is anything but a dysfunctional systemic condition or a puzzling choice. Instead, it is a perfectly sensible, as well as immensely profitable, if generally unchosen, arrangement for states and elites to be in—a proposition that, as we shall see in chapter 9, has important implications for the future of empire. Overextension, then, is an institutional alternative to independence and integration, arising not because of supremely irrational or supremely rational elite choice but because the relations between potential core states and potential peripheries favor but do not predetermine such an outcome.[40] A slight but significant modification of Doyle's argument may be closest to the mark: accordingly, empire formation does not presuppose a powerful metropole—in conjunction with a weak periphery, transnational forces that bridge the two, and a favorable international environment—but a relatively *weak* one.[41]

NONPUZZLES

Whatever its intrinsic merits, this notion of overextension is at least conceptually less self-contradictory than that generally proffered by International Relations (IR) theorists. In general, what they seem to have in mind when they invoke the concepts of overexpansion, overstretch, overreach, and the like is the relatively straightforward proposition that some states expand successfully and then, after meeting their match, are forced to retreat. Why such behavior should be a puzzle is mystifying in light of the standard assumptions in which such arguments are usually embedded. Under conditions of anarchy, imperfect information, and security dilemmas, we expect states(men) to act in the manner of differently endowed individuals in a Hobbesian state of nature—some are Davids, other are Goliaths—and to extend their reach, get beaten, and perhaps try again. No less important, when restated in such terms the puzzle becomes just another way of asking why wars take place when, as is almost always the case, one side must by definition lose. The IR overreach puzzle is in this sense just a specific instance of the question of why a weaker state would get involved in a war or engage in bellicose behavior that it is too weak to sustain—or, to put it most simply, why elites make bad choices. The question is surely legitimate on its own terms, so long as we do not proceed to answer it by arguing in circular fashion that "bad" elites are responsible for "bad" outcomes, and so long as we appreciate that choice is of marginal utility to the study of empires and empire formation.[42]

Consider in this light two influential theories that attempt to explain bad choices in terms of contextual factors that presumably prevent elites from making good choices. Charles Kupchan develops a complex explanation of why elites fail to respond to changes that subvert their imperial ambitions and instead just press ahead with expansion. His account boils down to "strategic culture," a set of values, norms, and beliefs formed as a means of imperial legitimation at the time of initial expansion but which acquires a life of its own and, in the manner of Stephen Van Evera's notion of "blowback," prevents elites from responding appropriately to the growing challenges confronting their expanded states.[43] Kupchan's suggestion that elites create the strategic culture that then proceeds to ensnare them seems persuasive but only at first glance. Recall that his elites, like the constructivist elites encountered in chapter 5, do not create strategic cultures from nothing. They have to counter, mold, or refashion existing values, beliefs, and norms. And if they can do so at time t, why not at time $t + n$, when experience and maturity should make them all the more capable of effecting cultural change? "Things" may have gotten in the way, but if things conveniently get in the way only at time $t + n$, and never at time t, clearly they amount to little more than dei ex machinis. To state that strategic culture assumes a life of its own and becomes impervious to elite attempts to change it is not to solve the problem but merely to restate it.

Snyder's answer to the question of overreach—that logrolling and coalition formation establish a proimperial momentum, whereas "myths of empire" sustain it even when empire is no longer in the state's interest—falls into the same trap.[44] As with Kupchan, it is unclear why elites, as the conceptual categories that they are, cannot abandon myths of empire when they cease to promote the interests of imperial coalitions. More important, it is equally unclear why rationally acting though dysfunctional coalitions should not break up—if not willfully and consciously, then because they rest on, to use a hoary Marxist term, irreconcilable contradictions. That coalitions retain their momentum, even when their original raison d'être proves to be subversive of their interests, is the real puzzle—the explanandum and not the explanans—precisely because the coalitions were assumed to be supportive of the interests of the coalition partners in the first place. The problem is similar to that involving strategic culture. Just as elites crafty enough to construct such a culture must be deemed crafty enough to deconstruct it, so too self-interested actors capable of forming coalitions and generating myths of empire must be assumed no less capable of withdrawing from coalitions and abandoning the myths, especially when something as obviously counterproductive as military defeat takes place. Coalitions may, of course, be rechristened "institutions" and these in turn may then be posited as being too "sticky" to permit a turning back of the clock. But this maneuver would be valid only if we assume that the original construction of coalitions and myths took place in the complete absence of obstructionist institutions, surely a far-fetched assumption.

LESS AS MORE

Why, then, do empires rise and fall? I can think of many answers, some better, some worse, and all more or less legitimate. Although a theory of everything is beyond our grasp, our relative ignorance is no cause for despair. More focused theoretical enterprises, such as providing plausible accounts of imperial emergence (or decline) via territorial expansion, regime change, elite formation, or structural transformation, should be possible. They too will be flawed, of course, but so what? Unless we choose to live in a postmodern epistemological universe, there is no reason that some incomplete theories should not seize a greater or more important or more interesting chunk of "everything" than others. After all, although we expect all theories to be flawed, we have no reason to expect all of them to be equally flawed.

The image of empires as structured systems is of particular relevance to these considerations, because it suggests why one commonplace way of looking at empire—that centered on imperial intent—is especially misleading. Although it may be inconceivable, perhaps even impossible, for atoms to align themselves in just the right manner to create a functioning computer, it is surely unnecessary for master planners to have planned and designed the vast majority of systems we encounter in the world. In the physical world all manner of systems—from galaxies to ponds to atoms—arose without evident design (but naturally, in accordance with "natural laws"). In the social world as well, societies, economies, polities, clans, nations, classes, and any number of other entities have arisen as a result of complex causal chains, historical conjunctures, contingencies, and perhaps in accordance with lawlike social science theories.[45]

Structures are not, as Rey Koslowski and Friedrich Kratochwil rightly argue, "immutable" but not, I submit, because they are simply "dependent for their reproduction on the practices of the actors," so that "fundamental change of the international system occurs when actors, through their practices, change the rules and norms constitutive of international interaction."[46] Koslowski and Kratochwil imply that structures in general and imperial structures in particular are what they are because of the actors implicated in them. This suggests that empire presupposes something akin to imperial intent—or imperialism and imperialists. But we have, as I have argued, no reason to think that empires must be, or even can be, purposefully designed. Nothing about the kind of authority that is exercised in different quadrants of figure 7.2 or the kind of core-periphery relations that exist at any stage of an empire's lifespan presupposes imperialism and only imperialism.

As with revolutions and nations, empires emerge whenever their defining characteristics come together as a cluster in some time or space. We can as easily imagine empire formation as the product of conscious imperialism as we can imagine it the consequence of circumstances involving neither imperial intent nor even imperial awareness. If so, just as there is no reason that nations should not emerge among peoples and polities expressly opposed or indifferent to nationalism, so too there is no reason that empires should not emerge among people and polities expressly opposed to empire and imperialism. In that case, the imperial relationship will, in all likelihood, be called something else—humanitarian intervention or peacekeeping, perhaps—but it will be imperial, despite all protestations to the contrary, so long as the defining characteristics are clustered appropriately. If, to bring us back to the introduction's epigraph, it walks like a duck and it talks like a duck, it's definitely a duck.

chapter 9. imperial futures

A final possibility awaits us in this, the final chapter. As I show here, an open-minded, conceptually attuned approach to empire formation can lead to the conclusion that the forces promoting empire—acquisition, elite union, war, dictatorial regimes, social differentiation, and excluded elites—are likely to be with us for some time to come. I also show that one can construct a theoretically plausible—because it is conceptually coherent—story of how the United States and Russia could acquire the status of imperial cores as a result of a variety of nonintentional forces. Such scenarios are, I stress, not predictions but only statements of possibility. The possible is neither necessary nor perhaps even probable; it definitely is not—as the conventional wisdom on the end of empires, the intrinsically benign nature of U.S. power, and the decrepit condition of Russian power, might insist—impossible. Indeed, if we grant that troops and trumpets are not the only way for imperial relationships to emerge, the picture, not unexpectedly, looks mixed.

WARS AND PEACE

Despite some fluctuations, most international sources of empire have declined in importance over the last two centuries. Land purchases became virtually impossible, as well as ideologically taboo, after the division of the world into a seamless web of self-styled national states, and dynastic unions became irrelevant with the introduction of effectively nonmonarchical regimes in all states. As to war, some scholars believe that it has become so destructive as to have outlived its usefulness.[1] The thought is appealing, but because the human capacity for destruction seems to be enormous, some skepticism may still be warranted.

Rather more compelling is, I believe, the argument that one traditional goal of war, territorial expansion, may have become significantly more difficult to attain and sustain. Because modern states serve as the international system's organizing principle, the inviolability of state boundaries is a generally accepted international norm, and even failed states are usually preferred to territorial division.[2] To be sure, norms do get violated and the reconfiguration of states does occur, but, as the fall of the USSR and Yugoslavia suggests, usually as a last resort. In any case, if and when aggressors threaten security and regional stability, great-power intervention or geopolitical balancing frequently suffices to stifle or keep expansion within reasonable limits. In presupposing conditions that globalization itself threatens to upset, however, this claim, as I show in a subsequent section, may be of diminishing relevance.

Another important argument for the increasing irrelevance of war is the democratic peace thesis.[3] Consider the proposition that "democracies do not fight" in conjunction with what seems to be an empirically verifiable trend—that more countries are becoming increasingly democratic—and it follows that the probability of war should decline accordingly.[4] This trend may or may not be secular, inevitable, and irreversible, but even if it is—and we have no way of proving the case one way or the other—the conclusion rests primarily on the validity of the thesis. If we take the thesis on its own terms, as being about democracy and not about rich states, friendly states, or the like, why, then, might it be that democracies do not, or should not, fight?[5] And what does it mean, theoretically, to make such a claim?

For starters, the thesis does not, and plausibly cannot, claim that democracies are intrinsically more humane, more peaceful, or less interventionist, because such dispositions should be displayed toward all countries regardless of regime type.[6] Instead, the historical record clearly shows that democratic elites have been perfectly capable of genocide, war, and gross interference. By the same token, democratic publics have been happily supportive of the genocides, wars, and bullying pursued by their democratically elected leaders. The United States, arguably the most democratic state of the nineteenth and twentieth centuries, illustrates the point. Even if their reasons for doing so were beyond reproach, Americans did massacre Indians, drop two atomic bombs on the Japanese, assist in the fire bombing of Dresden, provoke war with Mexico and Spain, gratuitously incinerate retreating Iraqi soldiers, and intervene—militarily, diplomatically, and surreptitiously—in scores of states. French and British behavior in their Asian and African empires was no less egregious, amounting to what, by today's standards, would have to be termed crimes against humanity.

To be sure, the democracies cannot compare with Hitler's warmongering and extermination of Jews, Gypsies, Slavs, and homosexuals, but the difference involves deep shades of gray, and not, alas, simple blacks and whites.

For the democratic peace thesis to make sense on its own terms, it must claim that something in, or about, the *relations* between and among democratic states keeps them from going to war with one another. To put the matter this way is to shift the focus of the inquiry from the impact that democratic regimes have on international relations to the norms informing those relations and thus to make a fairly straightforward liberal internationalist claim. The democratic thesis, then, is not so much that democracies do not fight but that democratic interstate norms prevent the outbreak of war among states that share in such norms. In turn, such a restatement of the problem permits us to ask whether democratic norms suffice to prevent war or whether they merely facilitate its prevention. If the former—if it is true that norms make all the difference—it follows that democratic states should be equally disinclined to fight internal wars with their populations, which must be assumed to share in the democratic norms of the state. Civil wars and large-scale violence should not occur within democracies—but of course they do.

But perhaps the norms informing interstate relations are special. And perhaps in such a setting norms do indeed suffice to prevent war. A counterfactual thought experiment will help clarify the issue.[7] Assume that, tomorrow, democratic norms become hegemonic in all interstate relations and that all existing state elites claim sincerely to adhere to them. This is not, I submit, an outlandish assumption in light of the virtually universal endorsement of all manner of international treaties on human rights. If democratic norms do suffice to prevent war, such an experiment would force us to conclude that— all other circumstances notwithstanding—war will cease the day after tomorrow. If, alternatively, democratic norms merely reduce the likelihood of war, even with their universal entrenchment war would still occur—precisely because of continuing disparities in power, wealth, status, and influence— although it would become less likely.

Obviously, no way of adjudicating these claims empirically exists. But we can evaluate them theoretically. If so, the second claim strikes me as being infinitely more plausible, precisely because the counterfactual reveals that theoretically the claim—if democracy, then no war—is structurally identical to that made by revolutionaries: it is predictive, deterministic, and indifferent to initial conditions. In short, it is a theory of everything that, like all such self-styled theories, is untenable theoretically.[8] In contrast, the claim that democratic norms facilitate peace makes no such extravagant claims, is intrinsically plausible, and therefore theoretically acceptable. But it pointedly does not insist that wars will end.

Finally, even if we accept the democratic peace thesis, we may still be in trouble. Edward Mansfield and Jack Snyder appear to have established a correlation between war and states-in-transition, whether toward democracy or authoritarianism.[9] Because no state is ever, completely and finally, democratic and because every democratic state is, *in reality*, always moving toward or away from democracy, Mansfield and Snyder have, effectively if unintentionally, undermined the conceptual underpinnings of the democratic peace thesis itself. If all democratic states really are democratizing states, that some fight whereas others do not cannot be the result of their democratizing status but presumably of something else—perhaps disparities in power, wealth, status, and influence.

BREAKDOWNS AND DIFFERENTIATION

Empires come into being in at least two other ways: as a result of regime change and regional differentiation. Both bode relatively well for empire. First, we have no reason to think that existing nondictatorial systems will never break down and become dictatorial and that all ongoing transitions to democracy will succeed. Quite the contrary, we know from history, from the extensive literature on democratic breakdowns, and from the transparent teleology of the concept of transition that democracies do end and that democratization can fail.[10] We also know that empires can have perfectly democratic cores and that perfectly democratic states can treat, and have treated, nondemocracies atrociously and democracies less than peacefully. Needless to say, the possibility of democratic breakdowns also casts doubt on the inevitability of the democratic peace, even if we accept the thesis as valid.

Consider the ongoing "transitions" in the former Soviet Union and east-central Europe. Although conventional wisdom has it that they are all democracies of sorts—albeit "fragile" ones—and that their democratic consolidation is the order of the day, a more rigorous institutional understanding of democracy suggests that these systems are protodemocracies at best and, as recent trends may confirm, stable nondemocracies—or to stand Fareed Zakaria's terminology on its head—"liberal authoritarianisms" at worst.[11] Civil war in Albania; financial collapse in Bulgaria; authoritarian trends in Slovakia, Croatia, Serbia, Bosnia, Belarus, Azerbaijan, Armenia, Russia, Ukraine, Uzbekistan, and Kyrgyzstan; as well as continued economic decline and an explosion of crime and social decay in virtually all the post-Soviet states suggest that most postcommunist countries have acquired the features of coherent systems with pathological properties that are likely to persist for the foreseeable future.[12] Indeed, this condition of "permanent crisis," which is systemic and not transitional, suggests that these states are actually becoming Eurasian versions of Pakistan, Nigeria, Zaire, Brazil, or Mexico.[13]

The second internal source of empire, differentiation, is especially likely in the near future. All that modernization is supposed to entail—industrialization, education, urbanization, and so on—not only occurs unevenly, thus creating pockets if not whole areas of backward development, but also leads to social differentiation and elite frustration. And if, as the history of modernization leads us to expect, these continue to breed ethnic assertiveness, regional patriotism, and communal identities, the probability should remain correspondingly high that distinct elites and populations, unsuccessful separatist movements, nondemocratic relations between cores and peripheries, and thus empires will emerge.[14]

Here too countervailing tendencies exist. Willfully or not, the core elites of empires have frequently pursued policies—such as assimilation, resettlement, and genocide—aimed at ending the core-periphery distinction. As we know from chapter 8, however, elites may not be capable of ending that distinction. Even if we believe that the logic of the modern bureaucratic state may be incompatible with that of empire, it does not follow that state elites actually have the capacity, wherewithal, or skills either to eliminate empire or to do so in a manner that will not aggravate core-periphery relations or even create core-periphery distinctions.[15] The literature on the crisis of the state in general and of the national state in particular provides ample grounds for paying heed to the limitations on elites.[16] This caveat is of particular relevance today, when the language of human rights and self-determination dominates international discourse, when identity may have become the key criterion of political loyalty, and when state attempts to deal with ethnic diversity are almost invariably represented as encroachments on cultural authenticity and thus become inducements to ethnic mobilization.

GLOBALIZATION

Finally, I wish to suggest that of all the forces facilitating empire at present, globalization may turn out to be the most powerful. To be sure, any claim involving globalization—and especially one as large as mine—runs the risk of incoherence, because the concept appears rapidly to have sunk to the level of a discourse or ideology on the one hand or a zoo on the other.[17] A few examples will illustrate the point. Anthony Giddens defines globalization—incomprehensibly, to my mind—as "concern[ing] the intersection of presence and absence, the interlacing of social events and social relations 'at distance' with local contextualities."[18] Only marginally less obscure is Richard Falk, who says that it is "a series of developments associated with the ongoing dynamic of economic restructuring at the global level."[19] Christine Chin and James Mittelman are a tad more helpful, claiming that globalization is "not only about a series of intensifications in the dynamics of capitalism (i.e. competition and accumulation), but also fundamentally about interactions—changes in different spheres of social activity, the ways that they compress time and space, and their varied impact on strata in zones of the world economy."[20] Ulrich Beck is least obscurantist, terming globalization a "process . . . that creates transnational social ties and spaces, promotes local cultures, and . . . brings third cultures to the surface."[21]

My own halfhearted stab at definitional clarity, in chapter 6, tried to apply Occam's razor to this conceptual mess and spoke only of the growth of forces across state boundaries (whether they also challenge boundaries and therefore the nation-state is a causal issue that, contrary to Beck, does not belong in the definition itself). Some such notion is, and should be, I believe, at the heart of the concept, because only such boundary-transgressing connotations squarely confront the institutional reality of the nation-state and thereby imply what may be an important problematic. So defined, however, globalization is neither all that new—representing instead a continuation of trends initiated in the nineteenth century and perhaps earlier—nor all that global, inasmuch as it is largely confined to North America, Western Europe, and parts of East Asia. Nor, finally, is it all that salutary, because it clearly has, almost by definition, the potential to be disruptive and destabilizing.[22]

With the many caveats about theoretical underdetermination fully in mind, I remain impressed by how remarkably easy it is to stand conventional wisdom on its head and argue that globalization can promote imperial forms of political and economic organization. First, inasmuch as globalization is modernization writ large, we can easily imagine that it too will proceed unevenly, thereby creating a variety of objective and subjective conditions that promote cultural solidarity, ethnic militance, and regional distinctions. Telecommunications, computerization, and the English language will also spread unevenly.

More important, even where they are fully implanted, they are just as likely to provoke resistance as to promote homogeneity.[23]

Second, and relatedly, although globalization may, as some economists suggest, lead to unprecedented economic growth and prosperity for all in the long run, it will also advantage the economically strong over the economically weak and thus reinforce the leading position of the developed parts of the world. The worldwide financial crisis of 1997–1999 has brought home, even to globalization's avatars, the fact that "emerging markets"—and their hapless populations—are especially vulnerable to the vagaries of international capital flows.[24] It is therefore inconceivable, for me at least, that the currently most advanced countries of the world will not continue to be in positions of relative and absolute primacy for many years to come. Consider that the "industrialized countries" (excluding the countries of the former Soviet Union and Eastern Europe) held 81.4 percent of the world's wealth in 1994, up from 77.3 percent in 1960. The share of world income owned by the richest 20 percent of the world's population increased from 70.2 percent in 1960 to 82.8 percent in 1990, while the corresponding share of the poorest 20 percent fell from 2.3 percent to 1.3 percent. These figures conceal an even greater disparity: the richest 358 individuals in the world possess as much wealth as 45 percent of the world's population.[25]

Third, and most important, globalization will radically undermine the state's ability to extract resources from internationally mobile capital as entrepreneurs "shop around" for the least burdensome countries for their assets and investments. Perhaps inevitably, the tax burden will continue to shift to the less mobile segments of the world's population, a trend that will once again enhance the value of fixed territory with fixed populations—and empires, as we know, are in the final analysis premised on some significant measure of territorial control.[26] The much vaunted information revolution will likely exacerbate these tendencies, on the one hand assisting global capital in its efforts to escape state taxation, on the other hand enabling the state to tax the residual populations.[27] Because the financial burdens states can impose have limits, states may resort to national appeals as a way of eliciting popular acquiescence in and compliance with government policy. States, in sum, may become weaker as a result of globalization, but they are also likely to become more territorial and more ideological.

Such developments have obvious implications for international relations. First, financially weak, nationally self-assertive, and territorially greedy states-(men) will not enhance stability. Worse, the emergence of a transnational business class with little loyalty to any state may impel policy elites to compensate for economic losses by practicing beggar-thy-neighbor policies and territorial aggrandizement, thereby undermining security. Second, the volatility and unpredictability that come with globalization will expose states to exogenously generated economic crises—witness the 1997–1998 financial crisis in Asia, Russia, Eastern Europe, and Latin America—and thus to instability, insecurity, and—once again—the search for national and territorial certainties. Third, in the resulting interstate competition for economic resources and territory, some states will be winners, whereas others will be losers, even if losing is a relative proposition. Imperial hierarchies are possible; hegemonic relationships are virtually inevitable. Fourth, as some states destabilize and others acquire power, revolutionary solutions to perceived problems and inequalities will appear both increasingly plausible and attractive to national elites. Radical systemic change of the sort already propagated by the International Monetary Fund and other transnational elites may indeed be the only option available to desperate states(men) forced to cope with international insecurity and the "betrayal of the intellectuals"—the transnational entrepreneurs—on the one hand and increasing popular demands on the other. And revolution, as Stephen Walt reminds us, intensifies security dilemmas, promotes conflict, and increases the possibility of war.[28]

A transnational entrepreneurial class is likely to develop into something resembling an international civil society—autonomous, well informed, and prosperous.[29] But whether such a stratum will share a commitment to democracy, human rights, social justice, and economic well-being for others, however, is at least an open question. Much will depend on the ability of states to co-opt members of this elite—on the order of, perhaps, medieval European aristocracies—and thereby integrate them into existing political orders. Inclusion may enhance the new aristocracy's bonds with the population at large, but, as inclusion will transpire on the new aristocracy's terms, it is unlikely to reduce its wealth, status, and power. Almost inevitably, some states—probably those that perform better in the international competition—will attract more of the new civil society than others, which will improve their international standing, promote hierarchies, and exacerbate global economic inequalities. Ralf Dahrendorf is right to suspect that democracy is unlikely to prosper under such conditions.[30] By making the vast majority of citizens subject to impersonal forces beyond their control, globalization may actually induce them to support authoritarianism and nationalist quick fixes to their woes.

Taken together, these trends suggest that globalization could actually promote imperial structures—hublike relationships between politically and economically dominant cores and their "colonies" on the periphery. Because globalization is not a force of nature, it will emanate from, and reinforce the centrality of, those states that already possess the greatest economic and political resources and are most capable of asserting themselves. Indeed, according to Robert Keohane and Joseph Nye, "the information revolution has not greatly decentralized or equalized power among states. If anything, it has had the opposite effect."[31] And because the resources that matter most in a globalized economic setting involve financial and information flows, globalization may promote the development of imperial networks with financial and information giants at their hubs.

IMPERIUM AMERICANUM?

The United States emerges as a leading candidate for just such a position of imperial dominance. Its conventional and nuclear capability is unparalleled and—as the costs of the ongoing revolution in military technology will be prohibitively high for all other states—is likely to remain vastly superior for some time to come.[32] America's economic size and dynamism and its communications capacity guarantee it a leading position in the global economy. The U.S. state, while currently "lean," is highly effective as an administrative, extractive, and policing mechanism.[33] The fetishization of "American leadership" provides the ideological underpinnings of empire.[34] To be sure, the accepted discourse generally speaks of unilateralism or isolationism, and not empire, but the words should not distract us from the concept and the referent it captures.[35]

The possibility of a U.S. empire is perfectly compatible with the likelihood that the United States may not, as the declinist literature once argued, be able to play the role of world hegemon: its resources may be too few and its domestic weaknesses may be too many to sustain hegemonic stability on a world scale.[36] But the incapacity of the United States to serve as an international hegemon has few, if any, implications for its ability to become involved in a set of imperial relationships closer to home and more directly in its backyard. Indeed, relative global weakness may even be the precondition of relative regional dominance over weaker societies, failed states, or dependent economies brought together by the United States and via the United States into a hublike imperial structure.

Nor is the possibility of an *imperium Americanum* undermined by Washington's promotion of democracy. Regardless of whether William Robinson is correct to argue that "the promotion of polyarchy in U.S. foreign policy is intended to suppress popular democratization, which is a threat to elite status quos and the structure of an asymmetric international order, and is thus an attempt to resolve crises of elite domination generated by globalizing pressures," the emergence and potential consolidation of democratic regimes is of little consequence to the relations between such regimes and a potential core.[37] Those relations can easily be hierarchical—that is to say, imperial—because we have no reason to suppose that democracies, even if peacefully inclined, cannot dominate one another and thereby become implicated in imperial structures.

The leading candidates for U.S. imperial rule are, not surprisingly, the countries of Latin America. They have been the objects of U.S. hegemony as well as of formal and informal empire in the past, and ingrained historical patterns, as expressions of path dependence, are not irrelevant to how subsequent relations may evolve. Ongoing developments hint at the emergence, or reemergence, of more or less hublike economic relationships—termed "investment clusters" by Barbara Stallings—between the United States and Argentina, Bolivia, Chile, Colombia, El Salvador, Mexico, and Venezuela. According to Stallings, "An economy is in the cluster of [another country] when the latter dominates annual investment flows, either through absolute dominance over a host country (with more than 50 percent of total investment) or relative dominance (where its investment exceeds the share of the next largest investor by at least 10 percent)."[38] The United States was also, as Peter Smith points out, "the largest single trading partner for every country of the region" by 1990.[39] Not surprisingly, although only 15 percent of U.S. trade was with Latin America in 1992, the latter's trade with the United States increased from 33 percent in 1980 to 43 percent in 1992. In turn, intra–Latin American trade accounted for only 17 percent of total Latin American trade.[40]

Very much in line with the nonintentionalist approach to empire formation adopted in this book, Smith explains "United States predominance" as resulting

in large part from a systemic retreat by extrahemispheric rivals. . . . This occurred not so much because the end of the Cold War provoked the United States to do anything particularly bold, innovative, or effective; it happened, instead, because outside powers withdrew from the Americas and directed their attention elsewhere. The European Community focused on the rehabilitation and reincorporation of East Europe; the Soviet Union withdrew and then collapsed, leaving Russia to cope with enormous domestic challenges; Japan, ever mindful of its relationship with the United States (and beset by its own economic problems), proved reluctant to accelerate involvement in the hemisphere; and China, despite its headlong rush toward economic growth, was not yet in any position to pursue an aggressive strategy toward Latin America. There were no strong competitors for the United States. As a result, U.S. supremacy in the Americas was uncontested and complete.[41]

Economic dominance does not yet spell empire, of course—especially because Latin American elites have managed to acquire substantial political autonomy in recent decades and such regional trade associations as Mercosur may disperse existing investment clusters—but they do suggest that proto-hub-like relationships are already a reality.

A political hub is also implicit—not "potential"—in the U.S. practices of applying its domestic laws to its southern neighbors, intervening militarily (as in Panama in 1989 and in Haiti in 1994) and, more generally, of compelling Latin elites to subordinate their own interests to such domestic U.S. concerns as immigration, terrorism, drugs, and human rights.[42] For such a hub to take definite shape, however, would require a substantial reduction in the power of local Latin American elites and states—perhaps as the result of financial crisis or a renewal and/or acceleration of revolutionary, terrorist, or armed opposition. The continued vitality of the Colombian Revolutionary Armed Forces and the National Liberation Army, the rebellion in Chiapas Province, and the seizure in 1997 of the Japanese embassy in Lima may be the last flickers of the rebelliousness of earlier decades; they may also be harbingers of things to come—especially if economic polarization, social immiseration, and political fragility continue in their present forms in Latin America.[43] Were a conjunction of economic dependence, political weakness, and growing U.S. intrusiveness to take place—hardly a preposterous eventuality in light of globalization's increasingly destabilizing consequences—a U.S. empire will have emerged in everything but name.

CREEPING REIMPERIALIZATION?

As with the preceding scenario, the case for empire formation in the former Soviet geopolitical space does not presuppose imperial intent, resting instead on continuing disparities in power, state capacity, and economic dependence within the context of a global environment that, in deterring linkages with the world, is likely to promote closer relations between Russia and its neighbors. Such a perspective provides, as I suggest here, not unpersuasive reasons to expect a Russian empire to reemerge.

The conventional wisdom would dispute this claim, typically arguing that, as the disastrous war in Chechnya presumably demonstrated, the Russian state is too weak to embark on such grandiose schemes.[44] Although the state *is* weak, of course, empire is still perfectly possible, because the view that weakness precludes empire suffers from several flaws. First, relative weakness, as we know, promotes nonintegration and thus is the precondition of empire. Second, even if this were not the case, the weakness argument is fixated on only one way for reimperialization to occur—by force. But as chapter 8 argued, forcible expansion is only one of many paths toward empire. That Russia may be weak militarily does not mean that a Russian empire cannot reemerge by other means—stealthily, even unintentionally. Indeed, Russia's relative clout, and its willingness to use it, was amply in evidence in Moscow's imposition in 1998 of sanctions and other punitive measures on Latvia for alleged discrimination against its Russian minority.

Third, Russian weakness is a relative notion. Russia's army may be demoralized, its stability may be fragile, and its economy may be in disarray, but those of the non-Russian states of the near abroad are even more so. Georgia, Tajikistan, Moldova, Armenia, and Azerbaijan are embroiled in, or suffering the consequences of, debilitating military conflicts; Estonia, Latvia, and Lithuania are ministates; geopolitical isolation may consign Turkmenistan, Kazakstan, Kyrgyzstan, and Uzbekistan to Russia's shadow; Belarus is uncertain about its independence; and Ukraine remains highly dependent on Russia economically.[45] Compared with the United States, Russia may be an underdeveloped state with nuclear arms; compared with its neighbors, Russia is a superpower. Although the Russian military failed in Chechnya, its non-Russian counterparts would have performed far worse, if only because they lack significant armed forces of any kind.[46] As the only post-Soviet state with a sizable army, Ukraine is barely able to feed, train, and equip the several hundred thousand soldiers in its ranks.[47] And we have no ground whatsoever for assuming that Ukrainian battle élan would even remotely approximate that of the Chechens.

Fourth, and most important, the possibility of reimperialization depends far less on the Russian elite's military intentions than on the relative state capacity and economic autonomy of Russia and its neighbors, and those are still largely the product of where states stood in the framework of totalitarian empire.[48] As I suggested in chapter 3, varying degrees of totalitarian control and imperial rule bequeathed states with profoundly different institutional legacies. Thus the east-central European satellites emerged from informal empire with more or less complete state apparatuses, bureaucracies, elites, armies, police forces, and courts and with more or less developed and minimally dependent economies. Russia inherited the bulk of the imperial state and its elites as well as a self-sufficient and resource-rich economy. The formally ruled non-Russian republics became independent without coherent states and with highly dependent economies, whereas their Communist Party old-boy networks retarded the formation of genuine elites. The Balts occupied an intermediate position between the east-central Europeans and the non-Russians.[49]

Russia's economic preponderance is reflected in its dominance of the total trade of most of its formerly Soviet neighbors. Ukraine, Belarus, Armenia, Georgia, Kyrgyzstan, Kazakstan, Tajikistan, and Uzbekistan are dependent on Russia for about half or more of their exports, imports, or both. Indeed, Kyrgyzstan's trade dependence, like Ukraine's energy dependence, is almost total.[50] Some energy-producing states may eventually be able to reduce that dependence, but most non-Russian successor states are likely to be married to Russia's economy for a long time to come. Just how intimate that marriage is was made painfully clear in the aftermath of Russia's financial crisis in 1998: all its neighbors in the near abroad experienced financial difficulties of their own, with the tremors reaching even the relatively independent Balts and east-central Europeans. Globalization is likely to deepen the non-Russian dependence on Russia, as the rigors of international competition and the ravages of financial breakdown force them to rely on traditional markets in and economic linkages with Russia. Seen in this light, the Ukrainian-Russian Accord on Economic Cooperation in the Years 1998–2007, which foresees a massive intensification of economic linkages, is as indicative of both sides' desire to establish normal relations as it is of their inability to integrate into the global economy.[51]

If relative state capacity and economic autonomy hold the key to the possibility of a post-Soviet imperial revival, it is hard to imagine how the east-central European states could be brought back into a Russian empire. They are independent, they are comparatively rich, they are economically independent, they are strategically important to the United States and Western Europe—and, as members of NATO and the European Union (EU), they will be part of Western Europe—and they are geographically distant from the former core. In stark contrast, the differences in state capacity and economic autonomy between Russia and its neighbors in the near abroad seem large enough to qualify as facilitating conditions of imperial reconstitution but not, I stress, of state building and integration.

If, as I suspect, Russia's neighbors are therefore destined for the kind of informal imperial rule formerly enjoyed by the east-central European satellites, the rapprochement in 1996–1998 between Russia and Belarus should be interpreted as the result of, above all, powerful systemic forces acting in conjunction with the megalomania of President Alyaksandr Lukashenka.[52] As what could be the first step toward some sort of imperial amalgam, the creeping reimperialization of Belarus may presage the future course of Russo-Ukrainian relations. Like Belarus, Ukraine remains highly dependent on Russia for energy, a variety of natural resources, investment, and military technology. Its emerging bourgeoisie is, like the comprador classes described by dependencia theorists, fixated on economic developments in Russia.[53] Ukraine's putative partners in the Commonwealth of Independent States—such as Moldova, Georgia, and Azerbaijan, with which Kyiv concluded something in the nature of an informal alliance in 1998—are too weak to offer significant balancing opportunities. And despite Warsaw's strong support of Ukraine, Polish elites will have no choice but increasingly to turn westward as they join Western European and Atlantic economic, political, and security structures.

In particular, NATO enlargement, while permanently removing Poland, the Czech Republic, and Hungary from Russia's "sphere of influence," will have two unintended proimperial side-effects.[54] It will, first, isolate Ukraine, Belarus, Moldova, and the Baltic states in a strategic no-man's land and, second, reinforce the plausibility of Russia's imperial ideology while highlighting the plight of Russian "abandoned brethren" in the Crimea, the Donbas, Latvia, and northeastern Estonia.[55] In turn, enlargement of the European Union—with the restrictions on population movement foreseen in the Schengen accords—will increase the economic isolation of these gray-zone states and thereby reinforce their dependence on Russia. Bereft of significant political and economic relations with the outside world, and so overwhelmingly fixated on Russia, Ukraine and its neighbors may have no choice but to engage in what Karen Dawisha calls "autocolonization."[56]

The proof of the imperial pudding will be in the reemergence of the three defining characteristics of empire. If, say, Russia, Belarus, and Ukraine remain distinct regions inhabited by culturally differentiated elites and populations; if political power is progressively transferred from Kyiv and Minsk to Moscow; and if, most important, Belarus and Ukraine come to be bound to Russia in a hublike political and economic structure, a post-Soviet Russian empire will indeed have emerged. Note that the first condition is already a reality, the second may be in the process of emerging as a consequence of the factors adduced in this chapter, and the third could—thanks to the expansion of NATO and the EU in the context of globalization—result from growing political and economic isolation from the West. And if such a scenario seems plausible for Belarus and Ukraine, it is equally plausible for most of the other Soviet successor states.

FROM EMPIRE TO LENIN?

As I stated at the outset, these scenarios are not inevitable. Moreover, I fully admit to the possibility of different outcomes. Contrary to the all-too-optimistic notion that the end of history, the evil empire, the cold war, and manifold other bad things must produce a world community of equal polities and societies, however, it is perfectly possible to recalibrate these premises by just a few degrees and project the unintentional emergence of imperial relations. Worse still, I have suggested that the emergent empires are likely to be not just any old polities but hierarchical systems centered on the United States and Russia. All this smacks of dreadfully unfashionable, if not downright old-fashioned, old thinking and, naturally enough, raises the specter of a renewed superpower competition.

But a renewed cold war is not in the cards. Although a U.S. empire is likely to be durable, I am far less confident about Russia's ability to sustain empire for more than the short term. The conventional wisdom is right to suggest that the Russian state may be too weak to act as an effective imperial hub; it is wrong only in claiming that the state could not acquire an empire, especially by nonimperialist means. Given the Russian state's inability to control its vast territory and raise resources from its obstreperous provinces, reimperialization will in all likelihood produce an imperial system suffering from extreme decay, one especially prone to both further disintegration and to collapse.[57]

No such weaknesses would appear to constrain the U.S. state, at least in the short term. Although the declinist literature typified by Paul Kennedy's writings points to the incapacity of the United States to maintain its relative economic dominance in a rapidly developing world, there is no reason to think, as I have already suggested, that decline and empire are mutually exclusive; indeed, the former may be a precondition of the latter.[58] If the imperium Americanum is to get its comeuppance, it will probably be for reasons external to the United States. Globalization may turn out to be a double-edged sword. If, as the crisis of 1997–1999 suggests, the emerging global economy proves to be less providential than its priests would have us believe—and capitalism has been known to have its troubles too—another crisis of capitalism may one day be upon us. At that time it may even be apposite to dust off our old copies of Lenin.

afterword

"The sun shone, having no alternative, on the nothing new." So begins Samuel Beckett's dreary comedy, *Murphy*.[1] One does not, I think, have to share Beckett's view of the world to suspect that choice-centered theories are probably trivial—if all they claim is that people make choices—or wrong—if they claim that choices are critical in deciding the course of events—or circular—if they insist that choices are the product of choosing.

I do not mean to suggest that choice is irrelevant and that we are merely the playthings of determinist forces. In the theoretically underdetermined world that we inhabit, there is, thankfully, as little reason to believe that causal laws drive us as that rational choice drives them. But I do think that Graham Greene got it just right in the following passage from *The Power and the Glory*:

"That's another thing I don't understand," the lieutenant said, "why you—of all people—should have stayed when the others ran."

"They didn't all run," the priest said.

"But why did you stay?"

"Once," the priest said, "I asked myself that. The fact is, a man isn't presented suddenly with two courses to follow: one good and one bad. He gets caught up. The first year—well, I didn't believe there was really any cause to run. Churches have been burnt before now. You know how often. It doesn't mean much. I thought I'd stay till next month, say, and see if things were better. Then—oh, you don't know how time can slip by. . . . Do you know I suddenly realized that I was the only priest left for miles around?"[2]

Among the many things that this book has attempted to demonstrate, foremost may be that we really know far less than we claim to know. I have suggested that this is an inescapable consequence of the fact that both theory and facts are grounded in concepts that are grounded in language that can never quite be pinned down. Thus theory is inevitably underdetermined and facts are inevitably overdetermined. By the same token, however, we do not know only that we know virtually nothing. Concepts can expand the realm of the theorizable and therefore knowable—but only if they are used, as Giovanni Sartori recommends, with care. Concepts *are* playthings, and, unlike revolutions, nations, and empires, they usually *are* the products of our choices. We can choose poorly, or we can choose less poorly. And the difference between less and more is, I submit, more than less.

notes

Preface

1. Alexander J. Motyl, "Why Empires Reemerge: Imperial Collapse and Imperial Revival in Comparative Perspective," *Comparative Politics* 31 (January 1999):127–45; "After Empire: Competing Discourses and Interstate Conflict in Postimperial Eastern Europe," in Barnett Rubin and Jack Snyder, eds., *Post-Soviet Political Order*, pp. 14–33 (London: Routledge, 1998); "Imperial Collapse and Revolutionary Change: Austria-Hungary, Tsarist Russia, and the Soviet Empire," in Jürgen Nautz and Richard Vahrenkamp, eds., *Die Wiener Jahrhundertwende*, pp. 813–32 (Vienna: Böhlau, 1993); "From Imperial Decay to Imperial Collapse: The Fall of the Soviet Empire in Comparative Perspective," in Richard Rudolph and David Good, eds., *Nationalism and Empire*, pp. 15–43 (New York: St. Martin's, 1991).

2. Theda Skocpol, *States and Social Revolutions* (Cambridge: Cambridge University Press, 1979).

3. David Stark and Laszlo Bruszt, *Postsocialist Pathways* (Cambridge: Cambridge University Press, 1998).

4. Giovanni Sartori, "Guidelines for Concept Analysis," in Giovanni Sartori, ed., *Social Science Concepts*, p. 15 (Beverly Hills, Calif.: Sage, 1984).

Introduction: Concepts and Theories

1. John R. Searle, *The Construction of Social Reality* (New York: Free Press, 1995), pp. 149–97; Peter Berger and Thomas Luckmann, *The Social Construction of Reality* (New York: Doubleday, 1966).

2. Giovanni Sartori, "Guidelines for Concept Analysis," in Giovanni Sartori, ed., *Social Science Concepts* (Beverly Hills, Calif.: Sage, 1984), p. 74.

3. Walter Carlsnaes, *The Concept of Ideology and Political Analysis* (Westport, Conn.: Greenwood, 1981), p. 5.

4. On "bundle theory" see Robert Audi, ed., *The Cambridge Dictionary of Philosophy* (Cambridge: Cambridge University Press, 1995), pp. 92–93.

5. On properties see Scott Gordon, *The History and Philosophy of Social Science* (London: Routledge, 1991), pp. 641–44.

6. Robert Cox, "Towards a Post-Hegemonic Conceptualization of World Order," in James Rosenau and Ernst-Otto Czempiel, eds., *Governance Without Governments: Order and Change in World Politics*, p. 133 (Cambridge: Cambridge University Press, 1992).

7. On conceptualism see H. H. Price, *Thinking and Experience* (Cambridge, Mass.: Harvard University Press, 1953); Audi, *Cambridge Dictionary*, p. 148. See also John Wilson, *Thinking with Concepts* (Cambridge: Cambridge University Press, 1963).

8. The painting analogy is suggested by Ernest Gellner, *Nations and Nationalism* (Ithaca, N.Y.: Cornell University Press, 1983), pp. 139–40.

9. Jonathan H. Turner, "Analytical Theorizing," in Anthony Giddens and Jonathan H. Turner, eds., *Social Theory Today*, pp. 156–94 (Cambridge: Polity Press, 1987); William Outhwaite, *Concept Formation in Social Science* (London: Routledge and Kegan Paul, 1983), pp. 151–155. On methodological holism see Audi, *Cambridge Dictionary*, pp. 335–36, 492; May Broadbeck, ed., *Readings in the Philosophy of the Social Sciences* (New York: Macmillan, 1968), pp. 245–335.

10. Daniel C. Dennett, *Consciousness Explained* (Boston: Little, Brown, 1991).

11. Jon Elster, *Nuts and Bolts for the Social Sciences* (Cambridge: Cambridge University Press, 1989); John Watkins, "Methodological Individualism and Social Tendencies," in Richard Boyd et al., eds., *The Philosophy of Science*, pp. 733–42 (Cambridge, Mass.: MIT Press, 1991).

12. Arthur Danto, *Narration and Knowledge* (New York: Columbia University Press, 1985), pp. 257–84; A. M. MacIver, "Levels of Explanation in History," in Broadbeck, *Readings*, pp. 304–16.

13. W. V. Quine, *Quiddities* (Cambridge, Mass.: Belknap, 1987), pp. 43–45. On defining characteristics see Sartori, "Guidelines for Concept Analysis," pp. 44–50.

14. Samuel P. Huntington, *Political Order in Changing Societies* (New Haven, Conn.: Yale University Press, 1968), pp. 55, 266, 274. The German translates as "And if they have not died, then they are still alive."

15. Charles Tilly, *From Mobilization to Revolution* (New York: Random House, 1978), pp. 189–200; Tilly, *European Revolutions, 1492–1992* (Oxford: Basil Blackwell, 1993), p. 5; Tilly, *Coercion, Capital, and European States, A.D. 990–1990* (Oxford: Basil Blackwell, 1990), pp. 1–2.

16. Nelson Goodman, *Fact, Fiction, and Forecast* (Cambridge, Mass.: Harvard University Press, 1983), pp 74–83.

17. See Christopher G. A. Bryant, "Conceptual Variation and Conceptual Relativism in the Social Sciences," in Diederick Raven et al., eds., *Cognitive Relativism and Social Science*, pp. 51–67 (New Brunswick, N.J.: Transaction, 1992).

18. Sartori, "Guidelines for Concept Analysis," pp. 35–44.

19. Giovanni Sartori, "Comparing and Miscomparing," *Journal of Theoretical Politics* 3 (1991):243–57.

20. Steven R. David, "Internal War: Causes and Cures," *World Politics* 49 (July 1997):552–76; Harry Eckstein, "On the Etiology of Internal Wars," in Clifford Paynton

and Robert Blackey, eds., *Why Revolution?* pp. 124–50 (Cambridge, Mass.: Schenkman, 1971).

21. Such reification may be symptomatic of a deeper problem. For better or worse, language is all we have to express ideas; if language fails to express certain thoughts, that is as much as to say that these thoughts cannot be expressed. If so, bemoaning the inadequacy of language makes little sense, when it might be more apposite to consider the possibility that, in purporting to transcend everyday language, the concepts involved actually have no meaning. Indeed, this incapacity to accept the constraints of human language may be why, as Alan Sokal and Jean Bricmont illustrate, postmodernists have a proclivity for incomprehensible mathematical and scientific metaphors that seem better equipped to get at what they cannot express linguistically. See Johannes Wetzel, "Krise in der Dromosphäre," *Die Zeit*, October 17, 1997, p. 15.

22. Friedrich Nietzsche, *On the Genealogy of Morals and Ecce Homo* (New York: Vintage, 1969), p. 80.

23. Russell Hardin, *One for All* (Princeton, N.J.: Princeton University Press, 1995), pp. 11–12.

24. Geoff Eley and Ronald Grigor Suny, "Introduction: From the Moment of Social History to the Work of Cultural Representation," in Geoff Eley and Ronald Grigor Suny, eds., *Becoming National: A Reader*, p. 10 (Oxford: Oxford University Press, 1996).

25. For a critique of this claim see Jeffrey C. Alexander, "The Centrality of the Classics," in Giddens and Turner, *Social Theory Today*, pp. 48–50.

26. Danto, *Narration and Knowledge*, pp. 1–16.

27. John A. Armstrong, *Nations Before Nationalism* (Chapel Hill: University of North Carolina Press, 1982), and "The Autonomy of Ethnic Identity," in Alexander J. Motyl, ed., *Thinking Theoretically About Soviet Nationalities*, p. 29 (New York: Columbia University Press, 1992).

28. Yael Tamir, "The Enigma of Nationalism," *World Politics* 47 (April 1995):424–25, 432.

29. On initial conditions see Ernst Nagel, *The Structure of Science*, 2d ed. (Indianapolis, Ind.: Hackett, 1977), pp. 30–32.

30. W. V. Quine, *Theories and Things* (Cambridge, Mass.: Belknap, 1981), p. 26.

31. See John D. Barrow, *Theories of Everything: The Quest for Ultimate Explanation* (New York: Fawcett Columbine, 1991), pp. 42–58.

32. Isolating necessary and facilitating conditions may, in the final analysis, be all that social science theories can do. For a trenchant critique of causal theory in general and of the utility of necessary, facilitating, and sufficient conditions in particular, see Ernest Sosa and Michael Tooley, "Introduction," in Ernest Sosa and Michael Tooley, eds., *Causation*, pp. 5–9 (Oxford: Oxford University Press, 1993).

33. Karl R. Popper, *Conjectures and Refutations* (London: Routledge and Kegan Paul, 1963), p. 115.

34. On theoretical underdetermination see W. V. Quine, *From a Logical Point of View* (Cambridge, Mass.: Harvard University Press, 1953), p. 43; Paul A. Roth, *Meaning and Method in the Social Sciences* (Ithaca, N.Y.: Cornell University Press, 1987).

35. Stephen Hawking, *A Brief History of Time* (New York: Bantam, 1988), pp. 10–11. See also Richard Feynman, *The Character of Physical Law* (New York: Modern Library, 1994), pp. 70–71.

36. Alexander, "Centrality of the Classics."

37. Alan Sokal, "Transgressing the Boundaries: Toward a Transformative Hermeneutics of Quantum Gravity," *Social Text* 18 (spring–summer 1996):217–52. See also Steven Weinberg, "Sokal's Hoax," *New York Review of Books*, August 8, 1996, pp. 11–15.

38. "L'Affaire Derrida," Letters to the Editor, *New York Review of Books*, February 11, 1993, pp. 44–45; "L'Affaire Derrida: Another Exchange," Letters to the Editor, *New York Review of Books*, March 25, 1993, pp. 65–67.

39. Gordon, *History and Philosophy of Social Science*, p. 651; Popper, *Conjectures and Refutations*, pp. 115–16.

40. For an excellent discussion of various ways in which theories may be evaluated, see David G. Wagner, *The Growth of Sociological Theories* (Beverly Hills, Calif.: Sage, 1984).

41. See Stephen Gaukroger, *Explanatory Structures* (Hassocks, Sussex, U.K.: Harvester, 1978); Imre Lakatos, "Falsification and the Methodology of Scientific Research Programmes," in Imre Lakatos and Alan Musgrave, eds., *Criticism and the Growth of Knowledge*, pp. 91–196 (Cambridge: Cambridge University Press, 1970).

42. Karl Popper, *The Logic of Scientific Discovery* (New York: Harper and Row, 1965), pp. 71–72.

43. Goodman, *Fact, Fiction, and Forecast*, p. 4.

44. James D. Fearon and David D. Laitin, "Explaining Interethnic Cooperation," *American Political Science Review* 90 (December 1996):716.

45. Ibid., 718.

46. Ibid., 718–19.

47. Jeffrey Friedman, ed., *The Rational Choice Controversy* (New Haven, Conn.: Yale University Press, 1996). See Roger Peterson, "The Rational Choice of Pathologies" (unpublished paper); and Karen Schweers Cook and Margaret Levi, eds., *The Limits of Rationality* (Chicago: University of Chicago Press, 1990).

48. Barry Posen, "The Security Dilemma and Ethnic Conflict," *Survival* 35 (spring 1993):30. James Fearon also treats ethnic groups as unitary actors, despite "much anecdotal evidence" suggesting "that in the case of ethnic conflict this assumption is violated empirically in ways that are highly significant." See his "Ethnic War as a Commitment Problem" (paper presented at the 1994 Annual Meeting of the American Political Science Association, September 2–5, 1994, New York, pp. 5–6).

49. Jack Snyder and Karen Ballentine, "Nationalism and the Marketplace of Ideas," *International Security* 21 (fall 1996):5–40.

50. Gordon, *History and Philosophy of Social Science*, p. 639. See also Turner, "Analytical Theorizing," pp. 161–67; Danto, *Narration and Knowledge*, pp. 137–41.

51. Albert Camus, *The Stranger* (New York: Vintage International, 1989), pp. 98–107.

52. Johan Galtung, *Theory and Methods of Social Research* (New York: Columbia University Press, 1969), p. 334.

53. Thomas A. Spragens Jr., *The Dilemma of Contemporary Political Theory* (New York: Dunellen, 1973), p. 155.

54. Quine, *Theories and Things*, pp. 71–72.

55. Roth, *Meaning and Method in the Social Sciences*, p. 19. See also Diederick Raven, "A Defense of Cognitive Relativism: Realism, Idealism, and Nominalism," in Raven et al., *Cognitive Relativism and Social Science*, pp. 117–19.

56. Quine, *Theories and Things*, pp. 21–22.

57. Paul Feyerabend, *Against Method* (London: Verso, 1988).

58. Douglas Chalmers, "Interpretive Frameworks: A Structure of Theory in Political Science" (unpublished paper, 1987, p. 45).

59. Jean-François Lyotard, *The Postmodern Condition: A Report on Knowledge* (Manchester, U.K.: Manchester University Press, 1984), p. xxiv; Donald N. McCloskey, *The Rhetoric of Economics* (Madison: University of Wisconsin Press, 1985); Berel Lang, *The Anatomy of Philosophical Style* (Oxford: Basil Blackwell, 1990); Daniel M. Hausman, ed., *The Philosophy of Economics*, 2d ed. (Cambridge: Cambridge University Press, 1994); William Connolly, *The Terms of Political Discourse* (Lexington, Mass.: Heath, 1974).

60. Gabriel A. Almond, *A Discipline Divided* (Beverly Hills, Calif.: Sage, 1990).

1. Revolutionary Change

1. Peter Weiss, *The Persecution and Assassination of Jean-Paul Marat as Performed by the Inmates of the Asylum of Charenton Under the Direction of the Marquis de Sade* (New York: Atheneum, 1981), p. 11.

2. N. N. Sukhanov, *The Russian Revolution, 1917* (London: Oxford University Press, 1955); François René de Chateaubriand, *The Memoirs of Chateaubriand* (New York: Knopf, 1961).

3. John Reed, *Ten Days That Shook the World* (New York: Bantam, 1987).

4. Andrew Arato, "Revolution, Restoration, and Legitimization: Ideological Problems of the Transition from State Socialism," in Michael Kennedy, ed., *Envisioning Eastern Europe*, pp. 185–86 (Ann Arbor: University of Michigan Press, 1994).

5. Mark Lilla, "A Tale of Two Reactions," *New York Review of Books*, May 14, 1998, p. 4.

6. Stan Taylor, *Social Science and Revolution* (New York: St. Martin's, 1984), p. 152.

7. Giovanni Sartori, "Guidelines for Concept Analysis," in Giovanni Sartori, ed., *Social Science Concepts* (Beverly Hills, Calif.: Sage, 1984), p. 41.

8. *Selected Readings from the Works of Mao Tsetung* (Beijing: Foreign Language Press, 1971), p. 30; Crane Brinton, *The Anatomy of Revolution* (New York: Vintage, 1965), pp. 17–18; Robert C. Tucker, ed., *The Marx-Engels Reader*, 2d ed.(New York: Norton, 1978), p. 164; Charles Tilly, *European Revolutions, 1492–1992* (Oxford: Basil Blackwell, 1993), p. 7.

9. See Mark Hagopian's excellent, though woefully underused *The Phenomenon of Revolution* (New York: Harper and Row, 1974).

10. Christoph Kotowski, "Revolution," in Sartori, *Social Science Concepts*, pp. 403–51.

11. See Alfred G. Cuzan and Richard J. Heggen, "A Micropolitical Explanation of the 1979 Nicaraguan Revolution," *Latin American Research Review* 17 (1982):157–70; John A. Booth, *The End and the Beginning: The Nicaraguan Revolution* (Boulder, Colo.: Westview, 1982); Donald C. Hodges, *Intellectual Foundations of the Nicaraguan Revolution* (Austin: University of Texas Press, 1986); Hans-Hermann Höhmann, ed., *Aufbruch im Osten Europas: Chancen für Demokratie und Marktwirtschaft nach dem Zerfall des Kommunismus* (Munich: Carl Hanser Verlag, 1993).

12. See Ian Kershaw and Moshe Lewin, eds., *Stalinism and Nazism: Dictatorships in Comparison* (Cambridge: Cambridge University Press, 1997).

13. See Ronald A. Francisco, "Theories of Protest and the Revolutions of 1989," *American Journal of Political Science* 37 (August 1993):663–80; Abraham Brumberg, ed., *Chronicle of a Revolution* (New York: Pantheon, 1990).

14. William H. Sewell Jr., "Historical Events as Transformations of Structures: Inventing Revolution at the Bastille," *Theory and Society* 25 (1996):844.

15. William Outhwaite, *Concept Formation in Social Science* (London: Routledge and Kegan Paul, 1983), p. 116.

16. Arato, "Revolution, Restoration, and Legitimization," pp. 190–91; Kotowski, "Revolution," p. 410; Theda Skocpol, *States and Social Revolutions* (Cambridge: Cambridge University Press, 1979), p. 4.

17. On the normative implications of revolutionary theory, see Sidney Hook, *Revolution, Reform, and Social Justice* (New York: New York University Press, 1975).

18. This is not an original definition. According to Samuel P. Huntington, "A revolution is a rapid, fundamental, and violent domestic change in the dominant values and myths of a society, in its political institutions, social structure, leadership, and government activity and policies" (*Political Order in Changing Societies* [New Haven, Conn.: Yale University Press, 1968], p. 264). Jack Goldstone writes, "I shall reserve the term 'revolution' for those cases where state breakdown is followed by substantial changes in political and social institutions and in the ideology used to justify those institutions" (*Revolution and Rebellion in the Early Modern World* [Berkeley: University of California Press, 1991], p. 10).

19. I shall sidestep the question of whether *A* and *A'* are the "same" entity. On the one hand, obviously they are not: thus the designation of prime. On the other hand, we can follow the change in defining characteristics within the boundaries established by the concept. I appreciate that, philosophically, the issues I have just touched upon are extremely complex but for the sake of brevity—and sanity?—will leave them unexplored.

20. For an excellent discussion of many of these issues, see Anthony D. Smith, *The Concept of Social Change* (London: Routledge and Kegan Paul, 1973).

21. On the public sphere see Craig Calhoun, "Civil Society and the Public Sphere," *Public Culture* 5 (1993):267–80.

22. This is, I know, an utterly unoriginal, dreadfully banal, and screamingly traditional division of "reality"—which, however, is probably as good as anything else.

23. Alexander Wendt has made this point in "Anarchy Is What States Make of It: The Social Construction of Power Politics," *International Organization* 46 (spring 1992):391–426.

24. Kotowski, "Revolution," pp. 443–47.

25. See Stephen E. Hanson, *Time and Revolution* (Chapel Hill: University of North Carolina Press, 1997).

26. Norman Cohn, *The Pursuit of the Millennium* (London: Secker and Warburg, 1957).

27. For a selection of Helmut Kohl's genuinely revolutionary writings, see *Deutschlands Zukunft in Europa: Reden und Beiträge des Bundeskanzlers* (Herford, Germany: Busse und Seewald, 1990). See also Marek Dąbrowski, ed., *The Gaidar Program: Lessons for Poland and Eastern Europe* (Warsaw: Friedrich-Ebert-Stiftung, 1993).

28. Quoted in David E. Sanger, "Indonesian Faceoff: Drawing Blood Without Bombs," *New York Times*, March 8, 1998, sec. 4, p. 1.

29. Jeffrey Sachs, *Poland's Jump to the Market Economy* (Cambridge, Mass.: MIT Press, 1994). The quintessential example of revolutionary hubris is, of course, V. I. Lenin's *What Is to Be Done?*

30. On the concept of transformation see Simone Schwanitz, *Transformationsforschung: Area Studies Versus Politikwissenschaft* (Berlin: Arbeitspapiere des Osteuropa-Instituts, 1997), no. 3; David Stark and Laszlo Bruszt, *Postsocialist Pathways* (Cambridge: Cambridge University Press, 1998).

31. Alfred Stepan, "Paths Toward Redemocratization: Theoretical and Comparative Considerations," in Guillermo O'Donnell et al., eds., *Transitions from Authoritarian Rule: Comparative Perspectives*, p. 71 (Baltimore, Md.: Johns Hopkins University Press, 1986).

32. Jürgen Kocka, "1945: Neubeginn oder Restauration?" in Carola Stern and Heinrich A. Winkler, eds., *Wendepunkte deutscher Geschichte, 1848–1990*, pp. 159–92 (Frankfurt am Main: Fischer Taschenbuch Verlag, 1994); Mikiso Hane, *Modern Japan* (Boulder, Colo.: Westview, 1986), pp. 341–74; Gary D. Allinson, *Japan's Postwar History* (Ithaca, N.Y.: Cornell University Press, 1997).

33. Norman M. Naimark, *The Russians in Germany* (Cambridge, Mass.: Belknap, 1995).

34. See Francis Fukuyama, "Liberal Democracy as a Global Phenomenon," *PS: Political Science and Politics* 24 (December 1991):659–64; Thomas J. Biersteker, "The 'Triumph' of Liberal Economic Ideas in the Developing World," in Barbara Stallings, ed., *Global Change, Regional Response*, pp. 174–96 (Cambridge: Cambridge University Press, 1995); Stephen Hanson and Willfried Spohn, eds., *Can Europe Work? Germany and the Reconstruction of Postcommunist Societies* (Seattle: University of Washington Press, 1995).

35. On resources see Amitai Etzioni, *A Comparative Analysis of Complex Organizations* (New York: Free Press, 1975); Ian Lustick, "Stability in Deeply Divided Societies: Consociationalism Versus Control," *World Politics* 31 (April 1979):324–44.

36. Timur Kuran, "Now Out of Never: The Element of Surprise in the East European Revolution of 1989," *World Politics* 44 (October 1991):7–48.

37. Stephan Haggard and Robert R. Kaufman, "Economic Adjustment and the Prospects for Democracy," in Stephan Haggard and Robert R. Kaufman, eds., *The Politics of Economic Adjustment*, p. 338 (Princeton, N.J.: Princeton University Press, 1992).

38. Leslie Armijo et al., "The Problems of Simultaneous Transition," in Larry Diamond and Marc F. Plattner, eds., *Economic Reform and Democracy*, pp. 228–29 (Baltimore, Md.: Johns Hopkins University Press, 1995). See also Arend Lijphart and Carlos H. Waisman, "The Design of Markets and Democracies: Generalizing Across Regions," in Arend Lijphart and Carlos H. Waisman, eds., *Institutional Design in New Democracies*, pp. 235–48 (Boulder, Colo.: Westview, 1996). For a dissenting view see M. Steven Fish, "Democratization's Requisites: The Postcommunist Experience," *Post-Soviet Affairs* 14 (1998):212–47.

39. Dennis P. Quinn and John T. Woolley, "Democracy and Risk and Return: Or How Democracy and Economic Growth Are Related" (unpublished manuscript, December 20, 1997).

40. Sachs, *Poland's Jump*, p. xiii. For a critique of Sachs see Jagdish Bhagwati, "Shock Treatments," *New Republic*, March 28, 1994, pp. 39–43.

41. John Mueller, "Democracy, Capitalism, and the End of Transition," in Michael Mandelbaum, ed., *Postcommunism: Four Perspectives*, p. 104 (New York: Council on Foreign Relations, 1996). See also Anders Aslund, "The Russian Road to the Market," *Current History* 94 (October 1995):314.

42. Otto Kirchheimer, "Confining Conditions and Revolutionary Breakthroughs," *American Political Science Review* 59 (December 1965):964–74.

43. Daniel Cohn-Bendit and Gabriel Cohn-Bendit, *Obsolete Communism: The Left-Wing Alternative* (New York: McGraw-Hill, 1968), p. 83.

44. Dietrich Harth, "Revolution und Mythos," in Dietrich Harth and Jan Assmann, eds., *Revolution und Mythos*, pp. 9–35 (Frankfurt am Main: Fischer Taschenbuch Verlag, 1992).

45. On how structures matter concretely see Richard E. Ericson, "The Structural Barrier to Transition: A Note on Input-Output Tables of Centrally Planned Economies" (unpublished manuscript, July 1996).

2. Revolutionary Bets

1. Crane Brinton, *The Anatomy of Revolution* (New York: Vintage, 1965); Lyford P. Edwards, *The Natural History of Revolutions* (Chicago: University of Chicago Press, 1927).

2. Ted Robert Gurr, *Why Men Rebel* (Princeton, N.J.: Princeton University Press, 1970); Samuel P. Huntington, *Political Order in Changing Societies* (New Haven, Conn.: Yale University Press, 1968); Chalmers Johnson, *Revolutionary Change* (Palo Alto, Calif.: Stanford University Press, 1982).

3. Theda Skocpol, *States and Social Revolutions* (Cambridge: Cambridge University Press, 1979); Ellen Kay Trimberger, *Revolution from Above* (New Brunswick, N.J.: Transaction, 1978); Jeffrey M. Paige, *Agrarian Revolution: Social Movements and Export Agri-*

culture in the Underdeveloped World (New York: Free Press, 1975); Barrington Moore Jr., *Social Origins of Dictatorship and Democracy* (Boston: Beacon, 1966); S. N. Eisenstadt, *Revolution and the Transformation of Societies* (New York: Free Press, 1978); Jack Goldstone, "Theories of Revolution: The Third Generation," *World Politics* 32 (April 1980):425–53.

4. Goldstone, "Theories of Revolution," p. 435. See also Goldstone, *Revolution and Rebellion in the Early Modern World* (Berkeley: University of California Press, 1991).

5. William H. Sewell Jr., "Historical Events as Transformations of Structures: Inventing Revolution at the Bastille," *Theory and Society* 25 (1996):841–81; Said Amir Arjomand, "Iran's Islamic Revolution in Comparative Perspective," *World Politics* 38 (April 1986):383–414; Ronald Grigor Suny, *The Revenge of the Past* (Palo Alto, Calif.: Stanford University Press, 1993); Jack Goldstone, "Ideology, Cultural Frameworks, and the Process of Revolution," *Theory and Society* 20 (August 1991):405–53.

6. Skocpol, *States and Social Revolutions*, p. x.

7. Ralf Dahrendorf, *Class and Class Conflict in Industrial Society* (Palo Alto, Calif.: Stanford University Press, 1959).

8. Skocpol, *States and Social Revolutions*, p. 29.

9. On the relationship between internal and external factors, see Kenneth N. Waltz, *Man, the State, and War* (New York: Columbia University Press, 1954).

10. Yale H. Ferguson and Richard W. Mansbach, *The State, Conceptual Chaos, and the Future of International Relations Theory* (Boulder, Colo.: Lynne Rienner, 1989).

11. Skocpol, *States and Social Revolutions*, pp. 24–33.

12. On the relative autonomy of the state see Ralph Miliband, *Marxism and Politics* (New York: Oxford University Press, 1977); Eric Nordlinger, *On the Autonomy of the Democratic State* (Cambridge, Mass.: Harvard University Press, 1981); Alfred Stepan, *The State and Society* (Princeton, N.J.: Princeton University Press, 1978).

13. Imre Lakatos, "Falsification and the Methodology of Scientific Research Programmes," in Imre Lakatos and Alan Musgrave, eds., *Criticism and the Growth of Knowledge*, pp. 91–196 (Cambridge: Cambridge University Press, 1970).

14. I thank Bridget Welsh for bringing this point to my attention.

15. Timur Kuran's concept of "preference falsification" plays a similar role in his theory of revolution. Because private preferences can be at variance with public preferences, "major revolutions are likely to come again and again as a surprise." That revolutions will continue to surprise scholars and contemporaries may be true but not for the reasons Kuran adduces. As we can never *really* know what someone's *real* private and public preferences are—public opinion polls may or may not be reflective of either—preference falsification is an empty signifier of little explanatory value. See Timur Kuran, "Now out of Never: The Element of Surprise in the East European Revolution of 1989," *World Politics* 44 (October 1991):47.

16. Skocpol, *States and Social Revolutions*, p. 4.

17. See Farideh Farhi, "State Disintegration and Urban-Based Revolutionary Crisis," *Comparative Political Studies* 21 (1988):231–56; Michael Tien-Lung Liu, "States and Urban Revolutions," *Theory and Society* 17 (1988):179–209.

18. On crises see James O'Connor, *The Meaning of Crisis* (Oxford: Basil Blackwell,

1987); Ekkart Zimmermann, "Crises and Crises Outcomes," *European Journal of Political Research* 7 (March 1979):67–115; Alexander J. Motyl, "Reassessing the Soviet Crisis: Big Problems, Muddling Through, Business as Usual," *Political Science Quarterly* 104 (1989):269–80.

19. Skocpol, *States and Social Revolutions*, p. xi.

20. Ibid., 3.

21. Ibid., 4.

22. Ibid., xi.

23. The literature on "events" is growing. See Susan Olzak, "Analysis of Events in the Study of Collective Action," *Annual Review of Sociology* 15 (1989):119–41; Larry Griffen, "Narrative, Event-Structure Analysis, and Causal Interpretation in Historical Sociology," *American Journal of Sociology* 98 (1993):1094–1133.

24. See David Easton, *The Analysis of Political Structure* (New York: Routledge, 1990); Mark Lichbach and Alan Zuckerman, eds., *Comparative Politics: Rationality, Culture, and Structure* (Cambridge: Cambridge University Press, 1997).

25. Nikki Keddie, "Can Revolutions Be Predicted; Can Their Causes Be Understood?" in Nikki R. Keddie, ed., *Debating Revolutions*, pp. 3–26 (New York: New York University Press, 1995).

26. Jack Goldstone, "Predicting Revolutions: Why We Could (and Should) Have Foreseen the Revolutions of 1989–91 in the U.S.S.R. and Eastern Europe," in Keddie, *Debating Revolutions*, pp. 39–64.

27. V. I. Lenin, *What Is to Be Done?*

28. Compare Lenin's *What Is to Be Done?* and Hitler's *Mein Kampf*. The similarities are striking.

29. From my point of view "counterrevolutionaries" are as revolutionary as "revolutionaries": they differ only with respect to direction. The former "reverse" the latter but are not, as a result, necessarily "regressive." See E. E. Rice, ed., *Revolution and Counter-Revolution* (Oxford: Basil Blackwell, 1991).

30. Alasdair MacIntyre, "Ideology, Social Science, and Revolution," *Comparative Politics* 5 (April 1973):321–42.

31. Karl Popper, *The Poverty of Historicism* (New York: Harper and Row, 1964), pp. 108–109.

32. Arthur Danto, *Narration and Knowledge* (New York: Columbia University Press, 1985), pp. 14–15.

33. Karl Popper, *The Logic of Scientific Discovery* (New York: Harper and Row, 1965); Nelson Goodman, *Fact, Fiction, and Forecast* (Cambridge, Mass.: Harvard University Press, 1983).

34. Charles Tilly, "Changing Forms of Revolution," in Rice, *Revolution and Counter-Revolution*, pp. 5–8.

35. Carl Hempel, *Aspects of Scientific Explanation and Other Essays in the Philosophy of Science* (New York: Free Press, 1965).

36. Wesley C. Salmon, "Four Decades of Scientific Explanation," in Philip Kitcher and Wesley C. Salmon, eds., *Scientific Explanation*, pp. 3–195 (Minneapolis: University of Minnesota Press, 1989).

37. May Broadbeck, "Explanation, Prediction, and 'Imperfect' Knowledge," in May Broadbeck, ed., *Readings in the Philosophy of the Social Sciences*, pp. 363–98 (New York: Macmillan, 1968).

38. See Bas C. Van Fraassen, *Laws and Symmetry* (Oxford: Clarendon, 1989).

39. John Dunn, "Revolution," in Terence Ball et al., eds., *Political Innovation and Conceptual Change*, pp. 333–56 (Cambridge: Cambridge University Press, 1989); Dietrich Harth, "Revolution und Mythos," in Dietrich Harth and Jan Assmann, eds., *Revolution und Mythos*, pp. 9–35 (Frankfurt am Main: Fischer Taschenbuch Verlag, 1992); William Connolly, *The Terms of Political Discourse* (Lexington, Mass.: Heath, 1974).

40. Christoph Kotowski, "Revolution," in Giovanni Sartori, ed., *Social Science Concepts* (Beverly Hills, Calif.: Sage, 1984), pp. 439–40.

41. Andreas Pickel and Helmut Wiesenthal, *The Grand Experiment* (Boulder, Colo.: Westview, 1997).

42. For an excellent critique of "theories of everything," see John D. Barrow, *Theories of Everything: The Quest for Ultimate Explanation* (New York: Fawcett Columbine, 1991).

43. See Stan Taylor, *Social Science and Revolution* (New York: St. Martin's, 1984), pp. 151–58.

44. Jürgen Habermas, *Vergangenheit als Zukunft* (Munich: Piper, 1993), p. 128.

45. Andreas Pickel, "Jump-Starting a Market Economy: A Critique of the Radical Strategy of Economic Reform," in Pickel and Wiesenthal, *Grand Experiment*, p. 72.

3. Revolutionary Losses

1. Georges Sorel, *Reflections on Violence* (New York: Collier, 1961).

2. Hannah Arendt, *On Revolution* (New York: Penguin, 1987); Stephen Walt, *Revolution and War* (Ithaca, N.Y.: Cornell University Press, 1996).

3. Kenneth N. Waltz, *Man, the State, and War* (New York: Columbia University Press, 1954).

4. See Anthony Giddens, *The Constitution of Society: Outline of the Theory of Structuration* (Cambridge, U.K.: Polity, 1984).

5. David Schoenbaum, *Hitler's Social Revolution* (New York: Norton, 1980).

6. Henri J. Barkey, *The State and the Industrialization Crisis in Turkey* (Boulder, Colo.: Westview, 1990), pp. 43–52; Bernard Lewis, *The Emergence of Modern Turkey*, 2d ed. (London: Oxford University Press, 1968); Şerif Mardin, "The Ottoman Empire," in Karen Barkey and Mark von Hagen, eds., *After Empire*, pp. 115–28 (Boulder, Colo.: Westview, 1997).

7. Ronald Grigor Suny, *The Revenge of the Past* (Palo Alto, Calif.: Stanford University Press, 1993).

8. Joseph Rothschild, *The Return to Diversity* (Oxford: Oxford University Press, 1989); Alexander Dallin, *German Rule in Russia, 1941–1945* (London: Macmillan, 1957).

9. Stephen Hanson and Willfried Spohn, eds., *Can Europe Work? Germany and the Reconstruction of Postcommunist Societies* (Seattle: University of Washington Press,

1995); M. Donald Hancock and Helga A. Welsh, eds., *German Unification: Processes and Outcomes* (Boulder, Colo.: Westview, 1994).

10. Daniela Dahn, *Westwärts und nicht vergessen* (Hamburg: Rowohlt, 1997).

11. Andreas Pickel, "Jump-Starting a Market Economy: A Critique of the Radical Strategy of Economic Reform," in Andreas Pickel and Helmut Wiesenthal, *The Grand Experiment* (Boulder, Colo.: Westview, 1997). p. 73; "Survey: Germany," *Economist*, November 9, 1996, pp. 6–16.

12. Compare the progress made by countries along the various dimensions measured by Freedom House. See Freedom House, *Nations in Transit: Civil Society, Democracy, and Markets in East Central Europe and the Newly Independent States* (New York: Freedom House, 1995); Adrian Karatnycky et al., eds., *Nations in Transit, 1997* (New Brunswick, N.J.: Transaction, 1997). See also Werner Weidenfeld, ed., *Central and Eastern Europe on the Way into the European Union* (Gütersloh, Germany: Bertelsmann Foundation, 1995).

13. See Alexander J. Motyl, "Structural Constraints and Starting Points: The Logic of Systemic Change in Ukraine and Russia," *Comparative Politics* 29 (July 1997):433–47.

14. Anders Aslund, "The Case for Radical Reform," in Larry Diamond and Marc F. Plattner, eds., *Economic Reform and Democracy*, p. 75 (Baltimore, Md.: Johns Hopkins University Press, 1995).

15. For a typical statement of the conventional wisdom, see Michael M. Weinstein, "Russia Is Not Poland, and That's Too Bad," *New York Times*, August 30, 1998, Week in Review sec., p. 5.

16. Goldman is quoted in "Comments and Discussion" of "The Unofficial Economy in Transition," by Simon Johnson, Daniel Kaufmann, and Andrei Shleifer, *Brookings Papers on Economic Activity*, no. 2 (1997):229.

17. For a different view see Anders Aslund, "Has Poland Been Useful as a Model for Russia?" in Aslund, ed., *Economic Transformation in Russia*, pp. 157–73 (New York: St. Martin's, 1994); Anders Aslund, "The Politics of the Economic Reform: Remaining Tasks," in Aslund, ed., *Russian Economic Reform at Risk*, pp. 194–201 (London: Pinter, 1995).

18. Rothschild, *Return to Diversity*; Romuald Misiunas and Rein Taagepera, *The Baltic States: Years of Dependence, 1940–80* (Berkeley: University of California Press, 1983); Suzanne Hruby, "The Church in Poland and Its Political Influence," *Journal of International Affairs* 36 (fall–winter 1982–83):317–28.

19. On the Czech Republic see World Bank, *World Development Report, 1996* (Washington, D.C.: World Bank, 1997), pp. 56–57; Jan Svejnar, ed., *The Czech Republic and Economic Transition in Eastern Europe* (San Diego, Calif.: Academic Press, 1995).

20. Samuel P. Huntington, *Political Order in Changing Societies* (New Haven, Conn.: Yale University Press, 1968).

21. Alexander J. Motyl, "Institutional Legacies and Reform Trajectories," in Karatnycky et al., *Nations in Transit, 1997*, pp. 17–22.

22. This argument is also developed in Alexander J. Motyl, *Dilemmas of Independence: Ukraine After Totalitarianism* (New York: Council on Foreign Relations, 1993), pp. 51–75.

23. See Michael Doyle, *Empires* (Ithaca, N.Y.: Cornell University Press, 1986), p. 40.

24. Maria Csanádi, "The Legacy of Party-States for the Transformation," *Communist Economies and Economic Transformations* 9 (March 1997):75.

25. Ibid., 78.

26. See Kazimierz Z. Poznanski, ed., *The Evolutionary Transition to Capitalism* (Boulder, Colo.: Westview, 1995); Jerry Hough, *Democratization and Revolution in the USSR, 1985-1991* (Washington, D.C.: Brookings Institution Press, 1997).

27. Anders Aslund, for example, writes that "if two people meet to exchange anything, a market exists." See "The Russian Road to the Market," *Current History* 94 (October 1995):314.

28. World Bank, *World Development Report, 1996*.

29. See Motyl, *Dilemmas of Independence*, pp. 51–75.

30. *Economist*, January 17, 1998, p. 98; Simon Stone and Oliver Weeks, "Prospects for the Georgian Economy," *CACP Briefing*, no. 15 (March 1998):1–6.

31. For a similar kind of thought experiment see Peter Berger and Thomas Luckmann, *The Social Construction of Reality* (New York: Doubleday, 1966), pp. 53–67.

32. Jürgen Habermas, *Vergangenheit als Zukunft* (Munich: Piper, 1993), p. 128.

33. David D. Laitin, *Identity in Formation* (Ithaca, N.Y.: Cornell University Press, 1998), pp. 21–24.

34. See Simon Johnson, Daniel Kaufmann, and Andrei Shleifer, "The Unofficial Economy in Transition," *Brookings Papers on Economic Activity*, no. 2 (1997):159–221.

35. Volodymyr Polokhalo calls the Ukrainian state "neototalitarian." See his "Vid Ukrainy komunistychno-totalitarnoi do Ukrainy neototalitarnoi?" *Politychna dumka*, no. 2 (1994):19. See also Ian McAllister, Stephen White, and Richard Rose, "Communists, Privilege, and Postcommunism in Russia," *International Politics* 34 (March 1997):79–95.

36. See Taras Kuzio, *Ukraine: Back from the Brink* (London: Institute for European Defence and Strategic Studies, 1995), pp. 20–23; Dominique Arel, "Ukraine: A Country Report," report prepared for the Minority Rights Group, New York, January 31, 1996.

37. Dmitrii Furman, "Ukraina i my," *Svobodnaia mysl'*, no. 1 (1995):69–83; Ella Zadorozhniuk and Dmitrii Furman, "Ukrainskie regiony i ukrainskaia politika," in Dmitrii Furman, ed., *Ukraina i Rossia*, pp. 88–129 (Moscow: Izdatel'stvo "Prava Cheloveka," 1997); Svitlana Kononchuk and Vyacheslav Pikhovshek, *The Dnipropetrovsk Family—2* (Kyiv: Ukrainian Center for Independent Political Research, 1997); *Dynamika elity* (Kyiv: Ahentstvo "Ukraina," 1998).

38. See Alexander J. Motyl, "State, Nation, and Elites in Independent Ukraine," in Taras Kuzio, ed., *Contemporary Ukraine*, pp. 3–16 (Armonk, N.Y.: Sharpe, 1998).

39. Jürgen Habermas, *The Theory of Communicative Action*, vol. 1 (Boston: Beacon, 1984); Craig Calhoun, ed., *Habermas and the Public Sphere* (Cambridge, Mass.: MIT Press, 1992).

40. Manfred Lohmann, "Das ukrainische Parteienspektrum und die Wahlen in der Ukraine vom 29. März 1998," *KAS/Auslands-Informationen* 14 (1998):44–71; *Ukraine Election Report*, April 10, 1998, pp. 1–4.

41. The Ukrainian left is hardly the monolith that it often appears to be. See Andrew Wilson, "The Ukrainian Left: In Transition to Social Democracy or Still in Thrall to the USSR?" *Europe-Asia Studies* 49 (November 1997):1293–1316.

42. Jewgenija Albaz, *Geheimimperium KGB* (Munich: DTV, 1992), pp. 239–70; Stephen M. Meyer, "The Military," in Timothy J. Colton and Robert Legvold, eds., *After the Soviet Union*, pp. 113–46 (New York: Norton, 1992); Eugene B. Rumer, *The Ideological Crisis in the Russian Military* (Santa Monica, Calif.: RAND, 1994); Renée de Nevers, *Russia's Strategic Renovation* (London: International Institute for Strategic Studies, 1994), Adelphi Paper 289.

43. See Lynn D. Nelson and Irina Y. Kuzes, *Radical Reform in Yeltsin's Russia* (Armonk, N.Y.: Sharpe, 1995); Padma Desai, "Russian Privatization: A Comparative Perspective," *Harriman Review* 8 (August 1995):1–34.

44. Consider the impressive political diversity documented by Michael McFaul and Nikolai Petrov, eds., *Previewing Russia's 1995 Parliamentary Elections* (Washington, D.C.: Carnegie Endowment, 1995).

45. See Lilia Shevtsova and Scott A. Bruckner, "Toward Stability or Crisis?" *Journal of Democracy* 8 (January 1997):12–26; Andrew Goodman, "Organized Change and Organized Crime: Explaining the Rise of Russian Organized Crime" (paper prepared for the 1998 Convention of the Association for the Study of the Nationalities, April 16–19, 1998, Columbia University, New York); Galina Luchterhandt, "Institutionalisierungsprozesse in der Politik seit der Verfassungsreform 1993," in Wolfgang Eichwede, ed., *Das neue Russland in Politik und Kultur*, pp. 26–35 (Bremen: Temmen, 1998).

46. Harry Eckstein et al., *Can Democracy Take Root in Post-Soviet Russia?* (Lanham, Md.: Rowman and Littlefield, 1998).

47. Leslie Dienes, "Energy and Mineral Exports from the Former USSR: Philosopher's Stone or Fool's Gold?" Donald W. Treadgold Papers, no. 18, August 1998, University of Washington, Seattle, p. 21. Peter Reddaway makes a similar point in "Russia on the Brink?" *New York Review of Books*, January 28, 1993, pp. 30–35, and "Desperation Time for Yeltsin's Clique," *New York Times*, January 13, 1995, p. A31.

48. Vladimir Shlapentokh, "Early Feudalism: The Best Parallel for Contemporary Russia," *Europe-Asia Studies* 48 (May 1996):393–411.

49. David Stark and Laszlo Bruszt, *Postsocialist Pathways* (Cambridge: Cambridge University Press, 1998), pp. 196–99.

50. James C. Scott, *Seeing Like a State* (New Haven, Conn.: Yale University Press, 1998); Karl Popper, *The Open Society and Its Enemies*, vol. 2 (London: Routledge and Kegan Paul, 1945).

51. For a prescient analysis see Philip Hanson, "What Sort of Capitalism Is Developing in Russia?" *Communist Economies and Economic Transformation* 9 (March 1997):27–42.

52. Dienes, "Energy and Mineral Exports," p. 33. Naturally, supporters of the theory underlying the policy of the International Monetary Fund will disagree and, not inappropriately, can blame any number of intervening variables for seeming theoretical failures. See Stanley Fischer, "Reforming World Finance," *Economist*, October 3, 1998, pp. 23–27.

4. National Inventions

1. Eric Hobsbawm, *Nations and Nationalism Since 1780* (Cambridge: Cambridge University Press, 1990); Eric Hobsbawm and Terence Ranger, eds., *The Invention of Tradition* (Cambridge: Cambridge University Press, 1992); Benedict Anderson, *Imagined Communities* (London: Verso, 1983).

2. Eric Hobsbawm, "Introduction: Inventing Traditions," in Hobsbawm and Ranger, *Invention of Tradition*, pp. 1–2. See also Eric Hobsbawm, "The New Threat to History," *New York Review of Books*, December 16, 1993, p. 63.

3. Anderson, *Imagined Communities*, p. 15.

4. *Merriam Webster's Collegiate Dictionary*, 10th ed. (Springfield, Mass.: Merriam Webster, 1963), pp. 578, 616.

5. See the excellent critique of the literature on invention and imagination by Yael Tamir, "The Enigma of Nationalism," *World Politics* 47 (April 1995):424–25, 432.

6. Ernest Gellner, *Nations and Nationalism* (Ithaca, N.Y.: Cornell University Press, 1983), p. 49.

7. Inasmuch as they must be *self-consciously* involved in inventing and imagining, however, elites clearly will be a select, and probably fairly small, group of people with unusual cognitive and/or affective skills. Intellectuals, writers, and political activists, precisely those individuals discussed by Miroslav Hroch, come to mind. See his *Social Preconditions of National Revival in Europe* (Cambridge: Cambridge University Press, 1985).

8. See Giovanni Sartori, "Guidelines for Concept Analysis," in Giovanni Sartori, ed., *Social Science Concepts* (Beverly Hills, Calif.: Sage, 1984), pp. 81–82.

9. John Searle, *The Construction of Social Reality* (New York: Free Press, 1995), pp. 79–126. See also Kenneth Russell Olson, *An Essay on Facts* (Palo Alto, Calif.: Center for the Study of Language and Information, 1987).

10. For an excellent example of this tendency see Robert B. Reich, "What Is a Nation?" *Political Science Quarterly* 106 (summer 1991):193–210. For an excellent analysis of this tendency see Walker Connor, "A Nation Is a Nation, Is a State, Is an Ethnic Group, Is a . . . ," *Ethnic and Racial Studies* 1 (1978):377–400.

11. Liah Greenfeld, *Nationalism: Five Roads to Modernity* (Cambridge: Harvard University Press, 1992), pp. 4–8; Rogers Brubaker, "Rethinking Nationhood," *Contention* 4 (fall 1994):3–14.

12. It is irrelevant for our purposes whether what I designate a lifeworld is identical with, or has all the theoretical overtones of, the concept discussed by Jürgen Habermas and other philosophers. On the concept of lifeworld see Donald M. Lowe, "Intentionality and the Method of History," in Maurice Natanson, ed., *Phenomenology and the Social Sciences*, vol. 2, pp. 103–30 (Evanston, Ill.: Northwestern University Press, 1973); Aron Gurwitsch, *Phenomenology and the Theory of Science* (Evanston, Ill.: Northwestern University Press, 1974), pp. 3–32; Jürgen Habermas, *Legitimation Crisis* (Boston: Beacon, 1975), pp. 10–11.

13. One could probably just as easily use Peter Berger and Thomas Luckmann's

(*The Social Construction of Reality* [New York: Doubleday, 1966], p. 65) notion of "primary knowledge."

14. Ibid., 98.

15. Hobsbawm, "Introduction: Inventing Traditions," p. 2.

16. Literary theory has much to say about the implication of readers in a text. See Jonathan Culler, *On Deconstruction: Theory and Criticism After Structuralism* (Ithaca, N.Y.: Cornell University Press, 1982), pp. 31–83.

17. Kurban Said, *Ali and Nino* (New York: Random House, 1970), pp. 43–44.

18. Claude Lévi-Strauss is obviously of relevance here. See Jonathan Culler, *Structuralist Poetics* (Ithaca, N.Y.: Cornell University Press, 1975), pp. 40–54.

19. The "new institutionalist" literature is enormous. For a summary of its basic arguments see Douglass North, *Institutions, Institutional Change, and Economic Performance* (Cambridge: Cambridge University Press, 1990).

20. Searle, *Construction of Social Reality*, p. 3.

21. F. A. Hayek, *The Counter-Revolution of Science* (Indianapolis, Ind.: Liberty Fund, 1979), pp. 149–50.

22. Smith's focus on *mythomoteurs* alerts us to the importance of a nation's having a place in time, whereas Barth's discussion of boundaries underscores a nation's difference from "the other" and therefore its place in space. Anthony Smith, *The Ethnic Origins of Nations* (Oxford: Basil Blackwell, 1986); Fredrik Barth, *Ethnic Groups and Boundaries* (Boston: Little, Brown, 1969). See also Crawford Young, *The Politics of Cultural Pluralism* (Madison: University of Wisconsin Press, 1976), pp. 41–44.

23. See Tom Bottomore and Patrick Goode, eds., *Austro-Marxism*, pp. 102–18 (Oxford: Clarendon, 1978).

24. Yaroslav Hrytsak, "Between Autonomy and Independence: Ukrainian Political Thought Prior [to] 1917" (unpublished manuscript, n.d.).

25. These two sets of propositions, one relating to a group's historicity, another to its otherness, do not exhaust the defining characteristics of a nation. A complete definition would entail more particulars about origins and otherness. Even so, this protodefinition has its uses. In particular, it permits us to differentiate nations from classes as well as to underscore the former's kinship with religious groups. The propositions characteristic of classes distinguish them from other classes but as a rule do not root them in historicist myths. (Some socialist theorists, however, such as Georges Sorel, did just that in the class-based ideologies they constructed.) In contrast, religious identity shares both characteristics with national identity, and it is, as a result, no surprise that the overlap between religious groups and nations is and has been historically great. See Pedro Ramet, ed., *Religion and Nationalism in Soviet and East European Politics* (Durham, N.C.: Duke University Press, 1989).

26. Mikhail A. Molchanov, "Borders of Identity: Ukraine's Political and Cultural Significance for Russia," *Canadian Slavonic Papers* 38 (March–June 1996):177–93; Serhy Yekelchyk, "The Location of Nation: Postcolonial Perspectives on Ukrainian Historical Debates," *Australian Slavonic and East European Studies* 11 (1997):161–84.

27. For an early statement of the ethnic-civic problematic, see Clifford Geertz, "The Integrative Revolution: Primordial Sentiments and Civil Politics in the New

States," in Jason L. Finkle and Richard W. Gable, eds., *Political Development and Social Change*, 2d ed., pp. 655–69 (New York: Wiley, 1971). On civic and ethnic nationalism see Liah Greenfeld, *Nationalism: Five Roads to Modernity* (Cambridge, Mass.: Harvard University Press, 1992), pp. 10–12.

28. See Peter Glotz, *Die falsche Normalisierung* (Frankfurt am Main: Suhrkamp, 1994).

29. Smith, *Ethnic Origins of Nations*, pp. 6–18.

30. Konstantin Symmons-Symonolewicz, *Modern Nationalism* (New York: Polish Institute of Arts and Sciences in America, 1968), p. 26. See also Lowell Barrington, "'Nation' and 'Nationalism': The Misuse of Key Concepts in Political Science," *PS: Political Science and Politics* 30 (December 1997):712–16.

31. John Breuilly, *Nationalism and the State* (Manchester, U.K.: Manchester University Press, 1985), p. 3.

32. Symmons-Symonolewicz, *Modern Nationalism*, pp. 27–28.

33. Michael Hechter, "Containing Nationalism" (unpublished manuscript, draft of November 25, 1997, chap. 1, p. 4).

34. Alexander J. Motyl, *Sovietology, Rationality, Nationality: Coming to Grips with Nationalism in the USSR* (New York: Columbia University Press, 1990), pp. 30–45.

35. Mark Hagopian, *Ideals and Ideologies of Modern Politics* (New York: Longman, 1985), pp. 2, 70. A classic view of nationalism as a thing of the mind is Hans Kohn, *The Idea of Nationalism* (New York: Macmillan, 1944).

36. Gellner, *Nations and Nationalism*, p. 1.

37. For a contrary view see Walker Connor, *The National Question in Marxist-Leninist Theory and Strategy* (Princeton, N.J.: Princeton University Press, 1984), p. 5. See also Peter Zwick, *National Communism* (Boulder, Colo.: Westview: 1983).

38. Elie Kedourie, *Nationalism* (London: Hutchinson, 1966).

39. Carlton Hayes, *Essays on Nationalism* (New York: Russell and Russell, 1966); Hobsbawm, *Nations and Nationalism Since 1780*.

40. Anthony D. Smith, *Theories of Nationalism* (London: Duckworth, 1971).

41. Gellner, *Nations and Nationalism*, pp. 35–38.

42. Greenfeld, *Nationalism*.

43. Andrea Chandler and Charles Furtado, eds., *Perestroika in the Soviet Republics* (Boulder, Colo.: Westview, 1992).

44. John A. Armstrong, *Nations Before Nationalism* (Chapel Hill: University of North Carolina Press, 1982). Although shocking to contemporary sensibilities, this claim is not original, having been made by Kohn, *Idea of Nationalism*, pp. 18–20.

5. National Weaknesses

1. Geoff Eley and Ronald Grigor Suny, "Introduction: From the Moment of Social History to the Work of Cultural Representation," in Geoff Eley and Ronald Grigor Suny, eds., *Becoming National: A Reader* (Oxford: Oxford University Press, 1996), p. 6.

2. David Laitin, "Transitions to Democracy and Territorial Integrity," in Adam Przeworski and Pranab Bardhan, eds., *Sustainable Democracy*, p. 20 (Cambridge: Cambridge University Press, 1995).

3. John A. Armstrong, "Whither Ukrainian Nationalism?" *Canadian Review of Studies in Nationalism* 23 (1996):111.

4. See the discussion in Anthony D. Smith, *The Ethnic Origins of Nations* (Oxford: Blackwell, 1986), pp. 7–18.

5. Ernest Gellner, *Nations and Nationalism* (Ithaca, N.Y.: Cornell University Press, 1983), pp. 39–52.

6. Like all typologies, this one is a construction that cannot claim to be definitive, because conceptual categories and theoretical approaches may be sliced in any number of equally useful ways. The number of types, for instance, could easily be increased, as could the number of dimensions. The terminology I propose may also be altered. Note too that these categories do not address the defining characteristics—or definition—of nations, because we have no reason to think that primordialism and constructivism must define nations differently. They could, in principle, accept identical definitions and still disagree fundamentally about questions relating to cause, time, and properties. Indeed, as Brubaker points out, most approaches rest on a "substantialist" ontology that conceives of nations as living human communities and not, as he would prefer, as discursive practices engaged in by humans. (Rogers Brubaker, *Nationalism Reframed* [Cambridge: Cambridge University Press, 1996], pp. 14–22.)

7. For a discussion of ideal types see Scott Gordon, *The History and Philosophy of Social Science* (London: Routledge, 1991), pp. 472–75.

8. As quoted in Raymond Pearson, "Fact, Fantasy, Fraud: Perceptions and Projections of National Revival," *Ethnic Studies* 10 (1993):44.

9. Brendan O'Leary, "On the Nature of Nationalism: An Appraisal of Ernest Gellner's Writings on Nationalism," *British Journal of Political Science* 27 (1997):192.

10. See Misha Glenny, *The Fall of Yugoslavia* (New York: Penguin, 1992); Robert D. Kaplan, *Balkan Ghosts: A Journey Through History* (New York: St. Martin's, 1993); Serge Schmemann, "Ethnic Battles Flaring in Former Soviet Fringe," *New York Times*, May 24, 1992, p. 10; Mark Danner, "America and the Bosnia Genocide," *New York Review of Books*, December 4, 1997, pp. 55–65; Leopold Senghor, *Négritude et humanisme* (Paris: Éditions de Seuil, 1964).

11. O'Leary, "On the Nature of Nationalism," p. 193; Smith, *Ethnic Origins of Nations*, p. 12; Anthony D. Smith, "Gastronomy or Geology? The Role of Nationalism in the Reconstruction of Nations," *Nations and Nationalism* 1 (March 1995):12.

12. Harold R. Isaacs, "Basic Group Identity: The Idols of the Tribe," in Nathan Glazer and Daniel P. Moynihan, eds., *Ethnicity*, pp. 29–52 (Cambridge, Mass.: Harvard University Press, 1975). See also H. Hoetink, *Two Variants in Caribbean Race Relations* (London: Oxford University Press, 1967); Arend Lijphart, *Democracy in Plural Societies* (New Haven, Conn.: Yale University Press, 1977), p. 17ff.

13. See such influential works as Raul Hilberg, *The Destruction of the European Jews* (New York: Holmes and Meier, 1985), pp. 5–7; Helen Fein, *Accounting for Genocide* (Chicago: University of Chicago Press, 1979), p. 4; Salo W. Baron, *The Russian Jew Un-*

der Tsars and Soviets (New York: Schocken, 1987). See also Alan S. Rosenbaum, ed., *Is the Holocaust Unique?* (Boulder, Colo.: Westview, 1996); Michael R. Marrus, *The Holocaust in History* (London: Weidenfeld and Nicolson, 1988), pp. 18–25.

14. Martin Bernal, *Black Athena*, 2 vols. (New Brunswick, N.J.: Rutgers University Press, 1987, 1991).

15. Donald L. Horowitz, *Ethnic Groups in Conflict* (Berkeley: University of California Press, 1985), pp. 78–83, 145–47; Pierre van den Berghe, "Race and Ethnicity: A Sociobiological Perspective," *Ethnic and Racial Studies* 1 (October 1978):401–11.

16. Samuel P. Huntington. *The Clash of Civilizations and the Remaking of World Order* (New York: Simon and Schuster, 1996), pp. 40–44.

17. For a sampling see G. John Ikenberry et al., "The West: Precious, Not Unique," Letters to the Editor, *Foreign Affairs* 76 (March–April 1997):162–65; "Cultural Explanations," *Economist*, November 9, 1996, pp. 23–26.

18. Gordon, *History and Philosophy of Social Science*, pp. 536–45; John R. Searle, *The Construction of Social Reality* (New York: Free Press, 1995); Peter Berger and Thomas Luckmann, *The Social Construction of Reality* (New York: Doubleday, 1966). See especially Frank J. Sulloway, "Darwinian Virtues," *New York Review of Books*, April 9, 1998, pp. 34–40.

19. On political culture see Gabriel A. Almond and Sidney Verba, eds., *The Civic Culture Revisited* (Beverly Hills, Calif.: Sage, 1989); Archie Brown, ed., *Political Culture and Communist Studies* (Houndmills, U.K.: Macmillan, 1984).

20. Liah Greenfeld, *Nationalism: Five Roads to Modernity* (Cambridge, Mass.: Harvard University Press, 1992).

21. Rogers Brubaker, *Citizenship and Nationhood in France and Germany* (Cambridge, Mass.: Harvard University Press, 1992).

22. Smith, *Ethnic Origins of Nations*.

23. Benedict Anderson, *Imagined Communities* (London: Verso, 1983).

24. Daniel Jonah Goldhagen, *Hitler's Willing Executioners: Ordinary Germans and the Holocaust* (New York: Vintage, 1996), p. 39.

25. See, in particular, Norman G. Finkelstein and Ruth Bettina Birn, *A Nation on Trial: The Goldhagen Thesis and Historical Truth* (New York: Henry Holt, 1998); Fritz Stern, "The Goldhagen Controversy," *Foreign Affairs* 75 (November–December 1996):128–38.

26. On the genetic fallacy see Peter A. Angeles, *A Dictionary of Philosophy* (London: Harper and Row, 1981), p. 100.

27. John Armstrong points to the same problem in his review essay of Greenfeld's book, *Nationalism: Five Roads to Modernity*, in *History and Theory* 33 (1994):83.

28. Goldhagen, *Hitler's Willing Executioners*, p. 482.

29. Eley and Suny, "Introduction," p. 8.

30. Ibid., 7.

31. Eric Hobsbawm, *Nations and Nationalism Since 1780* (Cambridge: Cambridge University Press, 1990), p. 10.

32. Greenfeld, *Nationalism*, p. 16.

33. Eley and Suny, "Introduction," p. 10.

34. This tendency is most tellingly in evidence in Eric Hobsbawm and Terence Ranger, eds., *The Invention of Tradition* (Cambridge: Cambridge University Press, 1992). See also Stuart J. Kaufman, "Spiraling to Ethnic War: Elites, Masses, and Moscow in Moldova's Civil War," *International Security* 21 (fall 1996):108–38; David A. Lake and Donald Rothchild, "Containing Fear: The Origins and Management of Ethnic Conflict," *International Security* 21 (fall 1996):41–75; Pearson, "Fact, Fantasy, Fraud," pp. 58–60.

35. Brubaker, *Nationalism Reframed*, p. 10.

36. Ibid., 61–67.

37. See Paul Boghossian, "Sokals Jux und seine Lehren," *Die Zeit*, January 31, 1997, p. 14–15; Thomas Assheuer, "Der Schnee von gestern," *Die Zeit*, August 13, 1998, p. 36.

38. The very early Eric Hobsbawm typifies this stance in *The Age of Revolution, 1789–1848* (New York: Mentor, 1962), pp. 163–77.

39. Gellner, *Nations and Nationalism*, pp. 56–57.

40. Searle, *Construction of Social Reality*, pp. 1–7; Berger and Luckmann, *Social Construction of Reality*; John A. Armstrong, "The Autonomy of Ethnic Identity," in Alexander J. Motyl, ed., *Thinking Theoretically About Soviet Nationalities* (New York: Columbia University Press, 1992), pp. 24–27.

41. Zygmunt Bauman, "Soil, Blood, and Identity," *Sociological Review* (1992):675. Hobsbawm insists that the nation "belongs exclusively to a particular, and historically recent, period" (*Nations and Nationalism Since 1870*, p. 9).

42. Gellner, *Nations and Nationalism*, p. 138.

43. On the rise and fall of totalitarianism see Abbott Gleason, *Totalitarianism: The Inner History of the Cold War* (New York: Oxford University Press, 1995); Alexander J. Motyl, "The End of Sovietology: From Soviet Studies to Post-Soviet Studies," in Alexander J. Motyl, ed., *The Post-Soviet Nations*, pp. 306–11 (New York: Columbia University Press, 1992).

44. William Connolly, *The Terms of Political Discourse* (Lexington, Mass.: Heath, 1974).

45. Systems seemed to lack the authoritative direction that "the state" was said to provide. In turn, the new institutionalism disaggregates the state into its component parts and thereby effectively "brings back" structures with functions. See Roy Macridis, "The Search for Focus," in Roy Macridis and Bernard Brown, eds., *Comparative Politics*, pp. 85–97 (Homewood, Ill.: Dorsey, 1972). See also Jeffrey Friedman, ed., *The Rational Choice Controversy* (New Haven, Conn.: Yale University Press, 1996).

46. Although the number of devastatingly critical reviews, by leading scholars of all political persuasions, of Goldhagen's book is breathtakingly large, it managed to become a finalist for the National Book Critics Circle Award. Go figure.

6. National Strengths

1. For a discussion of *ethnie*—which, as I have already suggested, are indistinguishable conceptually from nations—in ancient and medieval times, see Anthony D.

Smith, *The Ethnic Origins of Nations* (Oxford: Basil Blackwell, 1986). See also Lawrence J. Silberstein and Robert L. Cohn, eds., *The Other in Jewish Thought and History* (New York: New York University Press, 1994); Peter Garnsey and Richard Saller, *The Roman Empire: Economy, Society, and Culture* (Berkeley: University of California Press, 1987); Deno John Geanakoplos, *Byzantium: Church, Society, and Civilization Seen Through Contemporary Eyes* (Chicago: University of Chicago Press, 1984); Hugh Seton-Watson, *Nations and States* (London: Methuen, 1977); Susan Reynolds, *Kingdoms and Communities in Western Europe (900–1300)* (Oxford: Clarendon, 1984); Ivo Banac and Frank E. Sysyn, eds., Special issue: "Concepts of Nationhood in Early Modern Eastern Europe," *Harvard Ukrainian Studies* 10 (December 1986); Alfred Cobban, *The Nation-State and National Self-Determination*, rev. ed. (London: Collins, 1969); Hans Kohn, *Nationalism: Its Meaning and History*, rev. ed. (New York: Van Nostrand, 1971), pp. 11–15.

2. See Zygmunt Bauman, "Soil, Blood, and Identity," *Sociological Review* (1992):675–701.

3. Anthony D. Smith, *Theories of Nationalism* (London: Duckworth, 1971).

4. Joseph Rothschild discusses these points in *Ethnopolitics* (New York: Columbia University Press, 1981).

5. Contrary to Benedict Anderson (*Imagined Communities* [London: Verso, 1983]), print capitalism and the like make not *national* imaginings but broader and more expansive imaginings possible. Anderson's view rests on the unwarranted assumption that nations can be nations only if they consist of large numbers of people.

6. Karl Deutsch, *Nationalism and Social Communication* (Cambridge. Mass.: MIT Press, 1966).

7. Michael Hechter, *Internal Colonialism* (Berkeley: University of California Press, 1977).

8. Ernest Gellner, *Nations and Nationalism* (Ithaca, N.Y.: Cornell University Press, 1983), pp. 19–52.

9. See Michael Hechter, *Principles of Group Solidarity* (Berkeley: University of California Press, 1988); Russell Hardin, *One for All* (Princeton, N.J.: Princeton University Press, 1995).

10. See Paul Gilbert, *The Philosophy of Nationalism* (Boulder, Colo.: Westview, 1998), pp. 57–90.

11. See Liah Greenfeld's discussion of American nationalism in *Nationalism: Five Roads to Modernity* (Cambridge, Mass.: Harvard University Press, 1992), pp. 399–484.

12. "Survey: The World Economy," *Economist*, September 20, 1997, p. 7.

13. Ibid., 7–8.

14. Donald J. Puchala, "Western Europe," in Robert H. Jackson and Alan James, eds., *States in a Changing World*, p. 75 (Oxford: Clarendon, 1993); Michael Kidron and Ronald Segal, *The State of the World Atlas* (New York: Simon and Schuster, 1981), maps 26–27.

15. Linda Weiss, *The Myth of the Powerless State* (Ithaca, N.Y.: Cornell University Press, 1998).

16. Stephen D. Krasner, "Economic Interdependence and Independent Statehood," in Jackson and James, *States in a Changing World*, p. 318. See also Charles Tilly,

Coercion, Capital, and European States, A.D. *900–1990* (Oxford: Blackwell, 1990), pp. 96–126.

17. Ulrich Beck, "Capitalism Without Work," *Inter Nationes* (winter 1997–1998): 20–23.

18. "Wie wär's mit Selbstbestimmung?" (interview with Hans-Olaf Henkel and Ulrich Beck), *Die Zeit*, April 2, 1998, pp. 37–38.

19. Dennis P. Quinn and and John T. Woolley, "Democracy and Risk and Return: Or How Democracy and Economic Growth Are Related" (unpublished manuscript, December 20, 1997).

20. World Bank, *World Development Report, 1996* (Washington, D.C.: World Bank, 1997).

21. Nicos Poulantzas, *State, Power, Socialism* (London: Verso, 1980); Goran Therborn, *What Does the Ruling Class Do When It Rules?* (London: Verso, 1980); "The Economics of Antitrust," *Economist*, May 2, 1998, pp. 62–64.

22. For especially gloomy assessments see Jacques Attali, "The Crash of Western Civilization," *Foreign Policy* (summer 1997):54–64; Michel Chossudovsky, "Global Poverty in the Late Twentieth Century" (unpublished manuscript, Ottawa, 1998).

23. Carnegie Commission on Preventing Deadly Conflict, *Preventing Deadly Conflict* (New York: Carnegie Corporation of New York, 1997).

24. James Mayall, *Nationalism and International Society* (Cambridge: Cambridge University Press, 1990); Kenneth Waltz, *Theory of International Relations* (Reading, Mass.: Addison-Wesley, 1979).

25. Hendrik Spruyt, "Institutional Selection in International Relations: State Anarchy as Order," *International Organization* 48 (autumn 1994):556.

26. Ian Clark, *The Hierarchy of States* (Cambridge: Cambridge University Press, 1989), p. 18.

27. See Stephen D. Krasner, *International Regimes* (Ithaca, N.Y.: Cornell University Press, 1983); James Rosenau, *Turbulence in World Politics* (Princeton, N.J.: Princeton University Press, 1990), pp. 416–40.

28. Fiona Adamson and Alexander Cooley, "Institutionalizing Sovereignty: Systemic Change and Post-Imperial State-Building" (paper presented at the 1997 Convention of the American Political Science Association, August 28–31, 1997, Washington, D.C.).

29. See Robert Gilpin, *The Political Economy of International Relations* (Princeton, N.J.: Princeton University Press, 1987).

30. "Disappearing Taxes," *Economist*, May 31, 1997, pp. 21–23; Charles Lindblom, *Politics and Markets* (New York: Basic, 1977).

31. See Richard Rosecrance, *The Rise of the Trading State* (New York: Basic, 1986); "Little Countries: Small but Perfectly Formed," *Economist*, January 3, 1998, pp. 65–67.

32. Rosenau, *Turbulence in World Politics*, p. 405.

33. Wolfgang J. Mommsen, "The Varieties of the Nation State in Modern History," in Michael Mann, ed., *The Rise and Decline of the Nation State*, p. 226 (Oxford: Basil Blackwell, 1990).

34. Robert Keohane, ed., *Neorealism and Its Critics* (New York: Columbia University Press, 1986).

35. Martin Feldstein, "EMU and International Conflict," *Foreign Affairs* 76 (November–December 1997):60–73; Timothy Garton Ash, "Europe's Endangered Liberal Order," *Foreign Affairs* 77 (March–April 1998):51–65; "A Survey of EMU: An Awfully Big Adventure," *Economist*, April 11, 1998, pp. 7–8.

36. "Fanfare for the Euro," *Economist*, May 2, 1998, pp. 45–46; "The Ugly Side of European Politics," *Economist*, May 2, 1998, pp. 46–47; "Towards EMU: Kicking and Screaming into 1999," *Economist*, June 7, 1997, pp. 19–21; Oliver Schumacher, "Panzerknacker ohne Chance," *Die Zeit*, May 7, 1998, p. 3.

37. Maurice Obstfeld, "Europe's Gamble," *Brookings Papers on Economic Activity*, no. 2 (1997):300; "Towards EMU."

38. European Union, *Agenda 2000: Eine stärkere und erweiterte Union* (Brussels: Europäische Kommission, 1997).

39. Wolfgang Streeck, "Gewerkschaften zwischen Nationalstaat und Europäischer Union," in Dirk Messner, ed., *Die Zukunft des Staates und der Politik*, pp. 231–33 (Bonn: Dietz, 1998); Christian Wernicke, "Bonn bremst," *Die Zeit*, March 26, 1998, p. 3; "Survey: Germany," *Economist*, November 9, 1996, pp. 20–21.

40. Valerie Bunce, "State Collapse After State Socialism: A Comparison of the Soviet Union, Yugoslavia, and Czechoslovakia" (paper prepared for "Nationalism, Post-Communism and Ethnic Mobilization," conference, April 21–22, 1995, Cornell University, Ithaca, N.Y.).

41. William Wallace, *European-Atlantic Security Institutions: Current State and Future Prospects* (Ebenhausen, Germany: Stiftung Wissenschaft und Politik, 1994); David Gates, "Military Force Structures for European Security," in Armand Clesse et al., eds., *The International System After the Collapse of the East-West Order*, pp. 726–39 (Dordrecht, The Netherlands: Martinus Nijhoff, 1994); Peter Corterier, "NATO and the New Europe," in Clesse et al., *International System*, pp. 740–43.

42. Valérie Guérin-Sendelbach and Jacek Rulkowski, " 'Euro-Trio': France-Germany-Poland," *Aussenpolitik* 3 (1994):246–53.

43. Krasner, "Economic Interdependence" p. 319.

44. The assumption of elite ubiquity is widely held in most of the social science literature. Where elites come from is a question that has bedeviled scholars since the times of Plato and Aristotle. For a major contribution to the debate see Frank J. Sulloway, *Born to Rebel: Birth Order, Family Dynamics, and Creative Lives* (New York: Pantheon, 1996).

45. John Breuilly, *Nationalism and the State* (Manchester, U.K.: Manchester University Press, 1985)

46. Hurst Hannum, *Autonomy, Sovereignty, and Self-Determination: The Accommodation of Conflicting Rights* (Philadelphia: University of Pennsylvania Press, 1990); Simon Caney et al., eds., *National Rights, International Obligations* (Boulder, Colo.: Westview, 1996); Alexander J. Motyl, "Rites, Rituals, and Soviet-American Relations," in Robert Jervis and Seweryn Bialer, eds., *Soviet-American Relations After the Cold War*, pp. 183–96 (Durham, N.C.: Duke University Press, 1991).

47. On the relationship between nationalism and democracy, see Tatu Van-hanen, *The Process of Democratization: A Comparative Study of 147 States, 1980–88* (New York: Crane Russak, 1990), pp. 104–18; Alvin Rabushka and Kenneth A. Shep-sle, *Politics in Plural Societies* (Columbus, Ohio: Merrill, 1972); Arend Lijphart, "Po-litical Theories and the Explanation of Ethnic Conflict in the Western World," in Milton Esman, ed., *Ethnic Conflict in the Western World*, pp. 55–62 (Ithaca, N.Y.: Cor-nell University Press, 1977).

48. Robert H. Jackson and Alan James, "The Character of Independent State-hood," in Jackson and James, *States in a Changing World*, pp. 6–7.

7. Imperial Structures

1. Mark Beissinger, "The Persisting Ambiguity of Empire," *Post-Soviet Affairs* 11 (1995):155.

2. Soviet leaders were not the only ones to reject the imperial label; so too, and with equal vigor, did Sovietologists. One exception to this rule was Robert Conquest, ed., *The Last Empire* (Palo Alto, Calif.: Hoover Institution Press, 1986).

3. Michael Doyle, *Empires* (Ithaca, N.Y.: Cornell University Press, 1986), p. 45.

4. George Lichtheim, *Imperialism* (New York: Praeger, 1971), p. 5.

5. S. N. Eisenstadt, "Center-Periphery Relations in the Soviet Empire," in Alexan-der J. Motyl, ed., *Thinking Theoretically About Soviet Nationalities*, p. 206 (New York: Columbia University Press, 1992).

6. David A. Lake, "The Rise, Fall, and Future of the Russian Empire," in Karen Dawisha and Bruce Parrott, eds., *The End of Empire? The Transformation of the USSR in Comparative Perspective*, p. 34 (Armonk, N.Y.: Sharpe, 1997).

7. Geir Lundestad, *The American "Empire"* (Oslo: Norwegian University Press, 1990), p. 37.

8. Alexander Wendt and Daniel Friedheim, "Hierarchy Under Anarchy: Informal Empire and the East German State," *International Organization* 49 (autumn 1995):695.

9. This binary opposition is not, I emphasize, intended to imply that nonnatives are superior to natives or vice versa. As Sigmund Freud once said, sometimes a cigar is just a cigar.

10. Lenin, like many Marxists, made just this assumption, claiming that the eco-nomic subelite dictated to the political subelite. As subsequent research has shown, the picture is far more complicated, and Marxist attempts to defend that assumption have amounted to a profoundly regressive research program. See Carlo M. Cipolla, ed., *The Economic Decline of Empires* (London: Methuen, 1970).

11. On hegemony see Robert O. Keohane, *After Hegemony* (Princeton, N.J.: Prince-ton University Press, 1984).

12. See Clifford Geertz, *The Interpretation of Cultures* (New York: Basic, 1973).

13. Jean Gottmann, ed., *Centre and Periphery: Spatial Variation in Politics* (Beverly Hills, Calif.: Sage, 1980); Edward Shils, *Center and Periphery* (Chicago: University of Chicago Press, 1975).

14. See Anatol Lieven, *Chechnya: Tombstone of Russian Power* (New Haven, Conn.: Yale University Press, 1998); Gail W. Lapidus, "Contested Sovereignty: The Tragedy of Chechnya," *International Security* 23 (summer 1998):5–49.

15. See S. N. Eisenstadt, *The Political Systems of Empires* (Glencoe, N.Y.: Free Press, 1963).

16. Ronald Grigor Suny, "Russia, the Soviet Union, and Theories of Empire" (unpublished paper, March 14, 1996, p. 3).

17. Bruce Parrott, "Analyzing the Transformation of the Soviet Union in Comparative Perspective," in Dawisha and Parrott, *End of Empire?* p. 7.

18. Christopher Chase-Dunn and Thomas D. Hall, *Rise and Demise* (Boulder, Colo.: Westview, 1997), pp. 210–11.

19. Johan Galtung, "A Structural Theory of Imperialism," *Journal of Peace Research* 8 (1971):89. The ad copy for a computer program provides a neat illustration of this point:

> YOUR FAR-FLUNG EMPIRE:
> Your operation covers 60 countries.
> 10 languages.
> 49 currencies.
> 6 time zones.
> 4967 separate trade regulations.
> GATHERED TOGETHER:
> PeopleSoft enterprise software.
> (Advertisment for PeopleSoft, *Economist*, April 11, 1998, n.p.)

20. Some of these transportation networks are discussed and/or illustrated in Richard J. A. Talbert, ed., *Atlas of Classical History* (London: Routledge, 1985), pp. 51–53, 124–27; Martin Gilbert, *Soviet History Atlas* (London: Routledge and Kegan Paul, 1979), pp. 35–36; Paul Robert Magocsi, *Historical Atlas of East Central Europe* (Seattle: University of Washington Press, 1993), pp. 90–92.

21. I discuss "imperial decay," as the progressive weakening of the core-periphery relationship, in "From Imperial Decay to Imperial Collapse: The Fall of the Soviet Empire in Comparative Perspective," in Richard Rudolph and David Good, eds., *Nationalism and Empire*, pp. 15–43 (New York: St. Martin's, 1991).

22. See Richard Ericson, "Soviet Economic Structure and the National Question," in Alexander J. Motyl, ed., *The Post-Soviet Nations*, pp. 240–71 (New York: Columbia University Press, 1992).

23. Alexander J. Motyl, *Sovietology, Rationality, Nationality: Coming to Grips with Nationalism in the USSR* (New York: Columbia University Press, 1990), pp. 87–99.

24. Walter La Feber, *Inevitable Revolutions* (New York: Norton, 1993); Harold Molineu, *U.S. Policy Toward Latin America* (Boulder, Colo.: Westview, 1986).

25. See C. Wright Mills, *The Power Elite* (New York: Oxford University Press, 1959).

26. Peter H. Smith, *Talons of the Eagle* (New York: Oxford University Press, 1996), pp. 142–214.

27. David Easton, *A Framework for Political Analysis* (Englewood Cliffs, N.J.: Prentice Hall, 1965). See also Malcolm Waters, *Modern Sociological Theory* (London: Sage, 1994), pp. 131–72.

28. Robert Jervis, *System Effects: Complexity in Political and Social Life* (Princeton, N.J.: Princeton University Press, 1997), pp. 76–87.

29. Ibid., 177–91.

30. Jonathan Culler, *Structuralist Poetics* (Ithaca, N.Y.: Cornell University Press, 1975), p. 14.

31. David Easton, *The Analysis of Political Structure* (New York: Routledge, 1990); Waters, *Modern Sociological Theory*, pp. 92–129.

32. Easton, *Framework for Political Analysis*.

33. Robert Wesson, *The Imperial Order* (Berkeley: University of California Press, 1967), p. 36.

34. On associated characteristics see Giovanni Sartori, "Guidelines for Concept Analysis," in Giovanni Sartori, ed., *Social Science Concepts* (Beverly Hills, Calif.: Sage, 1984), pp. 32–33.

35. Bernard Lewis, *The Emergence of Modern Turkey*, 2d ed. (London: Oxford University Press, 1968); John A. Armstrong, "Mobilized Diaspora in Tsarist Russia: The Case of the Baltic Germans," in Jeremy Azrael, ed., *Soviet Nationality Policies and Practices*, pp. 63–104 (New York: Praeger, 1978); Hélène Carrère d'Encausse, *Decline of an Empire* (New York: Newsweek Books, 1979); Percival Spear, *A History of India*, vol. 2 (London: Penguin, 1990).

36. Charles Tilly raises similar points in "How Empires End," in Karen Barkey and Mark von Hagen, *After Empire*, pp. 1–11 (Boulder, Colo.: Westview, 1997).

37. Wendt and Friedheim, "Hierarchy Under Anarchy"; Doyle, *Empires*, p. 40.

38. Imanuel Geiss, "Great Powers and Empires: Historical Mechanisms of Their Making and Breaking," in Geir Lundestad, ed., *The Fall of Great Powers*, p. 34 (Oslo: Scandinavian University Press, 1994).

39. See the excellent essays by Rein Taagepera, "Patterns of Empire Growth and Decline: Context for Russia" (unpublished manuscript, March 25, 1995); "Size and Duration of Empires: Growth-Decline Curves, 600 B.C. to 600 A.D.," *Social Science History* 3 (October 1979):115–38; "Size and Duration of Empires: Systematics of Size," *Social Science Research* 7 (1978):108–27; "Size and Duration of Empires: Growth-Decline Curves, 3000 to 600 B.C.," *Social Science Research* 7 (1978):180–96.

40. See Joseph Tainter, *The Collapse of Complex Societies* (Cambridge: Cambridge University Press, 1988); Norman Yoffee and George L. Cowgill, eds., *The Collapse of Ancient States and Civilizations* (Tucson: University of Arizona Press, 1988); Chase-Dunn and Hall, *Rise and Demise*.

41. Warren Treadgold, *A History of the Byzantine State and Society* (Palo Alto, Calif.: Stanford University Press, 1997), pp. 102–46.

42. I develop this argument in *Imperial Ends: The Decay, Collapse, and Revival of Empires*, forthcoming.

43. One is reminded of Napoleon's comment, "On s'engage et puis on pense" (one acts and then one thinks).

44. Nonvoluntarist "declinists" fit the mold of Oswald Spengler, *The Decline of the West* (New York: Modern Library, 1962), or Paul Kennedy, *The Rise and Decline of the Great Powers* (New York: Vintage, 1987).

8. Imperial Trajectories

1. John Strachey, *The End of Empire* (New York: Praeger, 1959), p. 319.

2. David A. Lake, "The Rise, Fall, and Future of the Russian Empire," in Karen Dawisha and Bruce Parrott, eds., *The End of Empire? The Transformation of the USSR in Comparative Perspective* (Armonk, N.Y.: Sharpe, 1997), p. 40.

3. Yale Ferguson and Richard Mansbach, *The State, Conceptual Chaos, and the Future of International Relations Theory* (Boulder, Colo.: Lynne Rienner, 1989).

4. Yale Ferguson and Richard Mansbach, "Global Politics at the Turn of the Millenium: Changing Bases of 'Us' and 'Them'" (paper prepared for the Annual Meeting of the International Studies Association, March 18–21, 1998, Minneapolis, Minn., p. 17).

5. On the variety of imperial trajectories see Alexander J. Motyl, "From Imperial Decay to Imperial Collapse: The Fall of the Soviet Empire in Comparative Perspective," in Richard Rudolph and David Good, eds., *Nationalism and Empire*, pp. 15–43 (New York: St. Martin's, 1991).

6. For a dissenting opinion see David A. Lake, "Anarchy, Hierarchy, and the Variety of International Relations," *International Organization* 50 (winter 1996):1–33.

7. René Grousset, *The Empire of the Steppes* (New Brunswick, N.J.: Rutgers University Press, 1970), pp. 189–252; Eric Hobsbawm, *The Age of Empire, 1875–1914* (New York: Pantheon, 1987); John Keegan, *A History of Warfare* (New York: Knopf, 1994).

8. Johan Galtung, "A Structural Theory of Imperialism," *Journal of Peace Research* 8 (1971):81–117; Michael Doyle, *Empires* (Ithaca, N.Y.: Cornell University Press, 1986), p. 34.

9. See Alexander J. Motyl, *Sovietology, Rationality, Nationality: Coming to Grips with Nationalism in the USSR* (New York: Columbia University Press, 1990), pp. 72–86.

10. Geir Lundestad, *The American "Empire"* (Oslo: Norwegian University Press, 1990), p. 55.

11. Adam B. Ulam, *Expansion and Coexistence: The History of Soviet Foreign Policy, 1917–67* (New York: Praeger, 1968), pp. 364–65.

12. Robert Kann, *A History of the Habsburg Empire, 1526–1918* (Berkeley: University of California Press, 1974), p. 10.

13. See Allen Lynch, *Does Russia Have a Democratic Future?* (New York: Foreign Policy Association Headline Series, 1997), no. 313; Harry Eckstein et al., *Can Democracy Take Root in Post-Soviet Russia?* (Lanham, Md.: Rowman and Littlefield, 1998).

14. Quoted in Donald Kagan, *The Outbreak of the Peloponnesian War* (Ithaca, N.Y.: Cornell University Press, 1969), p. 42.

15. Ibid., 48.

16. See Charles Gati, ed., *The International Politics of Eastern Europe* (New York: Praeger, 1976).

17. Alexander J. Motyl, "Why Empires Reemerge: Imperial Collapse and Imperial Revival in Comparative Perspective," *Comparative Politics* 31 (January 1999):127–45.

18. Franz Ansprenger, *The Dissolution of the Colonial Empires* (London: Routledge, 1989).

19. Grousset, *Empire of the Steppes*, pp. 285–325; A. B. Bosworth, *Conquest and Empire: The Reign of Alexander the Great* (Cambridge: Cambridge University Press, 1988), pp. 229–58; Michael Hrushevsky, *A History of Ukraine* (New Haven, Conn.: Yale University Press, 1941), pp. 39–44.

20. Karl Deutsch, *Nationalism and Social Communication* (Cambridge, Mass.: MIT Press, 1966).

21. Ronald Grigor Suny, "Nation-Making, Nation-Breaking: The End of the Ottoman Empire and the Armenian Community" (unpublished paper, May 3, 1996).

22. See the meticulous tracking of the decline in the Native American population in John R. Swanton, *The Indian Tribes of North America* (Washington, D.C.: Smithsonian Institution, 1969). For excellent analyses see D. W. Meinig, *The Shaping of America*, vol. 2 (New Haven, Conn.: Yale University Press, 1993), pp. 78–103; Allen C. Lynch, "National Identity and U.S. Foreign Policy in a New World Order," *Romanian Journal of International Affairs* 3 (1997): 71–78.

23. Charles Tilly, ed., *The Formation of National States in Western Europe* (Princeton, N.J.: Princeton University Press, 1975).

24. Orest Subtelny, *Ukraine: A History* (Toronto: University of Toronto Press, 1988), pp. 38–41; Kann, *History of the Habsburg Empire*, pp. 54–101.

25. Motyl, "From Imperial Decay to Imperial Collapse."

26. David Good, *The Economic Rise of the Habsburg Empire, 1750–1914* (Berkeley: University of California Press, 1984); John Lukacs, *Budapest, 1900* (New York: Grove, 1990).

27. See Leo J. Moser, *The Chinese Mosaic: The Peoples and Provinces of China* (Boulder, Colo.: Westview, 1985).

28. Timothy Wickham-Crowley, *Guerrillas and Revolution in Latin America: A Comparative Study of Insurgents and Regimes Since 1956* (Princeton, N.J.: Princeton University Press, 1992).

29. Arnold J. Toynbee, *A Study of History*, 12 vols. (London: Oxford University Press, 1934–61); Oswald Spengler, *The Decline of the West* (New York: Modern Library, 1962); Arthur Danto, *Narration and Knowledge* (New York: Columbia University Press, 1985), pp. 1–16. See B. G. Brander, *Staring into Chaos: Explorations in the Decline of Western Civilization* (Dallas, Texas: Spence, 1998).

30. See Wolfgang J. Mommsen, *Theories of Imperialism* (New York: Random House, 1980).

31. See Martin Carnoy, *The State and Political Theory* (Princeton, N.J.: Princeton University Press, 1984); James A. Caporaso, ed., *The Elusive State* (Beverly Hills, Calif.: Sage, 1989).

32. Eugen Weber, *Peasants into Frenchmen* (Palo Alto, Calif.: Stanford University Press, 1976); Perry Anderson, *Lineages of the Absolutist State* (London: Verso, 1979).

33. Meinig, *Shaping of America*, pp. 222–428; Robert Leckie, *The Wars of America*, vol. 1 (New York: HarperPerennial, 1993).

34. Robert Gilpin, *War and Change in World Politics* (Cambridge: Cambridge University Press, 1981), pp. 106–55.

35. Ibid., 156–185; Lake, "Anarchy, Hierarchy," pp. 1–33.

36. Paul Kennedy, *The Rise and Decline of the Great Powers* (New York: Vintage, 1987).

37. Imanuel Geiss, "Great Powers and Empires: Historical Mechanisms of Their Making and Breaking," in Lundestad, *Fall of Great Powers*, pp. 33–34.

38. Lake, "Anarchy, Hierarchy," p. 20.

39. Geiss concurs with my skepticism ("Great Powers and Empires," p. 35).

40. See Charles A. Kupchan, *The Vulnerability of Empire* (Ithaca, N.Y.: Cornell University Press, 1994); Jack Snyder, *Myths of Empire* (Ithaca, N.Y.: Cornell University Press, 1991).

41. Doyle, *Empires*, p. 52.

42. Michael E. Brown, "The Causes and Regional Dimensions of Internal Conflict," in Michael E. Brown, ed., *The International Dimensions of Internal Conflict*, pp. 576–81 (Cambridge, Mass.: MIT Press, 1996).

43. Kupchan, *Vulnerability of Empire*, pp. 90–104; Snyder refers to Van Evera's work in *Myths of Empire*, p. 41.

44. Snyder, *Myths of Empire*, pp. 31–65.

45. See Robert Jervis, *System Effects: Complexity in Political and Social Life* (Princeton, N.J.: Princeton University Press, 1997), pp. 10–21.

46. Rey Koslowski and Friedrich V. Kratochwil, "Understanding Change in International Politics: The Soviet Empire's Demise and the International System," *International Organization* 48 (spring 1994):216.

9. Imperial Futures

1. John Mueller, *Retreat from Doomsday: The Obsolescence of Major War* (New York: Basic, 1989).

2. See Ian Lustick, *Unsettled States, Disputed Lands* (Ithaca, N.Y.: Cornell University Press, 1993).

3. Bruce Russett, *Grasping the Democratic Peace* (Princeton, N.J.: Princeton University Press, 1993); Michael Doyle, "Kant, Liberal Legacies, and Foreign Affairs," *Philosophy and Public Affairs* 12 (fall 1983):205–35; Miriam Fendius Elman, ed., *Paths to Peace: Is Democracy the Answer?* (Cambridge, Mass.: MIT Press, 1997).

4. Walter C. Clemens Jr., *Dynamics of International Relations* (Lanham, Md.: Rowman and Littlefield, 1998), p. 291.

5. Ibid., 282–88.

6. No less an authority than Immanuel Kant appears to disagree. See *Perpetual Peace and Other Essays* (Indianapolis, Ind.: Hackett, 1983).

7. Counterfactual conditionals cannot and do not corroborate some theory, T, because, as Nelson Goodman has shown, counterfactuals presuppose laws (or, in the case of the social sciences, theories). We are entitled to engage in what-if scenarios,

not because they provide additional evidence of the validity or invalidity of *T* but because a different theory, *T'*, permits us to consider what would have happened if some premise were different from the actual reality. See Goodman, *Fact, Fiction, and Forecast* (Cambridge, Mass.: Harvard University Press, 1983). See also Bruce Russett, "Counterfactuals About War and Its Absence," in Philip E. Tetlock and Aaron Belkin, eds., *Counterfactual Thought Experiments in World Politics*, pp. 171–86 (Princeton, N.J.: Princeton University Press, 1996).

8. This is precisely the point made by Spencer R. Weart in *Never at War: Why Democracies Will Not Fight One Another* (New Haven, Conn.: Yale University Press, 1998).

9. Edward D. Mansfield and Jack Snyder, "Democratization and the Danger of War," *International Security* 20 (summer 1995):5–38.

10. Juan Linz, *Crisis, Breakdown, and Reequilibration* (Baltimore, Md.: Johns Hopkins University Press, 1978); Valerie Bunce, "Should Transitologists Be Grounded?" *Slavic Review* 54 (spring 1995):111–27.

11. Fareed Zakaria, "The Rise of Illiberal Democracy," *Foreign Affairs* 76 (November–December 1997):22–43.

12. Alexander J. Motyl, "Institutional Legacies and Reform Trajectories," in Adrian Karatnycky et al., eds, *Nations in Transit, 1997*, pp. 17–22 (New Brunswick, N.J.: Transaction, 1997).

13. Mark Beissinger and Crawford Young have organized the first international conference on this theme, "Beyond State Crisis? The Quest for the Efficacious State in Africa and Eurasia," March 11–14, 1999, the University of Wisconsin–Madison.

14. Joseph Rothschild, *Ethnopolitics* (New York: Columbia University Press, 1981).

15. Ernest Gellner, *Nations and Nationalism* (Ithaca, N.Y.: Cornell University Press, 1983); Hendrik Spruyt, *The Sovereign State and Its Competitors* (Princeton, N.J.: Princeton University Press, 1994).

16. See Dirk Messner, ed., *Die Zukunft des Staates und der Politik* (Bonn: Dietz, 1998); Fritz W. Scharpf, "Die Handlungsfähigkeit des Staates am Ende des zwanzigsten Jahrhunderts," *Politische Vierteljahresschrift* 32 (1991):621–34; Linda Weiss, *The Myth of the Powerless State* (Ithaca, N.Y.: Cornell University Press, 1998).

17. On globalization as discourse see Barry K. Gills, ed., Special issue: "Globalization and the Politics of Resistance," *New Political Economy* 2 (March 1997).

18. Anthony Giddens, *Modernity and Self-Identity* (Palo Alto, Calif.: Stanford University Press, 1991), p. 21.

19. Richard Falk, "Resisting 'Globalization-from-Above' Through 'Globalization-from-Below,'" *New Political Economy* 2 (March 1997):17.

20. Christine N. B. Chin and James H. Mittelman, "Conceptualizing Resistance to Globalization," *New Political Economy* 2 (March 1997):26.

21. Ulrich Beck, *Was ist Globalisierung?* (Frankfurt am Main: Suhrkamp, 1997), p. 30.

22. See Rudolf Walther, "Weltbürger, gebt den Staat nicht auf!" *Die Zeit*, July 23, 1998, p. 35; Peter Beinart, "An Illusion for Our Time," *New Republic*, October 20, 1997, pp. 20–24.

23. Benjamin Barber, *Jihad Versus McWorld* (New York: Ballantine, 1995).

24. Joseph Kahn, "The Bear Draws Blood," *New York Times*, August 30, 1998, sec. 3, pp. 1, 5; David E. Sanger, "The Global Search for an Economic Parachute," *New York Times*, September 2, 1998, pp. 1, 11; "On the Edge," *Economist*, September 5, 1998, pp. 19–21.

25. Louis Emmerij, ed., *Economic and Social Development into the Twenty-First Century* (Washington, D.C.: Inter-American Development Bank, 1997); "Income Distribution," *Economist*, September 20, 1997, p. 116; "The Tap Runs Dry," *Economist*, May 31, 1997, pp. 21–23; John Baylis and Steve Smith, eds., *The Globalization of World Politics* (Oxford: Oxford University Press, 1997), p. 456; "Der Kollaps kommt" (interview with Dennis L. Meadows), *Die Zeit*, February 19, 1998, p. 25; Michel Chossudovsky, "Global Poverty in the Late Twentieth Century" (unpublished manuscript, Ottawa, 1998).

26. See Martin Rhodes, " 'Subversive Liberalism': Market Integration, Globalization and West European Welfare States," in William D. Coleman and Geoffrey R. D. Underhill, eds., *Regionalism and Global Economic Integration*, pp. 99–121 (London: Routledge, 1998); Richard Barnet and John Cavanaugh, *Global Dreams: Imperial Corporations and the New World Order* (New York: Simon and Schuster, 1994).

27. William A. Owens, "America's Information Edge," *Foreign Affairs* 75 (March–April 1996):20–36; Graciela Chichilnisky, "The Knowledge Revolution" (paper presented at "Governance and Sustainable Development," conference, October 8–10, 1997, Columbia University, New York).

28. Stephen Walt, *Revolution and War* (Ithaca, N.Y.: Cornell University Press, 1996), pp. 32–45.

29. See Meghnad Desai, "Global Governance," in Messner, *Die Zukunft des Staates*, pp. 341–42.

30. Ralf Dahrendorf, "An der Schwelle zum autoritären Jahrhundert," *Die Zeit*, November 14, 1997, p. 3. See also Lothar Brock, "Staatenwelt, Weltgesellschaft und Demokratie," in Messner, *Die Zukunft des Staates*, pp. 44–73.

31. Robert O. Keohane and Joseph S. Nye Jr., "Power and Independence in the Information Age," *Foreign Affairs* 77 (September–October 1998): 89.

32. "The Future of Warfare," *Economist*, March 8, 1997, pp. 21–24; Eliot A. Cohen, "A Revolution in Warfare," *Foreign Affairs* 75 (March–April 1996):37–54.

33. Fareed Zakaria, *From Wealth to Power* (Princeton, N.J.: Princeton University Press, 1998).

34. For a classic neoimperial statement see "The Price of American Leadership. Remarks by Samuel R. Berger, Assistant to the President for National Security Affairs," Office of the Press Secretary, The White House, May 1, 1998.

35. John Gerard Ruggie, *Winning the Peace* (New York: Columbia University Press, 1996), pp. 7–27.

36. See John Agnew, "Global Hegemony Versus National Economy: The United States in the New World Order," in George J. Demko and William B. Wood, eds., *Reordering the World* pp. 269–79 (Boulder, Colo.: Westview, 1994), and Stuart Corbridge, "Maximizing Entropy? New Geopolitical Orders and the Internationalization of Business," Demko and Wood, *Reordering the World*, pp. 281–300; Ivo H. Daalder, "The

United States and Military Intervention in Internal Conflict," in Michael E. Brown, ed., *The International Dimensions of Internal Conflict*, pp. 461–88 (Cambridge, Mass.: MIT Press, 1996). The declinist position has many critics. See Henry Nau, *The Myth of America's Decline* (Oxford: Oxford University Press, 1990); Joseph Nye, *Bound to Lead* (New York: Basic, 1991).

37. William I. Robinson, "Globalization, the World System, and 'Democracy Promotion' in U.S. Foreign Policy," *Theory and Society* 25 (1996):625.

38. Barbara Stallings, "The New International Context of Development," in Barbara Stallings, ed., *Global Change, Regional Response*, p. 360 (Cambridge: Cambridge University Press, 1995).

39. Peter H. Smith, *Talons of the Eagle* (New York: Oxford University Press, 1996), p. 225.

40. Stallings, "New International Context," p. 355.

41. Smith, *Talons of the Eagle*, p. 225.

42. Ibid., 263–91; Abraham F. Lowenthal, "Latin America and the United States in a New World: Prospects for Partnership," in Abraham F. Lowenthal and Gregory F. Treverton, eds., *Latin America in a New World*, pp. 237–46 (Boulder, Colo.: Westview, 1994).

43. David Schrieberg, "Dateline Latin America: The Growing Fury," *Foreign Policy* (spring 1997):161–75.

44. See Jack F. Matlock, "Dealing with a Russia in Turmoil," *Foreign Affairs* 75 (May–June 1996):38–51; Sherman Garnett, "Troubled Times for Russia," *IISS Strategic Survey, 1995–96* (Oxford: Oxford University Press, 1996), pp. 116–17.

45. Rajan Menon, "In the Shadow of the Bear: Security in Post-Soviet Central Asia," *International Security* 20 (summer 1995):149–81; Rajan Menon, "After Empire: Russia and the Southern 'Near Abroad,'" in Michael Mandelbaum, ed., *The New Russian Foreign Policy*, pp. 100–66 (New York: Council on Foreign Relations, 1998).

46. Hendrik Spruyt, "The Prospects for Neo-Imperial and Nonimperial Outcomes in the Former Soviet Space," in Karen Dawisha and Bruce Parrott, eds., *The End of Empire? The Transformation of the USSR in Comparative Perspective*, p. 327 (Armonk, N.Y.: Sharpe, 1997); Heinrich Tiller, "Die militärpolitische Entwicklung in den Nachfolgestaaten der ehemaligen Sowjetunion," in Hans-Hermann Höhmann, ed., *Zwischen Krise und Konsolidierung* (Munich: Carl Hanser Verlag, 1995), p. 352.

47. Tor Bukkvoll, *Ukraine and European Security* (London: Royal Institute of International Affairs, 1997), pp. 84–87; Anatoly S. Gritsenko, *Civil-Military Relations in Ukraine: A System Emerging from Chaos* (Groningen, The Netherlands: Centre for European Security Studies, 1997).

48. On state capacity see Walt, *Revolution and War*, pp. 21–22.

49. Motyl, "Institutional Legacies and Reform Trajectories."

50. Menon, "After Empire," p. 115; Margarita Mercedes Balmaceda, "Gas, Oil, and the Linkages Between Domestic and Foreign Policies: The Case of Ukraine," *Europe-Asia Studies* 50 (March 1998):257–86; Andrew Wilson and Igor Burakovsky, *The Ukrainian Economy Under Kuchma* (London: Royal Institute of International Affairs, 1996), pp. 32–37; Transcript, *Newsline*, RFE-RL, September 16, 1998, p. 3.

51. Roman Woronowycz, "Ukraine and Russia Initial Economic Cooperation Pact," *Ukrainian Weekly*, March 1, 1998, pp 1, 5.

52. See Taras Kuzio, "The East Slavic Conundrum: Unity or Divergence?" (unpublished paper, May 1996); Marc Nordberg and Taras Kuzio, "Nation and State Building: Historical Legacies and National Identities in Belarus and Ukraine" (unpublished paper).

53. For examples of this type of analysis see Fernando Henrique Cardozo and Enzo Faletto, *Dependency and Development in Latin America* (Berkeley: University of California Press, 1979); Andre Gunder Frank, *Latin America: Underdevelopment or Revolution?* (New York: Monthly Review, 1969).

54. Michael Mandelbaum, *NATO Expansion: A Bridge to the Nineteenth Century* (Chevy Chase, Md.: Center for Political and Strategic Studies, 1997).

55. Vera Tolz, "Conflicting 'Homeland Myths' and Nation-State Building in Postcommunist Russia," *Slavic Review* 57 (summer 1998):267–94; Olga Alexandrova, "Russland und sein 'nahes Ausland,'" in Hans-Hermann Höhmann, ed., *Zwischen Krise und Konsolidierung*, pp. 325, 330–33; "Vozroditsia li soiuz?" *Nezavisimaia gazeta—Stsenarii*, May 23, 1996, pp. 4–5; Alexander J. Motyl, "After Empire: Competing Discourses and Interstate Conflict in Postimperial Eastern Europe," in Barnett Rubin and Jack Snyder, eds., *Post-Soviet Political Order*, pp. 28–30 (London: Routledge, 1998); David D. Laitin, *Identity in Formation* (Ithaca, N.Y.: Cornell University Press, 1998); Chauncy D. Harris, "Ethnic Tensions in Areas of the Russian Diaspora," *Post-Soviet Geography* 34 (April 1993):233–38; Paul Kolstoe, *Russians in the Former Soviet Republics* (Bloomington: Indiana University Press, 1995); Leon Aron, "The Foreign Policy Doctrine of Postcommunist Russia and Its Domestic Context," in Mandelbaum, *New Russian Foreign Policy*, pp. 23–63.

56. Karen Dawisha, "Constructing and Deconstructing Empire in the Post-Soviet Space," in Dawisha and Parrott, *The End of Empire?* pp. 342–46.

57. See Alexander J. Motyl, "Why Empires Reemerge: Imperial Collapse and Imperial Revival in Comparative Perspective," *Comparative Politics* 31 (January 1999):127–45.

58. Paul Kennedy, *The Rise and Decline of the Great Powers* (New York: Vintage, 1987); William H. McNeill, "Introductory Historical Commentary," in Geir Lundestad, ed., *The Fall of Great Powers*, pp. 3–22 (Oslo: Scandinavian University Press, 1994).

Afterword

1. Samuel Beckett, *Murphy* (New York: Grove Weidenfeld, 1957), p. 1.

2. Graham Greene, *The Power and the Glory* (London: Penguin, 1971), p. 195.

bibliography

Adamson, Fiona and Alexander Cooley. "Institutionalizing Sovereignty: Systemic Change and Post-Imperial State-Building." Paper presented at the 1997 Convention of the American Political Science Association, August 28–31, 1997, Washington, D.C.

Agnew, John. "Global Hegemony Versus National Economy: The United States in the New World Order." In George J. Demko and William B. Wood, eds., *Reordering the World*. Boulder, Colo.: Westview, 1994.

Albaz, Jewgenija. *Geheimimperium KGB*. Munich: DTV, 1992.

Alexander, Jeffrey C. "The Centrality of the Classics." In Anthony Giddens and Jonathan H. Turner, eds., *Social Theory Today*. Cambridge, U.K.: Polity, 1987.

Alexandrova, Olga. "Russland und sein 'nahes Ausland.'" In Hans-Hermann Höhmann, ed., *Zwischen Krise und Konsolidierung*. Munich: Carl Hanser Verlag, 1995.

Allinson, Gary D. *Japan's Postwar History*. Ithaca, N.Y.: Cornell University Press, 1997.

Almond, Gabriel A. *A Discipline Divided*. Beverly Hills, Calif.: Sage, 1990.

Almond, Gabriel A. and Sidney Verba, eds. *The Civic Culture Revisited*. Beverly Hills, Calif.: Sage, 1989.

Anderson, Benedict. *Imagined Communities*. London: Verso, 1983.

Anderson, Perry. *Lineages of the Absolutist State*. London: Verso, 1979.

Angeles, Peter A. *A Dictionary of Philosophy*. London: Harper and Row, 1981.

Ansprenger, Franz. *The Dissolution of the Colonial Empires*. London: Routledge, 1989.

Arato, Andrew. "Revolution, Restoration, and Legitimization: Ideological Problems of the Transition from State Socialism." In Michael Kennedy, ed., *Envisioning Eastern Europe*. Ann Arbor: University of Michigan Press, 1994.

Arel, Dominique. "Ukraine: A Country Report." Prepared for the Minority Rights Group, New York, January 31, 1996.

Arendt, Hannah. *On Revolution*. New York: Penguin, 1987.

Arjomand, Said Amir. "Iran's Islamic Revolution in Comparative Perspective." *World Politics* 38 (April 1986):383–414.

Armijo, Elliott Leslie, Thomas J. Biersteker, and Abraham F. Lowenthal. "The Problems of Simultaneous Transition." In Larry Diamond and Marc F. Plattner, eds.,

Economic Reform and Democracy. Baltimore, Md.: Johns Hopkins University Press, 1995.

Armstrong, John A. "Mobilized Diaspora in Tsarist Russia: The Case of the Baltic Germans." In Jeremy Azrael, ed., *Soviet Nationality Policies and Practices*. New York: Praeger, 1978.

——. *Nations Before Nationalism*. Chapel Hill: University of North Carolina Press, 1982.

——. "The Autonomy of Ethnic Identity." In Alexander J. Motyl, ed., *Thinking Theoretically About Soviet Nationalities*. New York: Columbia University Press, 1992.

——. Review of *Nationalism: Five Roads to Modernity*, by Liah Greenfeld. *History and Theory* 33 (1994):79–95.

——. "Whither Ukrainian Nationalism?" *Canadian Review of Studies in Nationalism* 23 (1996):111–24.

Aron, Leon. "The Foreign Policy Doctrine of Postcommunist Russia and Its Domestic Context." In Michael Mandelbaum, ed., *The New Russian Foreign Policy*. New York: Council on Foreign Relations, 1998.

Ash, Timothy Garton. "Europe's Endangered Liberal Order." *Foreign Affairs* 77 (March–April 1998):51–65.

Aslund, Anders. "Has Poland Been Useful as a Model for Russia?" In Anders Aslund, ed., *Economic Transformation in Russia*. New York: St. Martin's, 1994.

——. "The Case for Radical Reform." In Larry Diamond and Marc F. Plattner, eds., *Economic Reform and Democracy*. Baltimore, Md.: Johns Hopkins University Press, 1995.

——. "The Politics of the Economic Reform: Remaining Tasks." In Anders Aslund, ed., *Russian Economic Reform at Risk*. London: Pinter, 1995.

——. "The Russian Road to the Market." *Current History* 94 (October 1995):311–16.

——, ed. *Economic Transformation in Russia*. New York: St. Martin's, 1994.

——, ed. *Russian Economic Reform at Risk*. London: Pinter, 1995.

Attali, Jacques. "The Crash of Western Civilization." *Foreign Policy* (summer 1997):54–64.

Audi, Robert, ed. *The Cambridge Dictionary of Philosophy*. Cambridge: Cambridge University Press, 1995.

Azrael, Jeremy, ed. *Soviet Nationality Policies and Practices*. New York: Praeger, 1978.

Ball, Terence, James Farr, and Russell L. Hanson, eds. *Political Innovation and Conceptual Change*. Cambridge: Cambridge University Press, 1989.

Balmaceda, Margarita Mercedes. "Gas, Oil, and the Linkages Between Domestic and Foreign Policies: The Case of Ukraine." *Europe-Asia Studies* 50 (March 1998): 257–86.

Banac, Ivo and Frank Sysyn, eds. Special issue: "Concepts of Nationhood in Early Modern Eastern Europe," *Harvard Ukrainian Studies* 10 (1986).

Barber, Benjamin *Jihad Versus McWorld*. New York: Ballantine, 1995.

Barkey, Henri J. *The State and the Industrialization Crisis in Turkey*. Boulder, Colo.: Westview, 1990.

Barkey, Karen and Mark von Hagen, eds. *After Empire*. Boulder, Colo.: Westview, 1997.

Barnet, Richard and John Cavanaugh. *Global Dreams: Imperial Corporations and the New World Order.* New York: Simon and Schuster, 1994.

Baron, Salo W. *The Russian Jew Under Tsars and Soviets.* New York: Schocken, 1987.

Barrington, Lowell. " 'Nation' and 'Nationalism': The Misuse of Key Concepts in Political Science." *PS: Political Science and Politics* 30 (December 1997):712–16.

Barrow, John D. *Theories of Everything: The Quest for Ultimate Explanation.* New York: Fawcett Columbine, 1991.

Barth, Fredrik. *Ethnic Groups and Boundaries.* Boston: Little, Brown, 1969.

Bauman, Zygmunt. "Soil, Blood, and Identity." *Sociological Review* (1992):675–701.

Baylis, John and Steve Smith, eds. *The Globalization of World Politics.* Oxford: Oxford University Press, 1997.

Beck, Ulrich. *Was ist Globalisierung?* Frankfurt am Main: Suhrkamp, 1997.

——. "Capitalism Without Work." *Inter Nationes* (winter 1997–1998):20–23.

Beinart, Peter. "An Illusion for Our Time." *New Republic,* October 20, 1997, pp. 20–24.

Beissinger, Mark. "The Persisting Ambiguity of Empire." *Post-Soviet Affairs* 11 (1995): 149–84.

Berger, Peter and Thomas Luckmann. *The Social Construction of Reality.* New York: Doubleday, 1966.

Bernal, Martin. *Black Athena.* 2 Vols. New Brunswick, N.J.: Rutgers University Press, 1987, 1991.

Bhagwati, Jagdish. "Shock Treatments." *New Republic,* March 28, 1994, pp. 39–43.

Biersteker, Thomas J. "The 'Triumph' of Liberal Economic Ideas in the Developing World." In Barbara Stallings, ed., *Global Change, Regional Response.* Cambridge: Cambridge University Press, 1995.

Boghossian, Paul. "Sokals Jux und seine Lehren." *Die Zeit,* January 31, 1997, pp. 14–15.

Booth, John A. *The End and the Beginning: The Nicaraguan Revolution.* Boulder, Colo.: Westview, 1982.

Bosworth, B. A. *Conquest and Empire: The Reign of Alexander the Great.* Cambridge: Cambridge University Press, 1988.

Bottomore, Tom and Patrick Goode, eds. *Austro-Marxism.* Oxford: Clarendon, 1978.

Boyd, Richard, Philip Gasper, and J. D. Trout, eds. *The Philosophy of Science.* Cambridge, Mass.: MIT Press, 1991.

Brander, B. G. *Staring into Chaos: Explorations in the Decline of Western Civilization.* Dallas, Texas: Spence, 1998.

Breuilly, John. *Nationalism and the State.* Manchester, U.K.: Manchester University Press, 1985.

Brinton, Crane. *The Anatomy of Revolution.* New York: Vintage, 1965.

Broadbeck, May. "Explanation, Prediction, and 'Imperfect' Knowledge." In May Broadbeck, ed., *Readings in the Philosophy of the Social Sciences.* New York: Macmillan, 1968.

——, ed., *Readings in the Philosophy of the Social Sciences.* New York: Macmillan, 1968.

Brock, Lothar. "Staatenwelt, Weltgesellschaft und Demokratie." In Dirk Messner, ed., *Die Zukunft des Staates und der Politik.* Bonn: Dietz, 1998.

Brown, Archie, ed. *Political Culture and Communist Studies.* Houndmills, U.K.: Macmillan, 1984.

Brown, Michael E. "The Causes and Regional Dimensions of Internal Conflict." In Michael E. Brown, ed., *The International Dimensions of Internal Conflict*. Cambridge, Mass.: MIT Press, 1996.

——, ed. *The International Dimensions of Internal Conflict*. Cambridge, Mass.: MIT Press, 1996.

Brubaker, Rogers. *Citizenship and Nationhood in France and Germany*. Cambridge, Mass.: Harvard University Press, 1992.

——. "Rethinking Nationhood." *Contention* 4 (fall 1994):3–14.

——. *Nationalism Reframed*. Cambridge: Cambridge University Press, 1996.

Brumberg, Abraham, ed. *Chronicle of a Revolution*. New York: Pantheon, 1990.

Bryant, Christopher G. A. "Conceptual Variation and Conceptual Relativism in the Social Sciences." In Diederick Raven, Lieteke van Vucht Tijssen, and Jan de Wolf, eds., *Cognitive Relativism and Social Science*. New Brunswick, N.J.: Transaction, 1992.

Bukkvoll, Tor. *Ukraine and European Security*. London: Royal Institute of International Affairs, 1997.

Bunce, Valerie. "Should Transitologists Be Grounded?" *Slavic Review* 54 (spring 1995):111–27.

——. "State Collapse After State Socialism: A Comparison of the Soviet Union, Yugoslavia, and Czechoslovakia." Paper prepared for "Nationalism, Post-Communism, and Ethnic Mobilization," conference, April 21–22, 1995, Cornell University, Ithaca, N.Y.

Calhoun, Craig. "Civil Society and the Public Sphere." *Public Culture* 5 (1993):267–80.

——, ed. *Habermas and the Public Sphere*. Cambridge, Mass.: MIT Press, 1992.

Caney, Simon, David George, and Peter Jones, eds. *National Rights, International Obligations*. Boulder, Colo.: Westview, 1996.

Caporaso, James A., ed. *The Elusive State*. Beverly Hills, Calif.: Sage, 1989.

Cardozo, Fernando Henrique and Enzo Faletto. *Dependency and Development in Latin America*. Berkeley: University of California Press, 1979.

Carlsnaes, Walter. *The Concept of Ideology and Political Analysis*. Westport, Conn.: Greenwood, 1981.

Carnegie Commission on Preventing Deadly Conflict. *Preventing Deadly Conflict*. New York: Carnegie Corporation of New York, 1997.

Carnoy, Martin. *The State and Political Theory*. Princeton, N.J.: Princeton University Press, 1984.

Carrère d'Encausse, Hélène. *Decline of an Empire*. New York: Newsweek Books, 1979.

Chalmers, Douglas. "Interpretive Frameworks: A Structure of Theory in Political Science." Unpublished paper, 1987.

Chandler, Andrea and Charles Furtado, eds. *Perestroika in the Soviet Republics*. Boulder, Colo.: Westview, 1992.

Chase-Dunn, Christopher and Thomas D. Hall. *Rise and Demise*. Boulder, Colo.: Westview, 1997.

Chateaubriand, François René de. *The Memoirs of Chateaubriand*. New York: Knopf, 1961.

Chichilnisky, Graciela. "The Knowledge Revolution." Paper presented at "Governance and Sustainable Development," conference, Columbia University, New York, October 8–10, 1997.

Chin, Christine N. B. and James H. Mittelman. "Conceptualizing Resistance to Globalization." *New Political Economy* 2 (March 1997):25–37.

Chossudovsky, Michel. "Global Poverty in the Late Twentieth Century." Unpublished manuscript, Ottawa, 1998.

Cipolla, Carlo M., ed. *The Economic Decline of Empires*. London: Methuen, 1970.

Clark, Ian. *The Hierarchy of States*. Cambridge: Cambridge University Press, 1989.

Clemens, Walter C. Jr. *Dynamics of International Relations*. Lanham, Md.: Rowman and Littlefield, 1998.

Clesse, Armand, Richard Cooper, and Yoshikazu Sakamoto, eds. *The International System after the Collapse of the East-West Order*. Dordrecht, The Netherlands: Martinus Nijhoff, 1994.

Cobban, Alfred. *The Nation-State and National Self-Determination*, rev. ed. London: Collins, 1969.

Cohen, Ariel. *Russian Imperialism*. Westport, Conn.: Praeger, 1996.

Cohen, Eliot A. "A Revolution in Warfare." *Foreign Affairs* 75 (March–April 1996):37–54.

Cohn, Norman. *The Pursuit of the Millennium*. London: Secker and Warburg, 1957.

Cohn-Bendit, Daniel and Gabriel Cohn-Bendit. *Obsolete Communism: The Left-Wing Alternative*. New York: McGraw-Hill, 1968.

Colton, Timothy J. and Robert Legvold, eds. *After the Soviet Union*. New York: Norton, 1992.

"Comments and Discussion" of "The Unofficial Economy in Transition," by Simon Johnson, Daniel Kaufmann, and Andrei Shleifer. *Brookings Papers on Economic Activity*, no. 2 (1997):222–30.

Connolly, William. *The Terms of Political Discourse*. Lexington, Mass.: Heath, 1974.

Connor, Walker. "A Nation Is a Nation, Is a State, Is an Ethnic Group, Is a . . . " *Ethnic and Racial Studies* 1 (1978):377–400.

——. *The National Question in Marxist-Leninist Theory and Strategy*. Princeton, N.J.: Princeton University Press, 1984.

Conquest, Robert, ed. *The Last Empire*. Palo Alto, Calif.: Hoover Institution Press, 1986.

Cook, Karen Schweers and Margaret Levi, eds. *The Limits of Rationality*. Chicago: University of Chicago Press, 1990.

Corbridge, Stuart. "Maximizing Entropy? New Geopolitical Orders and the Internationalization of Business." In George J. Demko and William B. Wood, eds., *Reordering the World*. Boulder, Colo.: Westview, 1994.

Corterier, Peter. "NATO and the New Europe." In Armand Clesse, Richard Cooper, and Yoshikazu Sakamoto, eds., *The International System after the Collapse of the East-West Order*. Dordrecht, The Netherlands: Martinus Nijhoff, 1994.

Cox, Robert. "Towards a Post-Hegemonic Conceptualization of World Order." In James Rosenau and Ernst-Otto Czempiel, eds., *Governance Without Governments: Order and Change in World Politics*. Cambridge: Cambridge University Press, 1992.

Csanádi, Maria. "The Legacy of Party-States for the Transformation." *Communist Economies and Economic Transformations* 9 (March 1997):61–85.

Culler, Jonathan. *Structuralist Poetics*. Ithaca, N.Y.: Cornell University Press, 1975.

——. *On Deconstruction: Theory and Criticism After Structuralism*. Ithaca, N.Y.: Cornell University Press, 1982.

Cuzan, Alfred and Richard J. Heggen. "A Micropolitical Explanation of the 1979 Nicaraguan Revolution." *Latin American Research Review* 17 (1982):157–70.

Daalder, Ivo H. "The United States and Military Intervention in Internal Conflict." In Michael E. Brown, ed., *The International Dimensions of Internal Conflict*. Cambridge, Mass.: MIT Press, 1996.

Dąbrowski, Marek, ed. *The Gaidar Program: Lessons for Poland and Eastern Europe*. Warsaw: Friedrich-Ebert-Stiftung, 1993.

Dahn, Daniela. *Westwärts und nicht vergessen*. Hamburg: Rowohlt, 1997.

Dahrendorf, Ralf. *Class and Class Conflict in Industrial Society*. Palo Alto, Calif.: Stanford University Press, 1959.

——. "An der Schwelle zum autoritären Jahrhundert." *Die Zeit*, November 14, 1997, p. 3.

Dallin, Alexander. *German Rule in Russia, 1941–1945*. London: Macmillan, 1957.

Danner, Mark. "America and the Bosnia Genocide." *New York Review of Books*, December 4, 1997, pp. 55–65.

Danto, Arthur. *Narration and Knowledge*. New York: Columbia University Press, 1985.

David, Steven R. "Internal War: Causes and Cures." *World Politics* 49 (July 1997):552–76.

Dawisha, Karen. "Constructing and Deconstructing Empire in the Post-Soviet Space." In Karen Dawisha and Bruce Parrott, eds., *The End of Empire? The Transformation of the USSR in Comparative Perspective*. Armonk, N.Y.: Sharpe, 1997.

Dawisha, Karen and Bruce Parrott, eds. *The End of Empire? The Transformation of the USSR in Comparative Perspective*. Armonk, N.Y.: Sharpe, 1997.

Demandt, Alexander, ed. *Das Ende der Weltreiche*. Munich: Beck, 1997.

Demko, George J. and William B. Wood, eds. *Reordering the World*. Boulder, Colo.: Westview, 1994.

de Nevers, Renée. *Russia's Strategic Renovation*. Adelphi Paper 289. London: International Institute for Strategic Studies, 1994.

Dennett, Daniel C. *Consciousness Explained*. Boston: Little, Brown, 1991.

Desai, Meghnad. "Global Governance." In Dirk Messner, *Die Zukunft des Staates und der Politik*. Bonn: Dietz, 1998.

Desai, Padma. "Russian Privatization: A Comparative Perspective." *Harriman Review* 8 (August 1995):1–34.

Deutsch, Karl. *Nationalism and Social Communication*. Cambridge, Mass.: MIT Press, 1966.

Diamond, Larry and Marc F. Plattner, eds. *Economic Reform and Democracy*. Baltimore, Md.: Johns Hopkins University Press, 1995.

Dienes, Leslie. "Energy and Mineral Exports from the Former USSR: Philosopher's Stone or Fool's Gold?" Donald W. Treadgold Papers, no. 18, August 1998, University of Washington, Seattle, 1998, p. 21.

BIBLIOGRAPHY 204 / 205

Doyle, Michael. "Kant, Liberal Legacies, and Foreign Affairs." *Philosophy and Public Affairs* 12 (fall 1983):205–35.

———. *Empires*. Ithaca, N.Y.: Cornell University Press, 1986.

Dunn, John. "Revolution." In Terence Ball, James Farr, and Russell L. Hanson, eds., *Political Innovation and Conceptual Change*. Cambridge: Cambridge University Press, 1989.

Dynamika elity. Kyiv: Ahentstvo "Ukraina," 1998.

Easton, David. *A Framework for Political Analysis*. Englewood Cliffs, N.J.: Prentice Hall, 1965.

———. *The Analysis of Political Structure*. New York: Routledge, 1990.

Eckstein, Harry. "On the Etiology of Internal Wars." In Clifford Paynton and Robert Blackey, eds., *Why Revolution?* Cambridge, Mass.: Schenkman, 1971.

Eckstein, Harry, Frederic J. Fleron Jr., Erik P. Hoffmann, and William M. Reisinger. *Can Democracy Take Root in Post-Soviet Russia?* Lanham, Md.: Rowman and Littlefield, 1998.

Edwards, Lyford P. *The Natural History of Revolutions*. Chicago: University of Chicago Press, 1927.

Eichwede, Wolfgang, ed. *Das neue Russland in Politik und Kultur*. Bremen: Temmen, 1998.

Eisenstadt, S. N. *The Political Systems of Empires*. Glencoe, N.Y.: Free Press, 1963.

———. *Revolution and the Transformation of Societies*. New York: Free Press, 1978.

———. "Center-Periphery Relations in the Soviet Empire." In Alexander J. Motyl, ed., *Thinking Theoretically About Soviet Nationalities*. New York: Columbia University Press, 1992.

Eley, Geoff and Ronald Grigor Suny. "Introduction: From the Moment of Social History to the Work of Cultural Representation." In Geoff Eley and Ronald Grigor Suny, eds., *Becoming National: A Reader*. Oxford: Oxford University Press, 1996.

Eley, Geoff and Ronald Grigor Suny, eds. *Becoming National: A Reader*. Oxford: Oxford University Press, 1996.

Elman, Miriam Fendius, ed. *Paths to Peace: Is Democracy the Answer?* Cambridge, Mass.: MIT Press, 1997.

Elster, Jon. *Nuts and Bolts for the Social Sciences*. Cambridge: Cambridge University Press, 1989.

Emmerij, Louis, ed. *Economic and Social Development into the Twenty-first Century*. Washington, D.C.: Inter-American Development Bank, 1997.

Ericson, Richard. "Soviet Economic Structure and the National Question." In Alexander J. Motyl, ed., *The Post-Soviet Nations*. New York: Columbia University Press, 1992.

———. "The Structural Barrier to Transition: A Note on Input-Output Tables of Centrally Planned Economies." Unpublished manuscript. July 1996.

Etzioni, Amitai. *A Comparative Analysis of Complex Organizations*. New York: Free Press, 1975.

European Union. *Agenda 2000: Eine stärkere und erweiterte Union*. Brussels: Europäische Kommission, 1997.

Falk, Richard. "Resisting 'Globalization-from-Above' Through 'Globalization-from-Below.'" *New Political Economy* 2 (March 1997):17–24.

Farhi, Farideh. "State Disintegration and Urban-Based Revolutionary Crisis." *Comparative Political Studies* 21 (1988):231–56.

Fearon, James D. "Ethnic War as a Commitment Problem." Paper presented at the 1994 Annual Meeting of the American Political Science Association, September 2–5, 1994, New York.

Fearon, James D. and David D. Laitin. "Explaining Interethnic Cooperation." *American Political Science Review* 90 (December 1996):715–35.

Fein, Helen. *Accounting for Genocide.* Chicago: University of Chicago Press, 1979.

Feldstein, Martin. "EMU and International Conflict." *Foreign Affairs* 76 (November–December 1997):60–73.

Ferguson, Yale H. and Richard W. Mansbach. *The State, Conceptual Chaos, and the Future of International Relations Theory.* Boulder, Colo.: Lynne Rienner, 1989.

——. "Global Politics at the Turn of the Millenium: Changing Bases of 'Us' and 'Them.'" Paper prepared for delivery at the Annual Meeting of the International Studies Association, March 18–21, 1998, Minneapolis, Minn.

Feyerabend, Paul. *Against Method.* London: Verso, 1988.

Feynman, Richard. *The Character of Physical Law.* New York: Modern Library, 1994.

Finkelstein, Norman G. and Ruth Bettina Birn. *A Nation on Trial: The Goldhagen Thesis and Historical Truth.* New York: Henry Holt, 1998.

Finkle, Jason L. and Richard W. Gable, eds. *Political Development amd Social Change,* 2d ed. New York: Wiley, 1971.

Fischer, Stanley. "Reforming World Finance." *Economist,* October 3, 1998, pp. 23–27.

Fish, M. Steven. "Democratization's Requisites: The Postcommunist Experience." *Post-Soviet Affairs* 14 (1998):212–47.

Francisco, Ronald A. "Theories of Protest and the Revolutions of 1989." *American Journal of Political Science* 37 (August 1993):663–80.

Frank, Andre Gunder. *Latin America: Underdevelopment or Revolution?* New York: Monthly Review, 1969.

Freedom House. *Nations in Transit: Civil Society, Democracy and Markets in East Central Europe and the Newly Independent States.* New York: Freedom House, 1995.

Friedman, Jeffrey, ed. *The Rational Choice Controversy.* New Haven, Conn.: Yale University Press, 1996.

Fukuyama, Francis. "Liberal Democracy as a Global Phenomenon." *PS: Political Science and Politics* 24 (December 1991):659–64.

Furman, Dmitrii. "Ukraina i my." *Svobodnaia mysl',* no. 1 (1995):69–83.

——, ed. *Ukraina i Rossia.* Moscow: Izdatel'stvo "Prava Cheloveka," 1997.

Galtung, Johan. *Theory and Methods of Social Research.* New York: Columbia University Press, 1969.

——. "A Structural Theory of Imperialism." *Journal of Peace Research* 8 (1971):81–117.

Garnett, Sherman. "Troubled Times for Russia." In *IISS Strategic Survey,* 1995–96. Oxford: Oxford University Press, 1996.

Garnsey Peter and Richard Saller. *The Roman Empire: Economy, Society, and Culture.* Berkeley: University of California Press, 1987.

Gates, David. "Military Force Structures for European Security." In Armand Clesse, Richard Cooper, and Yoshikazu Sakamoto, eds., *The International System After the Collapse of the East-West Order.* Dordrecht, The Netherlands: Martinus Nijhoff, 1994.

Gati, Charles, ed. *The International Politics of Eastern Europe.* New York: Praeger, 1976.

Gaukroger, Stephen. *Explanatory Structures.* Hassocks, Sussex, U.K.: Harvester, 1978.

Geanakoplos, Deno John. *Byzantium: Church, Society, and Civilization Seen Through Contemporary Eyes.* Chicago: University of Chicago Press, 1984.

Geertz, Clifford. "The Integrative Revolution: Primordial Sentiments and Civil Politics in the New States." In Jason L. Finkle and Richard W. Gable, eds., *Political Development amd Social Change,* 2d ed. New York: Wiley, 1971.

——. *The Interpretation of Cultures.* New York: Basic, 1973.

Geiss, Imanuel. "Great Powers and Empires: Historical Mechanisms of Their Making and Breaking." In Geir Lundestad, ed., *The Fall of Great Powers.* Oslo: Scandinavian University Press, 1994.

Gellner, Ernest. *Nations and Nationalism.* Ithaca, N.Y.: Cornell University Press, 1983.

Giddens, Anthony. *The Constitution of Society: Outline of the Theory of Structuration.* Cambridge, U.K.: Polity, 1984.

——. *Modernity and Self-Identity.* Palo Alto, Calif.: Stanford University Press, 1991.

Giddens, Anthony and Jonathan H. Turner, eds. *Social Theory Today.* Cambridge, U.K.: Polity, 1987.

Gilbert, Martin. *Soviet History Atlas.* London: Routledge and Kegan Paul, 1979.

Gilbert, Paul. *The Philosophy of Nationalism.* Boulder, Colo.: Westview, 1998.

Gilpin, Robert. *War and Change in World Politics.* Cambridge: Cambridge University Press, 1981.

——. *The Political Economy of International Relations.* Princeton, N.J.: Princeton University Press, 1987.

Glazer, Nathan and Daniel P. Moynihan, eds. *Ethnicity.* Cambridge, Mass.: Harvard University Press, 1975.

Gleason, Abbott. *Totalitarianism: The Inner History of the Cold War.* New York: Oxford University Press, 1995.

Glenny, Misha. *The Fall of Yugoslavia.* New York: Penguin, 1992.

Glotz, Peter. *Die falsche Normalisierung.* Frankfurt am Main: Suhrkamp, 1994.

Goldhagen, Daniel Jonah. *Hitler's Willing Executioners: Ordinary Germans and the Holocaust.* New York: Vintage, 1996.

Goldstone, Jack. "Theories of Revolution: The Third Generation." *World Politics* 32 (April 1980):425–53.

——. "Ideology, Cultural Frameworks, and the Process of Revolution." *Theory and Society* 20 (August 1991):405–53.

——. *Revolution and Rebellion in the Early Modern World.* Berkeley: University of California Press, 1991.

——. "Predicting Revolutions: Why We Could (and Should) Have Foreseen the Revolutions of 1989–91 in the U.S.S.R. and Eastern Europe." In Nikki R. Keddie, ed., *Debating Revolutions*. New York: New York University Press, 1995.

Good, David. *The Economic Rise of the Habsburg Empire, 1750–1914*. Berkeley: University of California Press, 1984.

Goodman, Andrew. "Organized Change and Organized Crime: Explaining the Rise of Russian Organized Crime." Paper prepared for the 1998 Convention of the Association for the Study of the Nationalities, Columbia University, April 16–19, 1998, New York.

Goodman, Nelson. *Fact, Fiction, and Forecast*. Cambridge, Mass.: Harvard University Press, 1983.

Gordon, Scott. *The History and Philosophy of Social Science*. London: Routledge, 1991.

Gottmann, Jean, ed. *Centre and Periphery: Spatial Variation in Politics*. Beverly Hills, Calif.: Sage, 1980.

Greenfeld, Liah. *Nationalism: Five Roads to Modernity*. Cambridge, Mass.: Harvard University Press, 1992.

Griffen, Larry. "Narrative, Event-Structure Analysis, and Causal Interpretation in Historical Sociology." *American Journal of Sociology* 98 (1993):1094–1133.

Gritsenko, Anatoly. *Civil-Military Relations in Ukraine: A System Emerging from Chaos*. Groningen, The Netherlands: Centre for European Security Studies, 1997.

Grousset, René. *The Empire of the Steppes*. New Brunswick, N.J.: Rutgers University Press, 1970.

Guérin-Sendelbach, Valérie and Jacek Rulkowski. "'Euro-Trio': France-Germany-Poland." *Aussenpolitik* 3 (1994):246–53.

Gurr, Ted Robert. *Why Men Rebel*. Princeton, N.J.: Princeton University Press, 1970.

Gurwitsch, Aron. *Phenomenology and the Theory of Science*. Evanston, Ill.: Northwestern University Press, 1974.

Habermas, Jürgen. *Legitimation Crisis*. Boston: Beacon, 1975.

——. *The Theory of Communicative Action*. Vol. 1. Boston: Beacon, 1984.

——. *Vergangenheit als Zukunft*. Munich: Piper, 1993.

Haggard, Stephan and Robert R. Kaufman. "Economic Adjustment and the Prospects for Democracy." In Stephan Haggard and Robert R. Kaufman, eds., *The Politics of Economic Adjustment*. Princeton, N.J.: Princeton University Press, 1992.

Hagopian, Mark. *The Phenomenon of Revolution*. New York: Harper and Row, 1974.

——. *Ideals and Ideologies of Modern Politics*. New York: Longman, 1985.

Hancock, M. Donald and Helga A. Welsh, eds. *German Unification: Processes and Outcomes*. Boulder, Colo.: Westview, 1994.

Hane, Mikiso. *Modern Japan*. Boulder, Colo.: Westview, 1986.

Hannum, Hurst. *Autonomy, Sovereignty, and Self-Determination: The Accommodation of Conflicting Rights*. Philadelphia: University of Pennsylvania Press, 1990.

Hanson, Philip. "What Sort of Capitalism Is Developing in Russia?" *Communist Economies and Economic Transformation* 9 (March 1997):27–42.

Hanson, Stephen E. *Time and Revolution*. Chapel Hill: University of North Carolina Press, 1997.

Hanson, Stephen and Willfried Spohn, eds. *Can Europe Work? Germany and the Reconstruction of Postcommunist Societies.* Seattle: University of Washington Press, 1995.

Hardin, Russell. *One for All.* Princeton, N.J.: Princeton University Press, 1995.

Harris, Chauncy D. "Ethnic Tensions in Areas of the Russian Diaspora." *Post-Soviet Geography* 34 (April 1993):233–38.

Harth, Dietrich. "Revolution und Mythos." In Dietrich Harth and Jan Assmann, eds., *Revolution und Mythos.* Frankfurt am Main: Fischer Taschenbuch Verlag, 1992.

——, and Jan Assmann, eds. *Revolution und Mythos.* Frankfurt am Main: Fischer Taschenbuch Verlag, 1992.

Hausman, Daniel M., ed. *The Philosophy of Economics,* 2d ed. Cambridge: Cambridge University Press, 1994.

Hawking, Stephen. *A Brief History of Time.* New York: Bantam, 1988.

Hayek, F. A. *The Counter-Revolution of Science.* Indianapolis: Liberty Fund, 1979.

Hayes, Carlton. *Essays on Nationalism.* New York: Russell and Russell, 1966.

Hechter, Michael. *Internal Colonialism.* Berkeley: University of California Press, 1977.

——. *Principles of Group Solidarity.* Berkeley: University of California Press, 1988.

——. "Containing Nationalism." Unpublished manuscript, November 25, 1997.

Hempel, Carl. *Aspects of Scientific Explanation and Other Essays in the Philosophy of Science.* New York: Free Press, 1965.

Hilberg, Raul. *The Destruction of the European Jews.* New York: Holmes and Meier, 1985.

Hobsbawm, Eric J. *The Age of Revolution, 1789–1848.* New York: Mentor, 1962.

——. *The Age of Empire, 1875–1914.* New York: Pantheon, 1987.

——. *Nations and Nationalism Since 1780.* Cambridge: Cambridge University Press, 1990.

——. "Introduction: Inventing Traditions." In Eric Hobsbawm and Terence Ranger, eds., *The Invention of Tradition.* Cambridge: Cambridge University Press, 1992.

——. "The New Threat to History." *New York Review of Books,* December 16, 1993, p. 63.

Hobsbawm, Eric and Terence Ranger, eds. *The Invention of Tradition.* Cambridge: Cambridge University Press, 1992.

Hodges, Donald C. *Intellectual Foundations of the Nicaraguan Revolution.* Austin: University of Texas Press, 1986.

Höhmann, Hans-Hermann, ed. *Aufbruch im Osten Europas: Chancen für Demokratie und Marktwirtschaft nach dem Zerfall des Kommunismus.* Munich: Carl Hanser Verlag, 1993.

——. *Zwischen Krise und Konsolidierung.* Munich: Carl Hanser Verlag, 1995.

Hoetink, H. *Two Variants in Caribbean Race Relations.* London: Oxford University Press, 1967.

Hook, Sidney. *Revolution, Reform, and Social Justice.* New York: New York University Press, 1975.

Horowitz, Donald L. *Ethnic Groups in Conflict.* Berkeley: University of California Press, 1985.

Hough, Jerry. *Democratization and Revolution in the USSR, 1985–1991.* Washington, D.C.: Brookings Institution Press, 1997.

Hroch, Miroslav. *Social Preconditions of National Revival in Europe.* Cambridge: Cambridge University Press, 1985.

Hruby, Suzanne. "The Church in Poland and Its Political Influence." *Journal of International Affairs* 36 (fall–winter 1982–83):317–28.

Hrushevsky, Michael. *A History of Ukraine.* New Haven, Conn.: Yale University Press, 1941.

Hrytsak, Yaroslav. "Between Autonomy and Independence: Ukrainian Political Thought Prior [to] 1917." Unpublished manuscript, n.d.

Huntington, Samuel. *Political Order in Changing Societies.* New Haven, Conn.: Yale University Press, 1968.

———. *The Clash of Civilizations and the Remaking of World Order.* New York: Simon and Schuster, 1996.

Ikenberry, G. John et al. "The West: Precious, Not Unique." Letters to the Editor. *Foreign Affairs* 76 (March–April 1997):162–65.

Isaacs, Harold R. "Basic Group Identity: The Idols of the Tribe." In Nathan Glazer and Daniel P. Moynihan, eds., *Ethnicity.* Cambridge, Mass.: Harvard University Press, 1975.

Jackson, Robert H. and Alan James. "The Character of Independent Statehood." In Robert H. Jackson and Alan James, eds., *States in a Changing World.* Oxford: Clarendon, 1993.

———, eds. *States in a Changing World.* Oxford: Clarendon, 1993.

Jervis, Robert. *System Effects: Complexity in Political and Social Life.* Princeton, N.J.: Princeton University Press, 1997.

Jervis, Robert and Seweryn Bialer, eds. *Soviet-American Relations After the Cold War.* Durham, N.C.: Duke University Press, 1991.

Johnson, Chalmers. *Revolutionary Change.* Palo Alto, Calif.: Stanford University Press, 1982.

Johnson, Simon, Daniel Kaufmann, and Andrei Shleifer. "The Unofficial Economy in Transition." *Brookings Papers on Economic Activity,* no. 2 (1997):159–239.

Kagan, Donald. *The Outbreak of the Peloponnesian War.* Ithaca, N.Y.: Cornell University Press, 1969.

Kann, Robert. *A History of the Habsburg Empire, 1526–1918.* Berkeley: University of California Press, 1974.

Kant, Immanuel. *Perpetual Peace and Other Essays.* Indianapolis, Ind.: Hackett, 1983.

Kaplan, Robert D. *Balkan Ghosts: A Journey Through History.* New York: St. Martin's, 1993.

Karatnycky, Adrian, Alexander J. Motyl, and Boris Shor, eds. *Nations in Transit, 1997.* New Brunswick, N.J.: Transaction, 1997.

Kaufman, Stuart J. "Spiraling to Ethnic War: Elites, Masses, and Moscow in Moldova's Civil War." *International Security* 21 (fall 1996):108–38.

Keddie, Nikki. "Can Revolutions Be Predicted; Can Their Causes Be Understood?" In Nikki R. Keddie, ed., *Debating Revolutions.* New York: New York University Press, 1995.

——, ed. *Debating Revolutions*. New York: New York University Press, 1995.

Kedourie, Elie. *Nationalism*. London: Hutchinson, 1966.

Keegan, John. *A History of Warfare*. New York: Knopf, 1994.

Kennedy, Michael, ed. *Envisioning Eastern Europe*. Ann Arbor: University of Michigan Press, 1994.

Kennedy, Paul. *The Rise and Decline of the Great Powers*. New York: Vintage, 1987.

Keohane, Robert O. *After Hegemony*. Princeton, N.J.: Princeton University Press, 1984.

——, ed. *Neorealism and Its Critics*. New York: Columbia University Press, 1986.

Keohane, Robert O. and Joseph S. Nye Jr. "Power and Independence in the Information Age." *Foreign Affairs*, 77 (September–October 1998):89.

Kershaw, Ian and Moshe Lewin, eds. *Stalinism and Nazism: Dictatorships in Comparison*. Cambridge: Cambridge University Press, 1997.

Kidron, Michael and Ronald Segal. *The State of the World Atlas*. New York: Simon and Schuster, 1981.

Kiernan, V. G. *Imperialism and Its Contradictions*. New York: Routledge, 1995.

Kirchheimer, Otto. "Confining Conditions and Revolutionary Breakthroughs." *American Political Science Review* 59 (December 1965):964–74.

Kitcher, Philip and Wesley C. Salmon, eds. *Scientific Explanation*. Minneapolis: University of Minnesota Press, 1989.

Kocka, Jürgen. "1945: Neubeginn oder Restauration?" In Carola Stern and Heinrich A. Winkler, eds., *Wendepunkte deutscher Geschichte, 1848–1990*. Frankfurt am Main: Fischer Taschenbuch Verlag, 1994.

Koebner, Richard. *Empire*. New York: Grosset and Dunlap, 1965.

Kohl, Helmut. *Deutschlands Zukunft in Europa: Reden und Beiträge des Bundeskanzlers*. Herford, Germany: Busse und Seewald, 1990.

Kohn, Hans. *The Idea of Nationalism*. New York: Macmillan, 1944.

——. *Nationalism: Its Meaning and History*, rev. ed. New York: Van Nostrand, 1971.

Kolstoe, Paul. *Russians in the Former Soviet Republics*. Bloomington: Indiana University Press, 1995.

Kononchuk, Svitlana and Vyacheslav Pikhovshek. *The Dnipropetrovsk Family—2*. Kyiv: Ukrainian Center for Independent Political Research, 1997.

Koslowski, Rey and Friedrich V. Kratochwil. "Understanding Change in International Politics: The Soviet Empire's Demise and the International System." *International Organization* 48 (Spring 1994):215–47.

Kotowski, Christoph. "Revolution." In Giovanni Sartori, ed., *Social Science Concepts*. Beverly Hills, Calif.: Sage, 1984.

Krasner, Stephen D. *International Regimes*. Ithaca, N.Y.: Cornell University Press, 1983.

——. "Economic Interdependence and Independent Statehood." In Robert H. Jackson and Allan James, eds., *States in a Changing World*. Oxford: Clarendon, 1993.

Kupchan, Charles A. *The Vulnerability of Empire*. Ithaca, N.Y.: Cornell University Press, 1994.

Kuran, Timur. "Now Out of Never: The Element of Surprise in the East European Revolution of 1989." *World Politics* 44 (October 1991):7–48.

Kuzio, Taras. *Ukraine: Back from the Brink*. London: Institute for European Defence and Strategic Studies, 1995.

——. "The East Slavic Conundrum: Unity or Divergence?" Unpublished paper, May 1996.

——, ed. *Contemporary Ukraine*. Armonk, N.Y.: Sharpe, 1998.

La Feber, Walter. *Inevitable Revolutions*. New York: Norton, 1993.

Laitin, David. "Transitions to Democracy and Territorial Integrity." In Adam Przeworski and Pranab Bardhan, eds., *Sustainable Democracy*. Cambridge: Cambridge University Press, 1995.

——. *Identity in Formation*. Ithaca, N.Y.: Cornell University Press, 1998.

Lakatos, Imre. "Falsification and the Methodology of Scientific Research Programmes." In Imre Lakatos and Alan Musgrave, eds., *Criticism and the Growth of Knowledge*. Cambridge: Cambridge University Press, 1970.

Lake, David A. "Anarchy, Hierarchy, and the Variety of International Relations." *International Organization* 50 (winter 1996):1–33.

——. "The Rise, Fall, and Future of the Russian Empire." In Karen Dawisha and Bruce Parrott, eds., *The End of Empire? The Transformation of the USSR in Comparative Perspective*. Armonk, N.Y.: Sharpe, 1997.

Lake, David A. and Donald Rothchild. "Containing Fear: The Origins and Management of Ethnic Conflict." *International Security* 21 (fall 1996):41–75.

Lang, Berel. *The Anatomy of Philosophical Style*. Oxford: Basil Blackwell, 1990.

Lapidus, Gail W. "Contested Sovereignty: The Tragedy of Chechnya." *International Security* 23 (summer 1998):5–49.

Leckie, Robert. *The Wars of America*. Vol. 1. New York: HarperPerennial, 1993.

Lewis, Bernard. *The Emergence of Modern Turkey*, 2d ed. London: Oxford University Press, 1968.

Lichbach, Mark and Alan Zuckerman, eds. *Comparative Politics: Rationality, Culture, and Structure*. Cambridge: Cambridge University Press, 1997.

Lichtheim, George. *Imperialism*. New York: Praeger, 1971.

Lieven, Anatol. *Chechnya: Tombstone of Russian Power*. New Haven, Conn.: Yale University Press, 1998.

Lijphart, Arend. *Democracy in Plural Societies*. New Haven, Conn.: Yale University Press, 1977.

——. "Political Theories and the Explanation of Ethnic Conflict in the Western World." In Milton Esman, ed., *Ethnic Conflict in the Western World*. Ithaca, N.Y.: Cornell University Press, 1977.

Lijphart, Arend and Carlos H. Waisman. "The Design of Markets and Democracies: Generalizing Across Regions." In Arend Lijphart and Carlos H. Waisman, eds., *Institutional Design in New Democracies*. Boulder, Colo.: Westview, 1996.

——, eds. *Institutional Design in New Democracies*. Boulder, Colo.: Westview, 1996.

Lilla, Mark. "A Tale of Two Reactions." *New York Review of Books*, May 14, 1998, pp. 4–7.

Lindblom, Charles. *Politics and Markets*. New York: Basic, 1977.

Linz, Juan. *Crisis, Breakdown, and Reequilibration*. Baltimore, Md.: Johns Hopkins University Press, 1978.

Lohmann, Manfred. "Das ukrainische Parteienspektrum und die Wahlen in der Ukraine vom 29. März 1998." *KAS/Auslands-Informationen* 14 (1998):44–71.

Lowe, Donald M. "Intentionality and the Method of History." In Maurice Natanson, ed. *Phenomenology and the Social Sciences*. Vol. 2. Evanston, Ill.: Northwestern University Press, 1973.

Lowenthal, Abraham F. "Latin America and the United States in a New World: Prospects for Partnership." In Abraham F. Lowenthal and Gregory F. Treverton, eds., *Latin America in a New World*. Boulder, Colo.: Westview, 1994.

Lowenthal, Abraham F. and Gregory F. Treverton, eds. *Latin America in a New World*. Boulder, Colo.: Westview, 1994.

Luchterhandt, Galina. "Institutionalisierungsprozesse in der Politik seit der Verfassungsreform 1993." In Wolfgang Eichwede, ed., *Das neue Russland in Politik und Kultur*. Bremen: Temmen, 1998.

Lukacs, John. *Budapest, 1900*. New York: Grove, 1990.

Lundestad, Geir. *The American "Empire."* Oslo: Norwegian University Press, 1990.

——, ed. *The Fall of Great Powers*. Oslo: Scandinavian University Press, 1994.

Lustick, Ian. "Stability in Deeply Divided Societies: Consociationalism Versus Control." *World Politics* 31 (April 1979):324–44.

——. *Unsettled States, Disputed Lands*. Ithaca, N.Y.: Cornell University Press, 1993.

Lynch, Allen. *Does Russia Have a Democratic Future?* New York: Foreign Policy Association Headline Series, no. 313, 1997.

——. "National Identity and U.S. Foreign Policy in a New World Order." *Romanian Journal of International Affairs* 3 (1997): 71–78.

Lyotard, Jean-François. *The Postmodern Condition: A Report on Knowledge*. Manchester, U.K.: Manchester University Press, 1984.

MacIntyre, Alasdair. "Ideology, Social Science, and Revolution." *Comparative Politics* 5 (April 1973):321–42.

MacIver, A. M. "Levels of Explanation in History." In May Broadbeck, ed., *Readings in the Philosophy of the Social Sciences*. New York: Macmillan, 1968.

Macridis, Roy. "The Search for Focus." In Roy Macridis and Bernard Brown, eds., *Comparative Politics*. Homewood, Ill.: Dorsey, 1972.

Magocsi, Paul Robert. *Historical Atlas of East Central Europe*. Seattle: University of Washington Press, 1993.

Mandelbaum, Michael. *NATO Expansion: A Bridge to the Nineteenth Century*. Chevy Chase, Md.: Center for Political and Strategic Studies, 1997.

——, ed. *Postcommunism: Four Perspectives*. New York: Council on Foreign Relations, 1996.

——, ed. *The New Russian Foreign Policy*. New York: Council on Foreign Relations, 1998.

Mann, Michael, ed. *The Rise and Decline of the Nation State*. Oxford: Basil Blackwell, 1990.

Mansfield, Edward D. and Jack Snyder. "Democratization and the Danger of War." *International Security* 20 (summer 1995):5–38.

Mardin, Şerif. "The Ottoman Empire." In Karen Barkey and Mark von Hagen, eds., *After Empire*. Boulder, Colo.: Westview, 1997.

Marrus, Michael R. *The Holocaust in History*. London: Weidenfeld and Nicolson, 1988.

Matlock, Jack F. "Dealing with a Russia in Turmoil." *Foreign Affairs* 75 (May–June 1996):38–51.

Mayall, James. *Nationalism and International Society*. Cambridge: Cambridge University Press, 1990.

McAllister, Ian, Stephen White, and Richard Rose. "Communists, Privilege, and Post-communism in Russia." *International Politics* 34 (March 1997):79–95.

McCloskey, Donald N. *The Rhetoric of Economics*. Madison: University of Wisconsin Press, 1985.

McFaul, Michael and Nikolai Petrov, eds. *Previewing Russia's 1995 Parliamentary Elections*. Washington, D.C.: Carnegie Endowment, 1995.

McNeill, William H. "Introductory Historical Commentary." In Geir Lundestad, ed., *The Fall of Great Powers*. Oslo: Scandinavian University Press, 1994.

Meinig, D. W. *The Shaping of America*. Vol. 2. New Haven, Conn.: Yale University Press, 1993.

Menon, Rajan. "In the Shadow of the Bear: Security in Post-Soviet Central Asia." *International Security* 20 (summer 1995):149–81.

———. "After Empire: Russia and the Southern 'Near Abroad.'" In Michael Mandelbaum, ed., *The New Russian Foreign Policy*. New York: Council on Foreign Relations, 1998.

Messner, Dirk, ed. *Die Zukunft des Staates und der Politik*. Bonn: Dietz, 1998.

Meyer, Stephen M. "The Military." In Timothy J. Colton and Robert Legvold, eds., *After the Soviet Union*. New York: Norton, 1992.

Miliband, Ralph. *Marxism and Politics*. New York: Oxford University Press, 1977.

Mills, C. Wright. *The Power Elite*. New York: Oxford University Press, 1959.

Misiunas, Romuald and Rein Taagepera. *The Baltic States: Years of Dependence, 1940–80*. Berkeley: University of California Press, 1983.

Molchanov, Mikhail A. "Borders of Identity: Ukraine's Political and Cultural Significance for Russia." *Canadian Slavonic Papers* 38 (March–June 1996):177–93.

Molineu, Harold. *U.S. Policy Toward Latin America*. Boulder, Colo.: Westview, 1986.

Mommsen, Wolfgang J. *Theories of Imperialism*. New York: Random House, 1980.

———. "The Varieties of the Nation State in Modern History." In Michael Mann, ed., *The Rise and Decline of the Nation State*. Oxford: Basil Blackwell, 1990.

Moore, Barrington Jr. *Social Origins of Dictatorship and Democracy*. Boston: Beacon, 1966.

Moser, Leo J. *The Chinese Mosaic: The Peoples and Provinces of China*. Boulder, Colo.: Westview, 1985.

Motyl, Alexander. "Reassessing the Soviet Crisis: Big Problems, Muddling Through, Business as Usual." *Political Science Quarterly* 104 (1989):269–80.

———. *Sovietology, Rationality, Nationality: Coming to Grips with Nationalism in the USSR*. New York: Columbia University Press, 1990.

———. "From Imperial Decay to Imperial Collapse: The Fall of the Soviet Empire in Comparative Perspective." In Richard Rudolph and David Good, eds., *Nationalism and Empire*. New York: St. Martin's, 1991.

———. "Rites, Rituals, and Soviet-American Relations." In Robert Jervis and Seweryn Bialer, eds., *Soviet-American Relations After the Cold War*. Durham, N.C.: Duke University Press, 1991.

———. "The End of Sovietology: From Soviet Studies to Post-Soviet Studies." In Alexander J. Motyl, ed., *The Post-Soviet Nations*. New York: Columbia University Press, 1992.

———. *Dilemmas of Independence: Ukraine After Totalitarianism*. New York: Council on Foreign Relations, 1993.

———. "Imperial Collapse and Revolutionary Change: Austria-Hungary, Tsarist Russia, and the Soviet Empire." In Jürgen Nautz and Richard Vahrenkamp, eds., *Die Wiener Jahrhundertwende*. Vienna: Böhlau, 1993.

———. *Imperial Ends: The Decay, Collapse, and Revival of Empires*. Forthcoming.

———. "Institutional Legacies and Reform Trajectories." In Adrian Karatnycky, Alexander J. Motyl, and Boris Shor, eds., *Nations in Transit, 1997*. New Brunswick, N.J.: Transaction, 1997.

———. "Structural Constraints and Starting Points: The Logic of Systemic Change in Ukraine and Russia." *Comparative Politics* 29 (July 1997):433–47.

———. "After Empire: Competing Discourses and Interstate Conflict in Post-Imperial Eastern Europe." In Barnett Rubin and Jack Snyder, eds., *Post-Soviet Political Order*. London: Routledge, 1998.

———. "State, Nation, and Elites in Independent Ukraine." In Taras Kuzio, ed., *Contemporary Ukraine*. Armonk, N.Y.: Sharpe, 1998.

———. "Why Empires Reemerge: Imperial Collapse and Imperial Revival in Comparative Perspective." *Comparative Politics* 31 (January 1999):127–45.

———, ed. *The Post-Soviet Nations*. New York: Columbia University Press, 1992.

———, ed. *Thinking Theoretically About Soviet Nationalities*. New York: Columbia University Press, 1992.

Mueller, John. *Retreat from Doomsday: The Obsolescence of Major War*. New York: Basic, 1989.

———. "Democracy, Capitalism, and the End of Transition." In Michael Mandelbaum, ed., *Postcommunism: Four Perspectives*. New York: Council on Foreign Relations, 1996.

Murrell, Peter. "Conservative Political Philosophy and the Strategy of Economic Transition." *East European Politics and Societies* 6 (winter 1992):3–16.

Nagel, Ernst. *The Structure of Science*, 2d ed. Indianapolis, Ind.: Hackett, 1977.

Naimark, Norman M. *The Russians in Germany*. Cambridge, Mass.: Belknap, 1995.

Natanson, Maurice, ed. *Phenomenology and the Social Sciences*. Vol. 2. Evanston, Ill.: Northwestern University Press, 1973.

Nau, Henry. *The Myth of America's Decline*. Oxford: Oxford University Press, 1990.

Nautz, Jürgen and Richard Vahrenkamp, eds. *Die Wiener Jahrhundertwende*. Vienna: Böhlau, 1993.

Nelson, Lynn D. and Irina Y. Kuzes. *Radical Reform in Yeltsin's Russia*. Armonk, N.Y.: Sharpe, 1995.

Nietzsche, Friedrich. *On the Genealogy of Morals and Ecce Homo*. New York: Vintage, 1969.

Nordberg, Marc and Taras Kuzio. "Nation and State Building, Historical Legacies and National Identities in Belarus and Ukraine." Unpublished paper.

Nordlinger, Eric. *On the Autonomy of the Democratic State.* Cambridge, Mass.: Harvard University Press, 1981.

North, Douglass. *Institutions, Institutional Change, and Economic Performance.* Cambridge: Cambridge University Press, 1990.

Nye, Joseph. *Bound to Lead.* New York: Basic, 1991.

Obstfeld, Maurice. "Europe's Gamble." *Brookings Papers on Economic Activity,* no. 2 (1997):241–300.

O'Connor, James. *The Meaning of Crisis.* Oxford: Basil Blackwell, 1987.

O'Donnell, Guillermo, Philippe C. Schmitter, and Laurence Whitehead, eds. *Transitions from Authoritarian Rule: Comparative Perspectives.* Baltimore, Md.: Johns Hopkins University Press, 1986.

O'Leary, Brendan. "On the Nature of Nationalism: An Appraisal of Ernest Gellner's Writings on Nationalism." *British Journal of Political Science* 27 (1997):191–222.

Olson, Kenneth Russell. *An Essay on Facts.* Palo Alto, Calif.: Center for the Study of Language and Information, 1987.

Olzak, Susan. "Analysis of Events in the Study of Collective Action." *Annual Review of Sociology* 15 (1989):119–41.

Outhwaite, William. *Concept Formation in Social Science.* London: Routledge and Kegan Paul, 1983.

Owens, William A. "America's Information Edge." *Foreign Affairs* 75 (March–April 1996):20–36.

Paige, Jeffrey M. *Agrarian Revolution: Social Movements and Export Agriculture in the Underdeveloped World.* New York: Free Press, 1975.

Parrott, Bruce. "Analyzing the Transformation of the Soviet Union in Comparative Perspective." In Karen Dawisha and Bruce Parrott, eds., *The End of Empire? The Transformation of the USSR in Comparative Perspective.* Armonk, N.Y.: Sharpe, 1997.

Paynton, Clifford and Robert Blackey, eds. *Why Revolution?* Cambridge, Mass.: Schenkman, 1971.

Pearson, Raymond. "Fact, Fantasy, Fraud: Perceptions and Projections of National Revival." *Ethnic Studies* 10 (1993):43–64.

Peterson, Roger. "The Rational Choice of Pathologies." Unpublished paper.

Pickel, Andreas and Helmut Wiesenthal. *The Grand Experiment.* Boulder, Colo.: Westview, 1997.

Polokhalo, Volodymyr. "Vid Ukrainy komunistychno-totalitarnoi do Ukrainy neototalitarnoi?" *Politychna dumka,* no. 2 (1994): 19.

Popper, Karl R. *The Open Society and Its Enemies.* Vol. 2. London: Routledge and Kegan Paul, 1945.

——. *Conjectures and Refutations.* London: Routledge and Kegan Paul, 1963.

——. *The Poverty of Historicism.* New York: Harper and Row, 1964.

——. *The Logic of Scientific Discovery.* New York: Harper and Row, 1965.

Posen, Barry. "The Security Dilemma and Ethnic Conflict." *Survival* 35 (spring 1993):27–47.

Poulantzas, Nicos. *State, Power, Socialism*. London: Verso, 1980.

Poznanski, Kazimierz Z., ed. *The Evolutionary Transition to Capitalism*. Boulder, Colo.: Westview, 1995.

Price, H. H. *Thinking and Experience*. Cambridge, Mass.: Harvard University Press, 1953.

Przeworski, Adam and Pranab Bardhan, eds. *Sustainable Democracy*. Cambridge: Cambridge University Press, 1995.

Puchala, Donald J. "Western Europe." In Robert H. Jackson and Alan James, eds., *States in a Changing World*. Oxford: Clarendon, 1993.

Quine, W. V. *From a Logical Point of View*. Cambridge, Mass.: Harvard University Press, 1953.

——. *Theories and Things*. Cambridge, Mass.: Belknap, 1981.

——. *Quiddities*. Cambridge, Mass.: Belknap, 1987.

Quinn, Dennis P. and John T. Woolley. "Democracy and Risk and Return: Or How Democracy and Economic Growth Are Related." Unpublished manuscript, December 20, 1997.

Rabushka, Alvin and Kenneth A. Shepsle. *Politics in Plural Societies*. Columbus, Ohio: Merrill, 1972.

Ramet, Pedro, ed. *Religion and Nationalism in Soviet and East European Politics*. Durham, N.C.: Duke University Press, 1989.

Raven, Diederick. "A Defense of Cognitive Relativism: Realism, Idealism, and Nominalism." In Diederick Raven, Lieteke van Vucht Tijssen, and Jan de Wolf, eds., *Cognitive Relativism and Social Science*. New Brunswick, N.J.: Transaction, 1992.

Raven, Diederick, Lieteke van Vucht Tijssen, and Jan de Wolf, eds. *Cognitive Relativism and Social Science*. New Brunswick, N.J.: Transaction, 1992.

Reddaway, Peter. "Russia on the Brink?" *New York Review of Books*, January 28, 1993, pp. 30–35.

Reed, John. *Ten Days That Shook the World*. New York: Bantam, 1987.

Reich, Robert B. "What Is a Nation?" *Political Science Quarterly* 106 (summer 1991):193–210.

Reynolds, Susan. *Kingdoms and Communities in Western Europe, 900–1300*. Oxford: Clarendon, 1984.

Rhodes, Martin. "'Subversive Liberalism': Market Integration, Globalization, and West European Welfare States." In William D. Coleman and Geoffrey R. D. Underhill, eds., *Regionalism and Global Economic Integration*. London: Routledge, 1998.

Rice, E. E., ed. *Revolution and Counter-Revolution*. Oxford: Basil Blackwell, 1991.

Robinson, William I. "Globalization, the World System, and 'Democracy Promotion' in U.S. Foreign Policy." *Theory and Society* 25 (1996):615–65.

Rosecrance, Richard. *The Rise of the Trading State*. New York: Basic, 1986.

Rosenau, James. *Turbulence in World Politics*. Princeton, N.J.: Princeton University Press, 1990.

Rosenau, James and Ernst-Otto Czempiel, eds. *Governance Without Governments: Order and Change in World Politics*. Cambridge: Cambridge University Press, 1992.

Rosenbaum, Alan S., ed. *Is the Holocaust Unique?* Boulder, Colo.: Westview, 1996.

Roth, Paul A. *Meaning and Method in the Social Sciences*. Ithaca, N.Y.: Cornell University Press, 1987.

Rothschild, Joseph. *Ethnopolitics*. New York: Columbia University Press, 1981.

———. *The Return to Diversity*. Oxford: Oxford University Press, 1989.

Rubin, Barnett and Jack Snyder, eds. *Post-Soviet Political Order*. London: Routledge, 1998.

Rudolph, Richard and David Good, eds. *Nationalism and Empire*. New York: St. Martin's, 1991.

Ruggie, John Gerard. *Winning the Peace*. New York: Columbia University Press, 1996.

Rumer, Eugene B. *The Ideological Crisis in the Russian Military*. Santa Monica, Calif.: RAND, 1994.

Russett, Bruce. *Grasping the Democratic Peace*. Princeton, N.J.: Princeton University Press, 1993.

———. "Counterfactuals About War and Its Absence." In Philip E. Tetlock and Aaron Belkin, eds., *Counterfactual Thought Experiments in World Politics*. Princeton, N.J.: Princeton University Press, 1996.

Sachs, Jeffrey. *Poland's Jump to the Market Economy*. Cambridge, Mass.: MIT Press, 1994.

Said, Kurban. *Ali and Nino*. New York: Random House, 1970.

Salmon, Wesley C. "Four Decades of Scientific Explanation." In Philip Kitcher and Wesley C. Salmon, eds., *Scientific Explanation*. Minneapolis: University of Minnesota Press, 1989.

Sartori, Giovanni. "Guidelines for Concept Analysis." In Giovanni Sartori, ed., *Social Science Concepts*. Beverly Hills, Calif.: Sage, 1984.

———. "Comparing and Miscomparing." *Journal of Theoretical Politics* 3 (1991):243–57.

———. "Totalitarianism, Model Mania, and Learning from Error." *Journal of Theoretical Politics* 5 (1993):5–22.

———, ed. *Social Science Concepts*. Beverly Hills, Calif.: Sage, 1984.

Scharpf, Fritz W. "Die Handlungsfähigkeit des Staates am Ende des zwanzigsten Jahrhunderts." *Politische Vierteljahresschrift* 32 (1991):621–34.

Schoenbaum, David. *Hitler's Social Revolution*. New York: Norton, 1980.

Schrieberg, David. "Dateline Latin America: The Growing Fury." *Foreign Policy* (spring 1997):161–75.

Schwanitz, Simone. *Transformationsforschung: Area Studies Versus Politikwissenschaft*. Berlin: Arbeitspapiere des Osteuropa-Instituts, 1997, no. 3.

Scott, James C. *Seeing Like a State* New Haven, Conn.: Yale University Press, 1998.

Searle, John R. *The Construction of Social Reality*. New York: Free Press, 1995.

Selected Readings from the Works of Mao Tsetung. Beijing: Foreign Language Press, 1971.

Senghor, Leopold. *Négritude et humanisme*. Paris: Éditions de Seuil, 1964.

Seton-Watson, Hugh. *Nations and States*. London: Methuen, 1977.

Sewell, William H. Jr. "Historical Events as Transformations of Structures: Inventing Revolution at the Bastille." *Theory and Society* 25 (1996):841–81.

Shevtsova, Lilia and Scott A. Bruckner. "Toward Stability or Crisis?" *Journal of Democracy* 8 (January 1997):12–26.

Shils, Edward. *Center and Periphery*. Chicago: University of Chicago Press, 1975.

Shlapentokh, Vladimir. "Early Feudalism: The Best Parallel for Contemporary Russia." *Europe-Asia Studies* 48 (May 1996):393–411.

Silberstein, Lawrence J. and Robert L. Cohn, eds. *The Other in Jewish Thought and History.* New York: New York University Press, 1994.

Sked, Alan. *The Decline and Fall of the Habsburg Empire, 1815–1918.* London: Longman, 1989.

Skocpol, Theda. *States and Social Revolutions.* Cambridge: Cambridge University Press, 1979.

Smith, Anthony D. *Theories of Nationalism.* London: Duckworth, 1971.

——. *The Concept of Social Change.* London: Routledge and Kegan Paul, 1973.

——. *The Ethnic Origins of Nations.* Oxford: Basil Blackwell, 1986.

——. "Gastronomy or Geology? The Role of Nationalism in the Reconstruction of Nations." *Nations and Nationalism* 1 (March 1995):3–23.

Smith, Peter H. *Talons of the Eagle.* New York: Oxford University Press, 1996.

Snyder, Jack. *Myths of Empire.* Ithaca, N.Y.: Cornell University Press, 1991.

Snyder, Jack and Karen Ballentine. "Nationalism and the Marketplace of Ideas." *International Security* 21 (fall 1996):5–40.

Sokal, Alan. "Transgressing the Boundaries: Toward a Transformative Hermeneutics of Quantum Gravity." *Social Text* 18 (spring–summer 1996):217–52.

Sorel, Georges. *Reflections on Violence.* New York: Collier, 1961.

Sosa, Ernest and Michael Tooley. "Introduction." In Ernest Sosa and Michael Tooley, eds., *Causation.* Oxford: Oxford University Press, 1993.

—, eds. *Causation.* Oxford: Oxford University Press, 1993.

Spear, Percival. *A History of India.* 2 Vols. London: Penguin, 1990.

Spengler, Oswald. *The Decline of the West.* New York: Modern Library, 1962.

Spragens, Thomas A. Jr. *The Dilemma of Contemporary Political Theory.* New York: Dunellen, 1973.

Spruyt, Hendrik. *The Sovereign State and Its Competitors.* Princeton, N.J.: Princeton University Press, 1994.

——. "Institutional Selection in International Relations: State Anarchy as Order." *International Organization* 48 (autumn 1994):527–57.

——. "The Prospects for Neo-Imperial and Nonimperial Outcomes in the Former Soviet Space." In Karen Dawisha and Bruce Parrott, eds., *The End of Empire? The Transformation of the USSR in Comparative Perspective.* Armonk, N.Y.: Sharpe, 1997.

Stallings, Barbara. "The New International Context of Development." In Barbara Stallings, ed., *Global Change, Regional Response.* Cambridge: Cambridge University Press, 1995.

——, ed. *Global Change, Regional Response.* Cambridge: Cambridge University Press, 1995.

Stark, David and Laszlo Bruszt. *Postsocialist Pathways.* Cambridge: Cambridge University Press, 1998.

Stepan, Alfred. *The State and Society.* Princeton, N.J.: Princeton University Press, 1978.

——. "Paths Toward Redemocratization: Theoretical and Comparative Considerations." In Guillermo O'Donnell, Philippe C. Schmitter, and Laurence Whitehead, eds., *Transitions from Authoritarian Rule: Comparative Perspectives*. Baltimore, Md.: Johns Hopkins University Press, 1986.

Stern, Carola and Heinrich A. Winkler, eds. *Wendepunkte deutscher Geschichte, 1848–1990*. Frankfurt am Main: Fischer Taschenbuch Verlag, 1994.

Stern, Fritz. "The Goldhagen Controversy." *Foreign Affairs* 75 (November–December 1996):128–38.

Stone, Simon and Oliver Weeks. "Prospects for the Georgian Economy." *CACP Briefing*, no. 15 (March 1998):1–6.

Strachey, John. *The End of Empire*. New York: Praeger, 1959.

Streeck, Wolfgang. "Gewerkschaften zwischen Nationalstaat und Europäischer Union." In Dirk Messner, ed., *Die Zukunft des Staates und der Politik*. Bonn: Dietz, 1998.

Subtelny, Orest. *Ukraine: A History*. Toronto: University of Toronto Press, 1988.

Sukhanov, N. N. *The Russian Revolution, 1917*. London: Oxford University Press, 1955.

Sulloway, Frank J. *Born to Rebel: Birth Order, Family Dynamics, and Creative Lives*. New York: Pantheon, 1996.

———. "Darwinian Virtues." *New York Review of Books*, April 9, 1998, pp. 34–40.

Suny, Ronald Grigor. *The Revenge of the Past*. Palo Alto, Calif.: Stanford University Press, 1993.

———. "Russia, the Soviet Union, and Theories of Empire." Unpublished paper, March 14, 1996.

———. "Nation-Making, Nation-Breaking: The End of the Ottoman Empire and the Armenian Community." Unpublished paper, May 3, 1996.

Svejnar, Jan, ed. *The Czech Republic and Economic Transition in Eastern Europe*. San Diego, Calif.: Academic Press, 1995.

Swanton, John R. *The Indian Tribes of North America*. Washington, D.C.: Smithsonian Institution, 1969.

Symmons-Symonolewicz, Konstantin. *Modern Nationalism*. New York: Polish Institute of Arts and Sciences in America, 1968.

Taagepera, Rein. "Size and Duration of Empires: Systematics of Size." *Social Science Research* 7 (1978):108–27.

———. "Size and Duration of Empires: Growth-Decline Curves, 3000 to 600 B.C." *Social Science Research* 7 (1978):180–96.

———. "Size and Duration of Empires: Growth-Decline Curves, 600 B.C. to 600 A.D." *Social Science History* 3 (October 1979):115–38.

———. "Patterns of Empire Growth and Decline: Context for Russia." Unpublished manuscript, March 25, 1995.

Tainter, Joseph. *The Collapse of Complex Societies*. Cambridge: Cambridge University Press, 1988.

Talbert, Richard J. A., ed. *Atlas of Classical History*. London: Routledge, 1985.

Tamir, Yael. "The Enigma of Nationalism." *World Politics* 47 (April 1995):418–40.

Taylor, Stan. *Social Science and Revolution*. New York: St. Martin's, 1984.

Tetlock, Philip E. and Aaron Belkin, eds. *Counterfactual Thought Experiments in World Politics*. Princeton, N.J.: Princeton University Press, 1996.

Therborn, Goran. *What Does the Ruling Class Do When It Rules?* London: Verso, 1980.

Tien-Lung Liu, Michael. "States and Urban Revolutions." *Theory and Society* 17 (1988):179–209.

Tiller, Heinrich. "Die militärpolitische Entwicklung in den Nachfolgestaaten der ehemaligen Sowjetunion." In Hans-Hermann Höhmann, ed., *Zwischen Krise und Konsolidierung*. Munich: Carl Hanser Verlag, 1995.

Tilly, Charles. *From Mobilization to Revolution*. New York: Random House, 1978.

——. *Coercion, Capital, and European States*, A.D. 990–1990. Oxford: Basil Blackwell, 1990.

——. "Changing Forms of Revolution." In E. E. Rice, ed., *Revolution and Counter-Revolution*. Oxford: Basil Blackwell, 1991.

——. *European Revolutions, 1492–1992*. Oxford: Basil Blackwell, 1993.

——. "How Empires End." In Karen Barkey and Mark von Hagen, eds., *After Empire*. Boulder, Colo.: Westview, 1997.

——, ed. *The Formation of National States in Western Europe*. Princeton, N.J.: Princeton University Press, 1975.

Tolz, Vera. "Conflicting 'Homeland Myths' and Nation-State Building in Postcommunist Russia." *Slavic Review* 57 (summer 1998):267–94.

Toynbee, Arnold J. *A Study of History*. 12 Vols. London: Oxford University Press, 1934–61.

Treadgold, Warren. *A History of the Byzantine State and Society*. Palo Alto, Calif.: Stanford University Press, 1997.

Trimberger, Ellen Kay. *Revolution from Above*. New Brunswick, N.J.: Transaction, 1978.

Tucker, Robert C., ed. *The Marx-Engels Reader*, 2d ed. New York: Norton, 1978.

Turner, Jonathan H. "Analytical Theorizing." In Anthony Giddens and Jonathan H. Turner, eds., *Social Theory Today*. Cambridge, U.K.: Polity, 1987.

Ulam, Adam B. *Expansion and Coexistence: The History of Soviet Foreign Policy, 1917–67*. New York: Praeger, 1968.

van den Berghe, Pierre. "Race and Ethnicity: A Sociobiological Perspective." *Ethnic and Racial Studies* 1 (October 1978):401–11.

Van Fraassen, Bas C. *Laws and Symmetry*. Oxford: Clarendon, 1989.

Vanhanen, Tatu. *The Process of Democratization: A Comparative Study of 147 States, 1980–88*. New York: Crane Russak, 1990.

Wagner, David G. *The Growth of Sociological Theories*. Beverly Hills, Calif.: Sage, 1984.

Wallace, William. *European-Atlantic Security Institutions: Current State and Future Prospects*. Ebenhausen, Germany: Stiftung Wissenschaft und Politik, 1994.

Walt, Stephen. *Revolution and War*. Ithaca, N.Y.: Cornell University Press, 1996.

Waltz, Kenneth N. *Man, the State, and War*. New York: Columbia University Press, 1954.

——. *Theory of International Relations*. Reading, Mass.: Addison-Wesley, 1979.

Waters, Malcolm. *Modern Sociological Theory*. London: Sage, 1994.

Watkins, John. "Methodological Individualism and Social Tendencies." In Richard Boyd, Philip Gasper, and J. D. Trout, eds., *The Philosophy of Science*. Cambridge, Mass.: MIT Press, 1991.

Weart, Spencer R. *Never at War: Why Democracies Will Not Fight One Another*. New Haven, Conn.: Yale University Press, 1998.

Weber, Eugen. *Peasants into Frenchmen*. Palo Alto, Calif.: Stanford University Press, 1976.

Weidenfeld, Werner, ed. *Central and Eastern Europe on the Way into the European Union*. Gütersloh, Germany: Bertelsmann Foundation, 1995.

Weinberg, Steven. "Sokal's Hoax." *New York Review of Books*, August 8, 1996, pp. 11–15.

Weiss, Linda. *The Myth of the Powerless State*. Ithaca, N.Y.: Cornell University Press, 1998.

Wendt, Alexander. "Anarchy Is What States Make of It: The Social Construction of Power Politics." *International Organization* 46 (spring 1992):391–426.

Wendt, Alexander and Daniel Friedheim. "Hierarchy Under Anarchy: Informal Empire and the East German State." *International Organization* 49 (autumn 1995):689–721.

Wesson, Robert. *The Imperial Order*. Berkeley: University of California Press, 1967.

Wetzel, Johannes. "Krise in der Dromosphäre." *Die Zeit*, October 17, 1997, p. 15.

Wickham-Crowley, Timothy. *Guerrillas and Revolution in Latin America: A Comparative Study of Insurgents and Regimes Since 1956*. Princeton, N.J.: Princeton University Press, 1992.

Wilson, Andrew. "The Ukrainian Left: In Transition to Social Democracy or Still in Thrall to the USSR?" *Europe-Asia Studies* 49 (November 1997):1293–1316.

Wilson, Andrew and Igor Burakovsky. *The Ukrainian Economy Under Kuchma*. London: Royal Institute of International Affairs, 1996.

Wilson, John. *Thinking with Concepts*. Cambridge: Cambridge University Press, 1963.

World Bank. *World Development Report, 1996*. Washington, D.C.: World Bank, 1997.

Yekelchyk, Serhy. "The Location of Nation: Postcolonial Perspectives on Ukrainian Historical Debates." *Australian Slavonic and East European Studies* 11 (1997):161–84.

Yoffee, Norman and George L. Cowgill, eds. *The Collapse of Ancient States and Civilizations*. Tucson: University of Arizona Press, 1988.

Young, Crawford. *The Politics of Cultural Pluralism*. Madison: University of Wisconsin Press, 1976.

Zadorozhniuk, Ella and Dmitrii Furman, "Ukrainskie regiony i ukrainskaia politika." In Dmitrii Furman, ed., *Ukraina i Rossia*. Moscow: Izdatel'stvo "Prava Cheloveka," 1997.

Zakaria, Fareed. "The Rise of Illiberal Democracy." *Foreign Affairs* 76 (November–December 1997):22–43.

———. *From Wealth to Power*. Princeton, N.J.: Princeton University Press, 1998.

Zimmermann, Ekkart. "Crises and Crises Outcomes." *European Journal of Political Research* 7 (March 1979):67–115.

Zwick, Peter. *National Communism*. Boulder, Colo.: Westview: 1983.

index